This book deals with both actual and potential terrorist attacks on the United States as well as natural disaster preparedness and management in the current era of global climate change. The topics of preparedness, critical infrastructure investments, and risk assessment are covered in detail. The author takes the reader beyond counter-terrorism statistics, better first responder equipment, and a fixation on FEMA grant proposals to a holistic analysis and implementation of mitigation, response, and recovery efforts. The recent Oklahoma tornadoes and the West Texas storage tank explosion show the unpredictability of disaster patterns, and the Boston Marathon bombings expose the difficulty in predicting and preventing attacks. Egli makes a compelling case for a culture of resilience by asserting a new focus on interagency collaboration, public-private partnerships, and collective action. Building upon the lessons of the 9/11 attacks, hurricane Katrina, and the Deepwater Horizon oil spill, the basic findings are supported by a creative mix of case studies, which include superstorm Sandy, cascading power outages, GPS and other system vulnerabilities, and Japan's Fukushima disaster with its sobering aftermath. This book will help a new generation of leaders understand the need for smart resilience.

Beyond the Storms

Strengthening Homeland Security and Disaster Management to Achieve Resilience

Dane S. Egli

M.E.Sharpe
Armonk, New York
London, England

Library of Congress Cataloging-in-Publication Data

Egli, Dane S., 1957-
  Beyond the storms : strengthening homeland security and disaster
management to achieve resilience / by Dane S. Egli.—First edition.
     pages cm
  Includes bibliographical references and index.
   ISBN 978-0-7656-4195-3 (cloth : alk. paper)—ISBN 978-0-7656-4196-0
(pbk. : alk. paper) 1. National security—United States. 2.
Terrorism—United States—Prevention. 3. Emergency management—United
States. 4. Civil defense—United States—Planning. I. Title.
   UA23.E393 2013
   363.34'80973—dc23
                                                            2013023093

Printed in the United States of America

The paper used in this publication meets the minimum requirements of
American National Standard for Information Sciences
Permanence of Paper for Printed Library Materials,
ANSI Z 39.48-1984.

~

SP (p)   10   9   8   7   6   5   4   3   2   1
IBT (c) 10   9   8   7   6   5   4   3   2   1

Soli Deo Gloria—
For being a faithful refuge in an uncertain world.

To the men and women in uniform,
For serving this country as first responders and service members to preserve our safety,
security, and freedoms.

To my parents, Cork and Connie Egli,
For leading the way with loving and resilient hearts.

Contents

List of Figures and Tables

TABLES

Foreword

Written with clarity and timely relevance, Dane Egli's *Beyond the Storms* is a very useful book on how the United States should respond to the natural disasters and various acts of terrorism that loom in our future. The author spells out a new pathway to national resilience in the face of disaster, using models and extended case studies to establish thoughtful and effective standards of response. In these historic times of extreme weather and national security complexities, I highly recommend the reading of this unique work.

There will never be a complex public policy crisis presented to this nation that can be resolved by a single government agency, a single private-sector firm, or a single nongovernmental organization. Hurricane Katrina and the Deepwater Horizon oil spill were not outliers. The complexity of our world is increasing exponentially, and the intersections of the natural and built environments are converging in ways that multiply the severity of impact in times of disaster. In the same manner, the intersection of powerful economic states, crumbling nation states, surging ethnic groups, fundamentalist religious groups, terrorist organizations, and transnational criminals (including cybercriminals) are converging and interacting in the global commons.

Traditional notions of political, social, economic, and cultural frameworks are changing in ways not seen before in modern history. Concepts of national sovereignty, the production of public and private goods, the functioning of capital markets, and, perhaps most important, the ability to identify and allocate the cost of risk are in a state of flux. Long-established norms for dealing with national crises are being challenged by the emancipation and ubiquity of information, the creation of new forms of value-added virtual innovations, and lightning-fast advances in earth, life, and data sciences that are not the property of governments.

In the face of these changes, it is clear the authorities, capabilities, capacities, competencies, or relationships of any single public or private agency are inadequate to mount a whole-of-government response or solve the problem independently. Now is the time to assess what we have learned in the early years of the twenty-first century, from Y2K to Fukushima to Superstorm Sandy. The United States needs to begin a *new* discussion that challenges our understanding of preparedness, disaster management, and functional resilience.

Beyond the Storms inspires that discussion by reintroducing basic theories of public goods, collective action, risk, and critical infrastructure resilience as a means to create not only a cause for action but a road map for action. It is a short work, but it is long on thinking about how to deal with the complex and inevitable problems of the future. We must recapture the desire to do hard things together, and this consequential work begins that process.

Thad Allen
Admiral, USCG (retired)

Preface

We can no longer afford to harden all vulnerable facilities or defend ourselves completely against future disasters. There are disruptive events coming—of increasing number and intensity—that will impose damages and dwarf the resources available to prevent or protect from their devastating impact. There has to be a better way.

As a nation, we must move *Beyond the Storms* of fixing things in response to the most recent crisis, establishing new government agencies, and frantically submitting emergency funding requests in a reactionary manner; instead, armed with a new sense of urgency, we must imbue our society with *resilient thinking*. This will require a fundamental shift from a preoccupation with preventing and protecting ourselves from emergencies we can never fully avoid, to a posture that innovatively mitigates, responds to, and recovers from inevitable disasters.

In 2012 alone, extreme weather affected every region of the country, from drought conditions in over 60 percent of the United States, catastrophic floods, Tropical Storm Debby in Florida, Hurricane Isaac in Louisiana, destructive wildfires on more than 9 million acres across 37 states, power outages affecting more than 3.4 million homes due to severe summer storms and deadly heat waves, to the historic landfall of Superstorm Sandy in the Northeast, the impact of disasters has been enormous (Kerry et al. 2012).

This text examines the most significant challenges to public-private efforts, including whole-of-government interagency coordination in support of national preparedness, and offers suggestions to improve safety and security across all domains. As this manuscript was being prepared for publication in the spring of 2013, the Boston Marathon bombings of April 15 rekindled memories of the 9/11 terrorist attack on the World Trade Center a dozen years before and renewed with stunning clarity the fear and vulnerability buried in America's collective consciousness. The central purpose of this book is to gain a better understanding of the current state of security and to identify gaps that will advance national-level policies in support of critical infrastructure resilience in the face of inevitable disasters. Linking the strategies of homeland security, disaster management, and community resilience to innovative approaches for wider national preparedness offers a potential roadmap for operationalizing intergovernmental and public-private collaboration. Such collaboration is vital to mitigate, respond to, and recover from the effects of complex problems of the twenty-first century—whether they prove to be extreme weather, environmental incidents, health pandemics, terrorism, or cyber attacks.

This initiative is based on an independent research project designed to uncover *what* the nation should consider in this era of growing complexity and uncertainty to significantly improve resilience. It is not an attempt to define *how* to carry out the proposed remedies or to uncover flashpoints or particular shortfalls inside government offices that are responsible for these missions. Rather, this is a serious effort—in the face of known and unknown threats—to complement and reinforce the ongoing resolve of public- and private-sector leaders striving to make the nation more secure.

The intended audience for this report is the constellation of students, planners, leaders, and decision makers in the public and private sector who are responsible for formulation and implementation of national and homeland security resilience and preparedness policy. Because this study offers insights regarding current and future disaster management and critical infrastructure protection (CIP) objectives, it also has utility for thought leaders who shape national, state, regional, and local policies.

The literature and policies supporting critical infrastructure resilience cover private-sector, cross-governmental, homeland security, academic, and commercial industry imperatives with a focus on the post–9/11 threat environment. *Collective action theory*[1] provides the theoretical underpinning for a unique view of resilience under the broad policy mandate of national preparedness—supporting homeland and national security relative to natural disasters, global terrorism, and health pandemics.

Expert interviews, document reviews, case studies, and other research conducted for this book shed light on the following policy, operational, and academic themes:

- the *current state of preparedness* based on policy directives to prevent, protect from, mitigate, respond to, and recover from disasters;
- an understanding of the *complexity and interdependencies* of critical infrastructures and global supply chains;
- the assertion of *resilience as a public good* enabled by collective action, interagency coordination, and public-private partnerships (PPPs);
- the ability of cross-governmental stakeholders to *implement policy* under current whole-of-nation interagency constructs; and
- potential *remedies to strengthen resilience and preparedness* in support of national-level safety, security, economic, and environmental objectives.

Major findings from this study show that:

- lessons on critical infrastructure protection point to broader strategic imperatives of *national preparedness and functional resilience*;
- awareness of America's *economic dependence upon critical infrastructures and global supply chains* is lacking across the general public;

- *interagency coordination and collective action* offer a systemic approach and practical utility to advance national preparedness;
- there is a need for a *comprehensive national framework* to implement existing policies, strengthen community resilience, and imbue a culture of preparedness;
- because of *extensive interdependencies across all infrastructure sectors,* potentially cascading impacts can occur when relatively local incidents trigger national-level degradation in services; and
- further study is needed to examine *regional dependencies and interdependencies,* operationalizing critical infrastructure resilence.

This study offers new insights into national preparedness—beyond predicting the next terrorist attack, protecting physical assets, and anticipating future hurricanes—by integrating collective-action precepts with interagency coordination across a mixture of agencies, departments, and organizations. Furthermore, it can serve a catalyzing role, bringing together multi-agency stakeholders to address disaster management and resilience policies, while supporting the American economy and global markets that depend upon the free flow of commerce. Most significantly, it provides the basis for the development of an implementation process that will help operationalize resilience policies.

ACKNOWLEDGMENTS

This study was made possible by the dedicated efforts of a host of people from the Johns Hopkins University Applied Physics Laboratory (JHU/APL), and external participants—primarily in Washington, DC; London, UK; the Port Authority of New York and New Jersey; and Ports of Los Angeles/Long Beach—who supported the research.

This project started as an independent study within JHU/APL's National Security Analysis and Homeland Protection Business Areas, under the supervision of Gregory Melcher and Dr. Jose Latimer, who were instrumental in shaping the direction of the study. I am grateful for the private-sector leaders and public officials who agreed to be interviewed or participated in discussion groups in support of this study; their input helped determine the state of critical infrastructure protection in the period since the September 11 attacks (2001), Hurricane Katrina (2005), and Superstorm Sandy (2012).

In particular, I want to thank Jonathon Cosgrove, Jared McKinney, and Claire Palmer, who provided invaluable research assistance, along with subject matter experts John Contestabile and Richard "DJ" Waddell from the JHU/APL staff, who reviewed the document and offered valuable insights.

Throughout this study, a variety of U.S. officials, British officials, and security experts from the public and private sectors were consulted, but the views expressed are derived from interviews, reports, policy documents, and case studies as distilled by the author. This volume is designed to serve as a catalyst for timely policy development, innovative disaster management, and improved preparedness at the local, regional, state, and national levels through a new focus on critical infrastructure resilience.

And for seeing the literary potential, I am grateful to my professional colleagues at JHU/APL, as well as the publishing team at M.E. Sharpe, including executive editor George Lobell, production editor Stacey Victor, and editorial coordinator Irene Bunnell.

NOTE

1. See Chapter 5 and the final case study (Figure A.14) for a description of collective action theory.

Beyond
the Storms

1 Introduction

> "As bad as Sandy was, future storms could be even worse. In fact, because of rising temperatures and sea levels, even a storm that's not as large as Sandy could—down the road—be even more destructive."
>
> Mayor Michael R. Bloomberg
> (New York City 2013a)

The future is uncertain. But trends indicate that storms and natural disasters will grow increasingly frequent and destructive. Terrorism, meanwhile, remains a persistent threat. We may be able to predict some storms and prevent some terrorist attacks, but perfect security is not achievable, especially in an open society. Nor can we afford to pursue it as in the past, with a primary focus on predicting the location of future intrusions or storms, hardening facilities, and targeting more terrorists.

Mayor Bloomberg of New York City, to take one prominent example, has recognized this reality. Bloomberg has proposed investing $20 billion in what has been called "managing the unavoidable" (Borenstein 2013). The plan, which seeks to make New York City more resilient to future storms and disasters, proposes everything from building new floodwalls to upgrading critical power and improving telecommunications infrastructures. The proposal is premised on the belief that Sandy-like storms will become more frequent in the future as the climate changes. The options, in Bloomberg's words, are either to "do nothing and expose ourselves to an increasing frequency of Sandy-like storms that do more and more damage," or to "make the investments necessary to build a stronger, more resilient New York—investments that will pay for themselves many times over in the years to come" (Russ 2013). In other words, resilience, not further emphasis on elusive prevention and physical protection programs—guns, gates, guards, and locks—is what is required to protect cities, populations, infrastructure, and commerce in the future.

Three trends, illustrated by examining New York City, indicate why Mayor Bloomberg is right—why resilience is essential: (1) infrequent "once-in-a-century" storms are likely to occur more frequently, (2) these storms are likely to adversely affect more Americans, and (3) these disasters are likely to cause exponentially more economic damage. To further explain these points, Hurricane Sandy, the worst hurricane to ever hit New York City, was at the time considered a once-in-seventy-year "loss event." The projected impacts of climate change—warmer temperatures and rising sea levels—could make Sandy a once-in-fifty-year disaster by mid-century. Increasing development in coastal areas, growing population concentrations in vulnerable coastal areas, and swelling waves due to rising sea levels have increased the number of people potentially affected—in the current example, 83 percent more New Yorkers are vulnerable to coastal flooding now than was previously calculated. Finally, rising sea levels and bigger storms could increase economic damages close to fivefold—in the case of a Sandy-like hurricane, an estimated $19 billion in damages to New York City would become something closer to $90 billion, and $65 billion in damages nationwide would become something closer to $300 billion (New York City 2013b; *USA Today* 2013).

Unless the trends reverse themselves, the economic cost of the disasters of the future, not to mention the incalculable toll of human suffering, will drastically increase. A posture focused primarily on defending the American fortress can do little to mitigate the inevitable disasters and extreme weather of the future. Storms will come. Hostile actors will avoid detection. Critical infrastructures will fail. The question is not if, but when. But America is not helpless in the face of the coming storms.

PURPOSE

In October 2012, just as weather forecasters were poised to declare the hurricane season over, Hurricane Sandy devastated the northeastern United States with historic impact. The tenth named hurricane of the 2012 season, Sandy became the largest Atlantic hurricane on record, with storm winds extending 1,100 miles in diameter. By the time it ended, the storm had caused 253 deaths and estimated damages of over $65 billion along a path that spanned a half-dozen countries in the Caribbean and a large swath of the East Coast of the United States. As catastrophic as Superstorm Sandy was, especially to the states of New Jersey and New York, it offers up significant lessons related to critical infrastructure, homeland security, and disaster management.

Moving beyond the post–9/11 focus on physical protection and focusing instead on the lessons of continuity and sustainability, this text addresses critical infrastructure *resilience*—the strategic imperative for those sailing through an ocean of unprecedented complexity and uncertainty. Such resilience requires a posture of learning and innovation that acknowledges the need to transform the way we think and act as a society with respect to national preparedness.

The occurrence of domestic and international disasters, among them flash floods, wildfires, terrorist attacks, oil spills, tornadoes, hurricanes, earthquakes, tsunamis, and pandemics, highlights the need for a greater understanding of the current state of cross-governmental and private sector coordination in preparedness and critical infrastructure resilience. By homeland security and emergency response standards, the year 2011 was truly historic and stands as a harbinger for those responsible for planning and disaster management: President Barack Obama signed 99 Stafford Act resolutions in response to state governors' requests for emergency assistance—14 of which cost the American taxpayer at least $1 billion each. In addition, there were 29 national-level emergency declarations and 25 Fire Management Assistance Grants

(FMAGs) disbursed. This study highlights the need for resilience within all systems and sectors as a public good, similar to requirements in force for safety, security, and environmental protection. With the expectation that the future will remain volatile, analysts and leaders must look *"Beyond the Storms"* of hurricanes, terrorist acts, and inevitable disasters to establish an enduring framework of preparedness and resilience.

Against this national security and homeland protection backdrop—with complex overlapping interests, uncoordinated players, and often fragmented policies—this study identifies the most critical variables and policy options that support improved critical infrastructure resilience. The most significant contribution of this study may be the empirically-based explanations, informed by contemporary case studies, of how current resilience and preparedness strategies link to efforts of local, state, regional, and federal governments and private companies and citizens. The text focuses on cross-governmental multi-agency collaboration because research findings suggest that significant improvements are possible by leveraging the benefits of interagency coordination, collective action, and public-private partnerships (PPPs).

According to the *National Security Strategy (NSS)*, "Our national security begins at home" (The White House 2010). Recognizing that our economic strength is inextricably linked to the global economy and underwrites our influence in the world, the *NSS* emphasizes the importance of a resilient society, forging new levels of international collaboration to "seize on the opportunities afforded by the world's interconnections." It is noteworthy that the *NSS* cites "resilience of our homeland" (along with military, intelligence, diplomacy, and security) among the most critical factors that will enable us to achieve our "national security capacity and be successful in the global marketplace." Furthermore, it refers to the importance of strengthening national capacity: "It is not simply about government action alone, but rather about the collective strength of the entire country." And resilience is a unifying thread that runs through the *NSS*, with the acknowledgment that "we will not be able to prevent every threat, so we must enhance resilience—the ability to adapt to changing conditions and prepare for, withstand, and rapidly recover from disruption"; we need to be coordinating across federal, state, local, tribal, territorial, regional, nongovernmental, and private-sector partners in a comprehensive "whole-of-nation" approach (The White House 2010).

Natural disasters continue their uncertain collisions with the human world, and terrorist elements remain intent on attacking U.S. interests; consequently, security and emergency planners study threats to the American homeland—including critical infrastructure—which cover air, land, maritime, cyber, and space domains, as well as global supply chains (Flynn 2007; McNicholas 2008). And since the terrorist attacks of September 11, 2001, and the aftermath of numerous natural disasters, officials struggle to set priorities among an unlimited number of potential disaster scenarios. Critical infrastructures are of particular concern because they are vulnerable to damage, disruption, or attack, and they play an essential role in the economic vitality of the nation (Congressional Research Service [CRS] 2007; The White House 2005, 2010).

Over the past decade, the United States has dramatically enhanced its focus on disaster management and intelligence capabilities—both foreign and domestic—to counter terrorism and prepare the homeland for natural disasters. However, threats and vulnerabilities to security, including critical infrastructures, continue to evolve. Notable events such as Hurricane Katrina (2005), the Deepwater Horizon Oil Spill in the Gulf of Mexico (2010), Hurricane Irene (2011), Japan's earthquake and tsunami (2011), Superstorm Sandy (2012), bombings in Boston (2013), and the devastating tornado in Oklahoma (2013), and even persistent piracy attacks in international waters highlight threats to vital infrastructures, fragile supply chains, and economic interests. The resulting losses and damage from the aforementioned disasters disrupted government and business functions, producing cascading effects far beyond their immediate physical location. Adversaries of America will no doubt study U.S. homeland vulnerabilities and attempt to exploit weaknesses in critical infrastructures and disaster response, underscoring the need to better understand the state of resilience and preparedness across the public and private sectors (Flynn 2007; The White House 2006, 2010; U.S. Government Accountability Office 2011b, 2011c).

Defining *resilience* is complicated by the fact that various disciplines employ the term in slightly different ways. It is used with different emphases in the fields of engineering, ecology, psychology, emergency response, disaster management, business, and public policy, oftentimes with little understanding of the primary actors and institutions involved in its application. As a useful reference and learning tool for strategic planners, policymakers, and students, this study offers a working definition of resilience that aligns with the most current policy directives and the deliberations of global innovators, thereby providing the basis for critical analysis of resilience variables. Resilience, then, is "the ability and capacity—of systems and people—to prepare for and adapt to changing conditions, and withstand and recover rapidly from disruptions, in order to maintain their core functions and integrity in the face of changing circumstances, including deliberate attacks, accidents, or naturally occurring threats or incidents" (The White House 2013b; Zolli and Healy 2012).

To help the reader understand the graphic realities of resilience successes and failures, and to underscore the challenges of improving strategic capacities in an uncertain and rapidly changing environment, this study draws from the details of contemporary case studies. Surveys of disasters from the not-too-distant past help to illuminate the efforts coordinated by various agencies, organizations, institutions, private-sector owners and operators, and other operational elements to achieve community resilience in the face of tragedy. The concepts of community resilience and regional preparedness are personalized for the reader through modern crises such as Superstorm Sandy, Hurricane Katrina, Japan's Fukushima nuclear disaster, regional power outages, and assessments of fragile dependencies upon supply chains and technologies such as the global positioning system (GPS).

INITIAL THEMES AND EXPECTATIONS

The topic of disaster preparedness is so broad and unbounded that, as a first step, the research proposal for this book needed some general direction and focus. A series of

10 broad topics emerged and are characterized as *initial themes and expectations* for this study. They are also captured in matrix form in Appendix E.

1. interagency coordination
2. international collaboration
3. private sector participation
4. information sharing
5. strategy implementation
6. systems integration
7. intelligence cooperation
8. governance and leadership
9. cross-domain solutions
10. concepts of operations

These 10 independent variables—along with major themes and definitions, collective action theory, and operationalizing questions—lay the groundwork for this study by identifying key references and potential linkages within the area of critical infrastructure resilience. A careful examination of these themes within the context of existing policies leads to the all-important next step: exploratory research across a defined field of study supported by a review of relevant policies, interviews with subject matter experts (SMEs), and an assessment of pertinent disaster management case studies.

Threats to critical infrastructure are not limited to natural disasters, as demonstrated by the terrorist attacks on the World Trade Center on September 11, 2001, the 2005 bombings of London's transit system, and the explosions that tore through the finish line of the 2013 Boston Marathon. In each case, to greater or lesser degrees, terrorists disrupted intermodal transportation, telecommunications, financial markets, and emergency services. The U.S. Government Accountability Office (GAO) has reported that our nation's critical infrastructure and key resources (CIKR)[1] remain vulnerable to a wide variety of threats (GAO 2007, 2012). Since the private sector owns and operates the majority of the nation's CIKR—banking and financial institutions, commercial facilities, telecommunications networks, transportation, and energy sectors—it is essential that the public and private sectors work together to protect and sustain these systems.

Collective action theory offers a useful tool to help identify and evaluate public and private issues and potential remedies within preparedness planning. This theory suggests that no single element within the public sector can secure our interests, and we must therefore rely upon the combined efforts of the public *and* private sectors. Such an approach recognizes that individuals (and organizations) are more likely to act on behalf of their collective interests if there are procedural or economic incentives (Page 2005; Kettl 2008).

To that end, this study examines the challenging questions that persist within the public and private sectors:

- What have we learned from major disasters such as the 9/11 terrorist attacks, Hurricanes Sandy and Irene, and the Japanese earthquake and tsunami?

- What would we do differently in disaster management with the benefit of lessons learned from major crises over the past decade?
- How can we galvanize the public through a national framework that helps operationalize resilience at the local and regional levels?
- With complex dependencies and interdependencies across the infrastructure sectors, what are the areas of greatest concern and what are the potential remedies for them?
- Leveraging collective action precepts, improved interagency coordination, and private-sector resources, how can we significantly recapitalize national infrastructures systems?
- Given our nation's central role in the global economy, what approaches are needed to forge more resilient supply chains?

STRUCTURE OF REPORT

By examining relevant policy documents and conducting case studies and interviews with SMEs, this study identifies key elements within the public and private sectors relative to critical infrastructure resilience and national preparedness policies. The selected case studies are exemplars of domestic and international events that occurred before, during, and after the promulgation of relevant national preparedness policies. They uncover the complex ligaments of the infrastructure sectors, as well as overlapping authorities and jurisdictions within the homeland security environment.

Chapter 2 of this book presents the central thesis of the study by asserting the strategic importance of critical infrastructure resilience, moving beyond routine planning, and asserting the case for a new approach to risk assessment and capabilities-based analyses.

Chapter 3 provides the background and assumptions for the study, offering historical context and a summary of the 16 infrastructure sectors, outlining foundational themes such as resilience, critical infrastructure protection (CIP), all-hazards approach, whole-of-nation, cross-domain solutions, globalized economy, cyber security, and an incident public-preparedness scale. It concludes by drawing lessons from unrestricted warfare literature.

Chapter 4 outlines the twenty-first century issues—including natural disasters, terrorist attacks, and pandemics—threatening homeland security, disaster management, and preparedness planning, along with the range of challenges from low-probability high-impact to high-probability low-impact events that inform resilience and preparedness policymaking.

Chapter 5 presents policy and literature reviews of collective action theory, interagency coordination, and the intersection of the two fields to help understand the means of expanding infrastructure and resilience investments within the context of whole-of-nation PPPs. It also includes a list of 12 overlapping themes to operationalize interagency coordination and collective action.

Chapter 6 explains the methodology of the study, starting with the problem definition, then describing qualitative data collection, the research and analysis approach, and challenges faced during this exploratory study.

Chapter 7 distills 93 major findings from the research—conducted over a six-month period—and frames the outcomes of the study in short paragraphs. These findings represent the most significant observations and empirical data from SME interviews, case studies, and document reviews, and serve to further inform the recommendations.

Chapter 8 contains 20 recommendations broken down into two general categories: strategic and operational. The 13 strategic and seven operational suggested remedies address gaps in the current fields of preparedness and resilience policy.

Finally, there are eight appendices that include the following supporting information: case study summaries; sample test questions and research topics; results of SME interviews; supporting remarks for major findings; initial themes and expectations; relevant external reports; SME interviewees; and a glossary of terms and acronyms. The book ends with an extensive list of references.

NOTE

1. CIKR are assets and systems—whether physical or virtual—so vital to the United States that "their destruction or incapacity would have a debilitating impact on national security, economic welfare, national public health, or any combination of those factors" (USA Patriot Act 2001, Section 1016e).

2 | Beyond the Storms

There is no safe harbor to avoid the impact of catastrophic events—*physical* disasters such as extreme weather, earthquakes, and terrorism, or those that are *virtual* such as chemical threats, infectious diseases, finance-related schemes, and the effects of electromagnetic pulses—and their direct or indirect consequences on the homeland. We face rapidly changing times, globally and nationally, marked by complexities and uncertainties that force us to make difficult decisions about homeland security and community preparedness (The White House 2010; Allen 2012). This book suggests a new approach that leverages whole-of-nation and private-sector capabilities to systematically strengthen preparedness, homeland security, and resilience.

The destabilizing impact of recent disasters has resulted in a reactionary posture that is not necessarily in the long-term interests of preparedness. Beyond the unquantifiable human costs associated with hazards, economic damages from natural disasters in the United States exceeded $55 billion in 2011 (National Academies 2012). In 2012, there were many different disasters, including Superstorm Sandy, lethal wildfires, regional droughts, domestic terrorism,[1] and the spread of West Nile virus. While we must address immediate crises and apply the lessons learned from 9/11, Hurricane Katrina, the Haiti earthquake, and the Deepwater Horizon oil spill, this study looks "beyond the storms" of pressing events to identify strategic opportunities that would make the nation better prepared and more secure through a new focus on long-term mitigation, response, and resilience.

IT'S MORE THAN CRITICAL INFRASTRUCTURE PROTECTION

This book documents the results of an exploratory study examining the state of preparedness in the United States. The initial focus of this study was *critical infrastructure protection* (CIP), but ultimately it extended to the broader concepts of preparedness and resilience, as the research pointed toward a different strategic view. It is clear that disaster management planners and leaders across public-private sectors understand how to build and protect infrastructures within their areas of responsibility; however, they appear to lack awareness of the challenges facing adjacent geographic or infrastructure sectors. Therefore, there is a need for a systematic approach to resilient thinking, integrated planning, and collective action at the national, regional, state, and local level.

Empirical data revealed a fragmented planning and risk assessment process, where agencies tend to focus narrowly on their areas of concern (ports, bridges, railways, tunnels, telecommunications, power, water, etc.), yet fail to recognize the complex interdependencies of the broader homeland security enterprise. Furthermore, when preparing budget requests or proposals for grant funding, submissions reflected this isolated approach that safeguarded a specific region or municipality at the expense of the collective good. Initial findings uncovered that while we live in an interconnected world of complex twenty-first-century vulnerabilities, we often employ twentieth-century ways of thinking and planning for security—allocating resources for physical protection based on the seniority of a congressional committee member, the best-written grant proposal, or a reactionary bias for "fixing things" to relieve the most immediate pain.

CURRENT STATE OF PREPAREDNESS

In the past century, catastrophic disasters have brought dramatic reminders that we need to better understand how to mitigate risk and improve critical infrastructure resilience. Studies of our current state of preparedness recognize that the majority of all critical infrastructures across 16 interdependent sectors are owned and operated locally or regionally by the private sector and often influenced by an uncoordinated mixture of investors, volunteers, nonprofit organizations, labor unions, and utilities; and the federal government is often hard-pressed—or simply unable—to make changes that might improve their coordination (Flynn 2007; National Infrastructure Advisory Council [NIAC] 2009).

It is increasingly clear that the nation needs a new resilience-based approach to critical infrastructure protection—one that can be integrated into the homeland security enterprise and build greater trust across public and private stakeholders. Real analytic models and action plans, not just government strategy documents, are needed to implement preparedness policies and incentivize the private sector to support policymaking, equity investments, cost recovery, new insurance markets, and legislative changes. Without such action, the nation's infrastructure will remain in its current state of disrepair (Allen 2012). Researchers and global innovators emphasize the futility of popular security habits (with a fixation on physical protection); they assert the need for new, more pragmatic, resilient approaches because current approaches have fallen short. (Zolli and Healy 2012).

There is a powerful call for a shift in disaster preparedness that places a stronger focus on resiliency. The statistics predict a looming challenge and general lack of understanding from a population that expects critical infrastructures to automatically serve their needs. For example, approximately 75 percent of the nation's GDP is fueled by our metro communities, and over 80 percent of the U.S. population is located in 11 mega-regions where new approaches to resilience thinking are needed most. The risk assessments and analytical frameworks that model infrastructure resilience in an interconnected environment must be developed to better understand these complex urban communities, as underscored by the cascading regional impacts caused by disasters such as Superstorm Sandy in October of 2012.

Now that federal funds are receding, there is a need for increased private-sector participation and for regional approaches that address the enduring mitigation challenges being faced by preparedness planners. The 90,000 local, regional, and state flood maps maintained by the Federal Emergency Management Agency (FEMA) are incomplete or outdated, as extreme weather conditions have revealed in recent years (U.S. Department of Homeland Security [DHS], Office of Inspector General [OIG] 2005); and corresponding products—risk maps—for regional disaster planning do not exist. Based on these shortfalls and the ongoing shift from a national top-down to a more local approach, *regional* action plans have been developed. They assert the following themes (GAO 2010; DomPrep 2012, 41; NIAC 2012b):

- reprioritizing based upon reduced grants and other federal assets;
- expanding participation of state, regional, and local assets;
- engaging small businesses, large corporations, and private investors;
- regionalizing planning, programs, structures, and processes;
- forging political consensus among local and regional leaders;
- expanding use of state fusion centers and all-hazards consortiums;
- increasing emphasis on public-private-academic partnerships;
- information sharing with all disaster management partners;
- leveraging the services of volunteer organizations and nonprofits; and
- emphasizing regional exercises, training, and education.

While these themes place a timely focus on the need to synchronize preparedness efforts at the regional level, are they sufficient to galvanize national- and state-level leaders and serve as a catalyst to refocus the country on functional resilience? This study attempts to answer that question.

A NATION AT RISK

The United States is at a critical juncture: many infrastructures are aging or failing, and current efforts to address the challenge are insufficient. America invests barely 2 percent of its GDP in infrastructure renewal and maintenance, one of the lowest figures among the world's industrialized nations. The following facts expose some of our demographic and infrastructure fault lines (GAO 2007; Gerencser et al. 2008; Byram 2009; Allen 2012; U.S. Department of the Treasury 2012; El Nasser 2012; American Society of Civil Engineers [ASCE] 2013):

- Using input from engineers in every state, the American Society of Civil Engineers (ASCE) gave the national infrastructure an overall grade of D-plus, a score influenced by failing areas such as aviation, drinking-water supply, roads, transit, and sewage treatment;
- the American population is migrating into the cities and approximately 75 percent of the GDP is derived from metro communities; 80 percent of the U.S. population is located within 11 mega-regions;
- 42 percent of the nation's urban highways are congested, costing our economy

more than $101 billion annually in lost time and fuel, while increasing emissions of harmful exhaust and pollution into the air;

- 38 percent of roads are in disrepair, and the United States must invest $225 billion per year over the next 50 years to maintain and enhance a decaying surface transportation system (but we are currently spending less than 40 percent of this amount);
- the United States operates 361 commercial sea and river ports and delivers over 20 million containers globally per year, supporting the world's largest trading commerce ($645 billion), yet there is no executive agent assigned to manage or integrate this dynamic global supply chain and its associated policies;
- the Army Corps of Engineers estimates that more than 95 percent of overseas trade produced or consumed by the United States moves through our nation's commercial ports, but our ports are in danger of losing their competitive advantage due to the slow and very complex process of critical dredging projects;
- by 2020, every major U.S. container port is projected to be handling at least double the volume it was designed to handle, and by 2040, this figure is projected to triple;
- over the next 20 years, railroads are projected to need nearly $200 billion in investments to accommodate increased freight traffic;
- over 25 percent of the nation's bridges are considered structurally deficient;
- there are approximately 85,000 dams in the country, averaging over 50 years old, and 4,000 of them are considered structurally at risk; and
- the United States has more than 500 major urban public transit operators, 66,000 chemical plants, 2,800 electric plants, 104 nuclear power plants, 1,600 municipal wastewater facilities, 2 million miles of pipelines, 87,000 food processing plants, and 5,000 public airports that are owned and operated *independently*; however, they are highly *interdependent* in their functional capabilities.

In light of these infrastructure flashpoints, and the need for America to sustain— or restore—its edge in the global economy, two Harvard Business School leaders proposed an eight-point "transformational" plan to face systemic national-level challenges. Topics like immigration, taxation, trade, regulation, energy, and a sustainable federal budget were addressed in the "U.S. Competitiveness Project," with the need to "improve infrastructure" (especially roads, ports, telecoms, and energy systems) making the middle of the list. They urged that policies and funding be linked directly to the stimulation of economic growth and emphasized "new mechanisms" such as public-private partnerships to "raise the rate of investments" (Porter and Rivkin 2012).

THE ISSUE OF OUR DAY

This sampling of facts bespeaks a menacing challenge that must be addressed with a sense of urgency; otherwise, infrastructure systems will continue to erode along with public safety and security. Many observers believe that this challenge—to dramatically transform how we secure and maintain our critical infrastructure through a posture of resilience—is the "issue of our day." As the Greatest Generation confronted the threats from Germany and Japan in World War II and proceeded to build the domestic infrastructure system that has been enjoyed for the past 60 years, the current generation also faces defining challenges. There is a need for a comparable resolve in taking on today's serious concerns—including economic austerity, natural disasters, and global security threats—to forge a culture of preparedness and invest wisely in critical infrastructure resilience.

Globalization and expanded markets have unwittingly introduced the potential for greater cascading hazards. Many of the freedoms that accompany technology and social networking advancements have in fact made us more vulnerable. This study reinforces observations made since the Y2K scare 13 years ago, when spending by the U.S. government and commercial industry to predict and prevent adverse impacts on critical infrastructures exceeded $100 billion. Since then, the lessons of globalization and cyber security suggest that vulnerabilities from "system complexity" have expanded at a faster pace than our means of mitigating them. Furthermore, interconnected infrastructure systems, while offering greater speed and efficiency, now present larger targets for potential exploitation by criminals and terrorists because networked architectures are operated in an open society (Mussington 2002). The qualities of speed, access, and anonymity that make these robust systems so effective also make them more vulnerable to nefarious elements.

How do we better understand these uncertainties and leverage the complex changes in our society to our advantage in building resilience at the local, regional, state, and national level? How do we integrate the benefits of social, behavioral, physical, and engineering sciences to support resilience-related research and policy development? And how do we recognize that the same asymmetric[3] forces (and actions by our adversaries) that make our world more dangerous may contain the ingredients we need to make it safer?[4] Clearly, our homeland security strategists need to consider new ways to introduce resilience into the way we plan and execute security (NIAC 2010).

Threats to our physical and virtual security are complex, new, and growing. They demand a new approach to how we prepare for attacks and sustain our infrastructure, as well as how we mitigate, respond to, and recover from crises. Many of the threats we face *cannot* be deterred or countered simply because the provision of civil liberties and a free society are paramount in the United States. The idea that complete physical security is normal, or even achievable with enough Transportation Security Administration (TSA) agents or Customs and Border Protection (CBP) officers, is an illusion that is consuming our finite economic resources.[5] Our focus must be fixed on building a new vision of twenty-first-century resilience in the face of uncertain and complex risks (Flynn and Burke 2012).

HOPE AND HUBRIS

This new vision starts with a careful examination of cultural mind-sets and deeply held attitudes toward emergency hazards. All disasters are personal, and the first priority in preparedness planning is an *individual* responsibility. According to FEMA guidelines, people should be self-sufficient for 72 hours after a disaster strikes if evacuating, and longer if sheltering-in-place (Insurance Institute for Business and Home Safety [IIBHS] 2012). Experts emphasize that America will never truly mitigate the harsh impact of disasters until the public takes personal ownership for the preparations necessary to respond to and recover from emergencies (DHS 2008, 2009; FEMA 2011).

The challenge of raising public awareness about preparation *before* a disaster strikes is manifested in the prevailing attitude of "It won't happen to me," or "We'll just deal with it when the time comes." While clearly a dangerous reaction, as learned from hurricanes Katrina, Irene, and Sandy, this type of thinking can also be linked to difficult economic times. A society struggling with poverty and unemployment is focused on financial survival and therefore is less likely to spend essential money (or even discretionary funds) on insurance or redundant systems that don't have an immediate return on investment or help "pay the bills." Yet, research indicates there is a 4:1 ratio associated with preventive action supporting infrastructure: For every dollar spent now on resilience-building and disaster preparedness, we can avoid at least $4 in future losses. However, an investment in resilience is often considered an "invisible" payoff, because if built and maintained properly, infrastructure works as planned and life continues uninterrupted (ASCE 2009; Kerry, Lautenberg, and Gillibrand 2012).

In addition to an attitude of denial, many people simply refuse to take ownership for individual preparation because they believe that "it's the government's responsibility," and "FEMA will take care of us." This attitude must be changed through a combination of initiatives at the local, regional, state, and national levels (Kettl 2004). Because extreme weather, terrorist attacks, and health epidemics are inevitable, citizens should rely less upon outside assistance and depend more upon their personal resources, enabling communities to be better prepared for future disasters. Additionally, rather than creating a new program that would add another financial burden to already-struggling small business communities and families, a system of rewards or incentives for the general public should be put into place to encourage resilience-supporting actions within existing daily priorities and resources. Although federal funds are needed to implement some programs, many requirements can—and should—be accomplished at the state level (American Red Cross 2010; GAO 2010; DHS 2012; DomPrep 2012).

Moving beyond human factors to an all-domain context (land, maritime, air, space, and cyber), the next section introduces a framework that draws upon the current pillars of national preparedness (prevent, protect, mitigate, respond, and recover), offering a continuum of options from infrastructure protection to functional continuity under a broad umbrella of resilience (Figure 2.1). This framework suggests a view of resilience that helps define the planning variables involved in national preparedness. There is an important distinction between protection, which focuses on the *threats,* and continuity, which focuses on *resuming operations* despite the consequences. In this framework, both objectives are enabled through the operating principles of *resilience.* And while prevention and protection may be the preferred options in many cases, they are not always possible. Therefore, an increased focus is needed on mitigation, response, and recovery (Congressional Research Service [CRS] 2012).

Figure 2.1 Resilience Framework

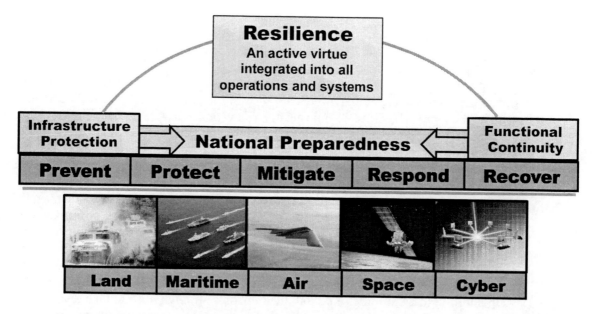

Sources: Images from: Space: Los Angeles Air Force Base, MILSATCOM Systems Directorate Awards Production Contract for Fourth AEHF Satellite, http://www.losangeles.af.mil/news/story.asp?id=123235593. Sea: Wikimedia Commons, Fleet 5 nations, http://commons.wikimedia.org/wiki/File:Fleet_5_nations.jpg. Land: DVIDSHUB (Flickr username), October 1, 2011, Vehicle down, http://www.flickr.com/photos/dvids/6207823230/. Cyber: (cropped) Wikimedia Commons, National-Cyber-Range-DARPA thumb, http://commons.wikimedia.org/wiki/File:National-Cyber-Range-DARPA_thumb.jpg. Air: http://www.af.mil/shared/media/photodb/photos/030814-F-QG253-105.jpg.

Understanding Resilience

Resilience, in a physical and structural sense, is "the ability to prepare for and adapt to changing conditions, and withstand and recover rapidly from disruptions" (The White House 2013b) However, the broader concept of resilience originated in the ecological and social sciences, where it is critical for survival and growth within complex systems. Research on these systems suggests that they evolve perpetually through an "adaptive cycle" of growth, crisis, transformation, and renewal. Resilience is not only the ability to recover from disasters and flex instead of snapping; it is also the ability to *get stronger* as a result of adversity (Gunderson, Holling, and Ludwig 2002). For the purposes of this study, resilience is "the ability and capacity—of systems and people—to prepare for and adapt to changing conditions, and withstand and recover rapidly from disruptions, in order to maintain their core functions and integrity in the face of changing circumstances, including deliberate attacks, accidents, or naturally occurring threats or incidents" (Zolli and Healy 2012; The White House 2013b).

The traditional view of physical security and infrastructure protection involves preparing for risks and dangers we do not know about, hardening facilities against a potential attack, and adding more redundancies and defensive layers to the system; it is analogous to an individual saving money in case of an unanticipated job loss. However, resilience suggests a different type of preparedness—the kind that, in addition to simply saving money, would involve learning new skills to establish a broader network and land a better job in the face of a layoff (Cooper-Ramo 2009). In the case of critical infrastructure, rather than "fixing things" or adding more safeguards through the congressional appropriations and authorization process, we should systematically evaluate where and how we can make optimal investments to rebound from a disaster and, in some cases, pre-position recovery resources and have trained response teams on standby.

Taking a resilient approach to pandemic threats, we might elect to rely upon more economical foreign suppliers for certain medical vaccines rather than create a new source in this country, because the threat has such a low probability of occurring (despite its potentially high consequence); or perhaps, we might focus on an agile and cost-effective health care system that is more resilient in the face of extreme medical emergencies (O'Rourke 2007; Cooper-Ramo 2009). Some architects might design a "zombie-proof house" that (1) is structurally secure; (2) has limited openings on the perimeter that are all lockable and impenetrable; (3) is capable of generating its own energy, food, and water; and (4) can manage its waste plan for real-world disasters, such as surviving when power and water are cut off. Infrastructure resilience stretches our imaginations to consider what designs might be required for extreme circumstances, taking the ideas of "off the grid" and "sustainability" to new levels (*Economist* 2012c, 14).

Among the various perspectives on resilience held by engineers and social scientists, the Multidisciplinary Center for Earthquake Engineering Research (MCEER) offers common actions to achieve resilience across all infrastructure sectors (Bruneau et al. 2003):

- Robustness: the inherent strength or resistance in a system to withstand external demands without degradation or loss of functionality;
- Redundancy: system properties that allow for alternative options, choices, and substitutions under stress;
- Resourcefulness: the capacity to mobilize needed resources and services during emergencies and disasters; and
- Rapidity: the speed with which disruption can be overcome and safety, services, and financial stability restored.

These traditional measures signal the need for more innovative thinking that goes beyond simply investing in more "guns, gates, guards, and locks" in order to protect physical structures. We must identify the capabilities needed to mitigate the impact of, and respond to, *inevitable* hazards. Oftentimes, it is nearly impossible to determine the risk of hazards because there is too much uncertainty to quantify the threats, vulnerabilities, or consequences. The variables in the equation can be so complex that this information is, at times, unknowable (Cooper-Ramo 2009, Zolli and Healy 2012).

Therefore, the best return on investment—and source of confidence—across interdependent supply chains, infrastructure sectors, and interconnected systems is not a fortress-protection mentality but an investment in *functional resilience*; such an investment imbues communities with a level of confident anticipation and personal preparation for inevitable disasters looming over the horizon. In a post-9/11, post-Sandy, post-H1N1 environment, we should no longer be surprised by disastrous interruptions to our otherwise normal lives; rather, we should anticipate and even expect them. We should prepare with a resilient mind-set even if it does not come naturally.

THE WAY AHEAD: FUNCTIONAL RESILIENCE

Functional resilience is a broad term used in building codes, environmental design, and civil engineering that involves making systems more durable and disaster-resistant through agile and adaptive approaches. Beyond extending the effective life of systems, functional resilience allows them to operate more efficiently, demanding fewer resources for repair and emergency response because flexibility is incorporated into the initial design (Gunderson, Holling, and Light 1995). The comprehensive application of this concept to preparedness and critical infrastructure resilience, along with the necessary assessment tools, has yet to be realized. There is encouraging work under way that includes computational models, operations research, and human factors, but there is a need to operationalize functional resilience in a coordinated and systematic manner.

The principles of functional resilience complement existing public policies. The fundamental objective of national preparedness is to take a holistic approach, focusing on systemic investments that enable the enterprise to absorb the impact of a disaster event without losing the capacity to function. The supporting taxonomy, focused on large-scale optimization, must identify the essential capabilities of the national infrastructure system so that limited fiscal resources can be invested wisely (Homeland Security Council 2007; GAO 2010; The White House 2013b).

Building on this concept of functional resilience, how might we build a framework that is useful across local, state, and federal equities within the homeland? First, a plan of such magnitude must operate in parallel with traditional physical protection, because there will always be mission-essential locations that need to be hardened against and protected from disaster. Second, it requires a capabilities-based approach with standard assessment criteria to determine where functions are assessed and located on the continuum of preparedness (between protection and continuity). The following questions arise: What functions[6] are so essential such that there is no tolerance for degradation; which ones can withstand disruption and some period of recovery; and which fall somewhere in between, with a mixture of functional capabilities? The criteria needed to make these judgments must be developed by mapping the unique interdependencies of each geographic region, identifying the appropriate independent variables, and leveraging the tools of both qualitative and quantitative research.

The goal is to better understand the nature of risk based upon essential functional requirements rather than on uncertain physical threats. Therefore, working with researchers, owners/operators, and policymakers, we need to introduce an effective framework (see Figure 2.1) that is adaptable and scalable to various geographic and infrastructure areas. Instead of a policy document that tries to fit all scenarios (and will likely be ignored by planners if not clearly relevant), guidance should take the form of a general model that is scalable, recognizing that credible threat information is often unavailable. By introducing a framework or model that can be applied across the range of functions and capabilities as general guidance, state and local authorities can better implement critical infrastructure and key resources (CIKR) and disaster management requirements. The utility of this resource will be demonstrated by how well future decisions are made regarding (1) maintenance and repair priorities and (2) strategic funding in order to strengthen preparedness and sustain critical infrastructure resilience (NIAC 2004a; Homeland Security Council 2007; National Research Council [NRC] 2011; DomPrep 2012, 13).

This framework (or resilience implementation process will offer the ability to align local, state, regional, and federal resiliency priorities in an integrated fashion, supporting the greater good rather than the special projects of political officials. For example, the Port of Los Angeles (POLA) moves more containers than any other maritime port in the country. It provides intermodal access to 14 major freight hubs across the nation and invests approximately $1 million per day in capital improvements. How should the POLA and local ports (with 88 different municipalities) best invest their scarce resources at such a critical transportation hub in the country? The question should be answered against a measurable set of capabilities-based criteria designed to achieve functional resilience in the face of certain and uncertain risks.

MANY CREATIVE IDEAS AND PARTNERS AVAILABLE

The encouraging news is that we are not alone. There are international partners who face similar challenges and are willing to share information, as well as professional forums to draw upon academia, public-private partnerships (PPPs), and the experience of commercial industry to improve preparedness. We can no longer afford—financially, technologically, or environmentally—to take a unilateral approach toward preparedness when facing a globalized system of interdependent supply chains and infrastructure sectors (NIAC 2004a; GAO 2010).

In the global context, the annual meeting of the World Economic Forum in Davos, Switzerland, held in January 2013, was attended by a diverse group of business and policy leaders seeking to address vexing problems in the international arena. Among their top issues—indeed, the overall theme and subject of the keynote address—was the idea of *dynamic resilience*. The upbeat title was muddied somewhat by the uncertainty of what resilience actually requires, especially when it is set against the backdrop of a struggling global economy, "moving sideways at best," from threats of social unrest to killer bacteria to deadly natural disasters that appear to be growing in frequency and cost" (Applegate 2013). While international leaders recognize the vital role of resilience in future safety and stability, we still lack a clear path forward to operationalize this elusive concept.

This study provides a new taxonomy of resilience initiatives that will help the nation and its leaders understand how to:

1. make the case more clearly to policymakers and senior decision makers,
2. leverage the capabilities of international partners,
3. incentivize investments from private equity sources,
4. start mapping infrastructure dependencies and interdependencies, and
5. build a capabilities-based model to advance the concept of functional resilience.

Below are some exemplars that help inform the efforts of preparedness planners in the public and private sectors:

- Military studies on unrestricted, irregular, and unconventional conflict provide a useful body of literature because of the similarities to complex and asymmetric factors that exist within critical infrastructure resilience and all-hazards environments.
- Academic institutions and Homeland Security Centers of Excellence across the country are actively studying and testing many of the issues surrounding preparedness and critical infrastructure resilience, generating research-based models to help inform strategic and operational planning.
- After the attacks of 9/11, aviation transportation was grounded for three full days as a security precaution, and the maritime ports—with the exception of the Ports of Los Angeles/Long Beach (POLALB), California—were closed, disrupting vital commerce and trade. Actions by the POLALB provide an example for centers of intermodal activity and complex interdependencies during future incidents, where advanced planning communications among emergency management, law enforcement, port authority, regulators, labor unions, and congressional leaders allowed increased security and sustained port operations to occur simultaneously.
- Counterparts to Homeland Security and FEMA planners in the British Cabinet Office's Civil Contingencies Secretariat have successfully implemented "business continuity" strategies with the private sector by leveraging the relationships that small and medium-sized enterprises already trust and rely upon: suppliers, customers, banks, insurance companies, professional organizations, and distributors.
- UK officials conduct an annual National Risk Assessment (since 2005) and publish an unclassified National Risk Register of Civil Emergencies to explain—in terms that are clear to the general public—what an emergency is and the types of risks (natural hazards and terrorist threats) that government planners are prepared for; and they offer online resources to summarize how the public should prepare for such eventualities.
- Recognizing a general lack of awareness about resilience and an attitude that "it won't happen to me, and if it does, we'll just deal with it when the time comes," UK officials have engaged a global publisher to prepare a 2012 text titled

Business Continuity for Dummies, forming an author's group from members of the private sector. This text is supported by the industries that work with small businesses and includes ideas that can be used by businesses lacking funds for a large-scale resiliency effort.

- The Australian National Security Strategy (ANSS) includes among their four strategic national security objectives the need to "ensure a safe and resilient population" and "secure our assets, infrastructure, and institutions." One of the eight pillars to support these objectives is "strengthening resilience" across their society. Recognizing "it is not possible to eliminate all risks to national security," they place an emphasis on PPPs and building community cohesion in order to "respond and recover quickly" to restore essential services (ANSS 2013).

- A thought-provoking book, *The Age of the Unthinkable,* by Joshua Cooper-Ramo (2009), offers some timely ideas about resilience, emphasizing that it requires a study of "complex adaptive systems"—allowing learning to continue during extreme danger—and has to be built into our systems in advance, like a strong immune response before flu season. The enemy can use small events to trigger big changes (like 9/11), so we need to establish a response system that is always on duty, protecting against and decreasing our susceptibility to disease.

- Israel's Ministry of Homefront Defense offers unique lessons from a society that embraces resilience at all levels; emphasizing that "when we shut down physically or economically, the enemy wins."

THE IMPLEMENTATION CHALLENGE: PUBLIC-PRIVATE PARTNERSHIPS

The key to the implementation of any local-, state-, regional-, or national-level policies in support of critical infrastructure resilience, preparedness, or business continuity is *leveraging the utility of public-private partnerships.* While many of the strategies and policies that inform these public policy challenges originate from federal- or state-level agencies, most disaster management and emergency response activity occurs at the local level among private-sector owners and operators. And since the majority of critical infrastructures are managed by the private sector, the greatest advancements in community resilience will stem from the actions of private-sector stakeholders (Kettl 2008; Brashear and Jones 2010).

In studying business continuity, there are three major private-sector concerns:

1. revenue disruption
2. supply-chain security
3. workforce protection

The private sector needs to know its public and private partners, understand their needs and expectations, and determine what can be mutually shared to support resilience before, during, and after a disaster. The first step for both parties is to get their own house in order and ensure internal steps have been taken to achieve accreditation through program evaluations and testing. In other words, before developing partnerships, public- and private-sector organizations must first demonstrate organic resilience (within their agency or company), so they come to the relationship with the ability to collectively advance preparedness (DomPrep 2012, 27).

Strategic policies and national strategies assert the importance of expanding PPPs and acknowledge the need to incentivize venture capitalists in supporting infrastructure improvements and disaster preparedness; however, few details have emerged in academia, think tanks, or public policies identifying *how* to incentivize these communities, infuse private-sector investments, or significantly expand PPPs. Private industry is in the business of making money by seeking investments that will reduce risk, decrease staffing needs, and provide a reliable flow of revenue in the current fiscal climate. As the public sector seeks to remove barriers and incentivize the private sector to increase participation in joint ventures and partnerships, there will be a natural resistance to collaborate and share information within the commercial industry: Anything that could provide competitors with a market advantage goes against the private sector's interests.

Industry is very reluctant to provide the government with proprietary business information regarding the performance of their operations and safety successes or failures. There is a great fear that such information might be diverted knowingly or unknowingly to the hands of regulators or their competitors, even though this same information is essential for productivity analyses and modeling efforts to counter the spread of disease (Reich 2002). For example, the Ports of Los Angeles/Long Beach (POLALB) place their economic survival and sustained prosperity on shipping traffic in general, and container flow in particular. During a natural or human-made disaster, these ports—and their market investors and customers—will go to great lengths to avoid closure and the subsequent rerouting of cargo commodities to other West Coast ports such as those in Seattle and Oakland (to the north) or Ensenada and San Diego (to the south). Such disruptions translate into lost revenue in the near term and potential lost market share in the long term if those shipping companies choose not to return. (Orosz 2012).

To help put this issue in context for both government planners and commercial industry, consider the economic impact of a port strike and the amount of revenue the private sector can lose. Estimates can vary widely, but experts claim that an 11-day lockout at ports on the West Coast in 2002 cost the local economy approximately $1 billion per day. More recently, in December 2012, this situation surfaced in POLALB, where a strike by union clerical workers resulted in the closure of 10 terminals at the nation's busiest port complex, costing billions of dollars over a two-week period and forcing some ships to sail to other West Coast ports to offload their cargo (Plumer 2012). Not only will dockworkers refuse to cross picket lines established by union workers who are striking for a new contract, but private companies will not share information that would in any way weaken their market position with other ports. When preparedness or resiliency policy is developed, policymakers must look at both the national interests as well as local economic realities that drive industry decisions. For example, rerouting of shipping-container traffic from POLALB (Figure 2.2) to another West Coast port-of-entry may support national policy objectives, but it's not likely to be a model that the ports will support (Orosz 2012).

Figure 2.2 Ports of Los Angeles/Long Beach, California

Source: Madlyinlovewithlife (Flickr username), February 7, 2009, Cargo Cranes, Port of Los Angeles, California. Image, http://www.flickr.com/photos/madlyinlovewithlife/6044091310/.

A NATIONAL CALL TO ACTION

The major findings from this study underscore areas that must be addressed by the nation at the local, regional, state, and federal levels if we are to establish a culture of preparedness within our public and private institutions. In general terms, this can be accomplished through awareness, planning, resource allocation, and strong leadership (O'Rourke 2007):

- Awareness: Leverage the public education process to expand awareness about disasters and knowledge of critical infrastructures. To accomplish this, use school curricula, the national network of some 350 science museums and centers, public media coverage, and professional societies and associations.
- Planning: Employ the proven value of training and exercises that help build relationships in emergency management networks. Reveal weaknesses and provide the groundwork for information-sharing and lessons learned. Allow

for the testing of data fusion, collaborative planning tools, and computational models. Run multiple scenarios in a training environment that allows operators to identify patterns and adjust concepts of operations (CONOPS). Conduct planning that supports the replacement of infrastructure; for example, when replacing a bridge, make it more earthquake resistant, more blast resistant, and increase standoff distances from piers.

- Resource Allocation: Recognize that financial resources and political commitment are needed to invest in continuity and critical infrastructure resilience. As assessments are made and functional capabilities are identified in geographic areas, there will be cross-disciplinary projects that need the budgetary support of the public and private sectors.

- Leadership: Apply the essential ingredient—and oftentimes most elusive quality—of strong leadership in defining and promoting resilient initiatives; implement public policy guidance and provide more timely information to decision makers.

Building upon these broad themes, a team of analysts and operational planners are taking steps to address significant challenges in more actionable terms. These efforts will serve as a catalyst among public- and private-sector leaders to support community resilience and operationalize *critical infrastructure resilience:*

1. Systematic *risk-mapping* of infrastructure dependencies and interdependencies in specific geographic areas will help leaders understand *what* the essential elements of preparedness and resilience are for a complex intermodal system. By employing scenario-based analyses, one can visualize the potential impact of a disaster and conduct a link analysis to understand connectedness between and among critical infrastructures. The outcome of this effort will be a risk map that identifies intermodal connectedness, single points of failure, and supporting interdependencies.

2. Another key objective is developing a *functional resilience framework,* using an integrated approach that helps planners identify *how* to proceed, as well as how to prioritize capability based on criticality and capabilities. Drawing from both qualitative and quantitative assessment criteria, along with the outputs of the risk mapping effort, business rules and mitigating actions will be identified that allow emergency planners to focus on the most important functional areas. This process will offer a tool that can be generalized or adapted to other communities in a scalable and flexible manner. The graphic representation of the framework will serve as a point of clarity to planners and practitioners who must begin to understand this approach as it applies to critical infrastructure resilience.

3. Equally important is the formulation of an *action plan* to operationalize the outcomes from the first two phases, providing planners with leading indicators as to *where and when* events must be executed. During this phase, policymakers attempt to forge a consensus among private- and public-sector leaders

regarding discrete projects, and implementation efforts. The outcome of this phase will be a roadmap that synchronizes the efforts necessary to achieve increased resilience, and it may suggest the need for new developments in governance, concepts of operations, and systems.

This study also asserts the importance of collective action in addressing national-level preparedness through expanded interagency coordination and increased private-sector participation. Building upon functional continuity, preparedness, and disaster management principles (Figure 2.1), there is a need to better understand resilience as an organizing principle to address national preparedness imperatives. Clearly, further research is required to generate new data and models for understanding complex adaptive systems. A systematic mapping of local, regional, state, and national capabilities-based requirements—based on a functional decomposition of all infrastructure dependencies and interdependencies—is needed. As this study highlights, such research should be a high federal priority and be pursued aggressively with an all-hazards, intergovernmental, regional approach to achieve preparedness and resilience objectives.

The findings of this study align with other major policies and initiatives, including Presidential Policy Directive 8 (PPD-8), Presidential Policy Directive 21 (PPD-21), the report *Disaster Resilience: A National Imperative* (National Academies 2012), and the STRONG Act legislation (Kerry, Lautenberg, and Gillibrand 2012). These references have emerged since August 2012, and represent a unique opportunity to build a "resiliency consensus" among public- and private-sector planners. While these documents contain many strong recommendations, they *will not make a difference* when the next disaster strikes critical infrastructure systems unless leaders agree to collectively join with cross-government interagency, private-sector, and academic actors to form a coalition of like-minded innovators. Disaster management planners must be willing to move beyond the immediate budget crisis and pressure to react to the most recent disaster, and team with others to resource, operationalize, and measure resilience. However, it will require extraordinary resolve and leadership to forge a consensus among a disparate group of leaders to bridge the current divide between collective action and individual rhetoric.

The following chapters lay the groundwork for a new approach to critical infrastructure resilience, summarizing basic assumptions, the threats landscape, and salient policies to understand the intersection of collective action and interagency coordination.

Notes

1. One nongovernmental organization (NGO) estimates there were 1,274 antigovernment groups at the end of 2011, up from 131 groups four years earlier (*Economist* 2012a, 27).

2. Asymmetric forces refer to a military action that does not attempt to match the size of an adversary, but exploits weaknesses of the larger force, employing small, elusive, unconventional, and high-tech methods to destabilize and surprise the opponent.

3. Our enemies have learned innovative ways to engage in twenty-first-century guerrilla warfare with asymmetric tactics. They have leveraged the technology of cell phones, explosives, and text messages

to evolve the design of improvised explosive devices (IEDs), and U.S. Special Forces have adjusted with innovative countermeasures.

4. The 9/11 hijackers spent less than $1 million to attack the United States; attempts to prevent similar future attacks (in police, airport security, and monitoring systems) cost Americans $1 million *an hour.*

5. Within the CIKR and resilience context, the analysis expands beyond simply physical or single-sector locations to include *function:* the purpose for which something is designed; a specified role, action, or capability.

3 Background and Assumptions

Figure 3.1 National Preparedness Strategic Context

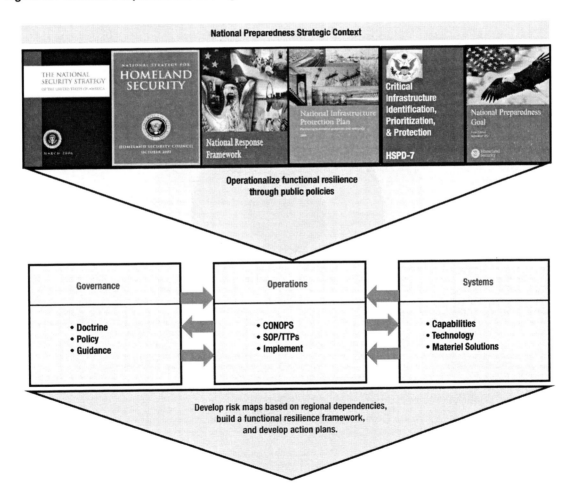

Source: Images from the U.S. Dept. of Homeland Security, http://www.dhs.gov.

This chapter provides 11 essential background themes and assumptions to shape the conceptual boundaries of this project. Assumptions offer effective "explanations and antecedents" (Friedman 1984), and they are basic "facts and ideals" which inform the body of work and help assess causal variables within individual case studies (George and Bennet 2005, 139). Once assumptions are established for qualitative measures at the basic level, one can construct secondary-level dimensions, "building upon these preliminary structures" (Goertz 2006, 35).

Beyond the Storms focuses primarily upon distilling the strategic themes facing the nation in preparedness and resilience implementation through collective action, public-private collaboration, and interagency coordination. The author derived these assumptions and background topics from a comprehensive review of primary preparedness and disaster management literature sources. These themes establish the fundamental premise for the relationships between the findings (Chapter 7), recommendations (Chapter 8), case studies (Appendix A), SME interviews (Appendix C), and initial themes and expectations (Appendix E), and represent the starting point for the study of resilience at the local, regional, state, or national level.

NATIONAL PREPAREDNESS STRATEGIC CONTEXT

This framework (Figure 3.1) offers the strategic context for examination of planning variables within the national preparedness policy environment. It establishes a taxonomy of governance, operations, and systems from which to discuss relevant strategies and categorize the issues that emerge while attempting to operationalize local-, regional-, state-, and national-level policy guidance.

Publications such as the *National Strategy for Homeland Security (NSHS), National Preparedness Report (NPR), National Response Framework (NRF)*, and *National Infrastructure Protection Plan (NIPP)* are strategic documents that inform our planning and implementation efforts across the homeland security enterprise, from local- to national-level policymakers. If prepared with familiar terms of reference and the heuristics[1] of all-hazard, cross-domain, public-private partnerships, they provide an approach to operationalize national preparedness and resilience in support of security, safety, economic, and environmental priorities. And the goal is to prevent, protect from, mitigate, respond to, and recover from disasters of any kind. Our collective efforts (government, industry, academia, commerce, etc.) are carried out within an existing and emerging disaster management community-of-interest, which is informed by a collective approach.

Preparedness and resilience planning and policy variables are placed into one of three categories: (1) *governance*, (2) *operations*, and (3) *systems. Governance* (doctrine, policy, and guidance) establishes the boundaries within which the public and private sectors must function. *Operations* (Concept of Operations/CONOPS, Standard Operating Procedures/SOP, Operational Plans/OPLANS, and Tactics, Techniques and Procedures) enable the implementation of preparedness policies, bridging across and enabling execution of the adjacent categories. *Systems* (capabilities, prototypes, and visualizations)—the place where business and industry engage the marketplace—allow us to apply technology to the problem at the operational and tactical level.[2]

The strategic imperatives that must be operationalized typically bridge all three areas because systems support operations, and operations support governance in a complementary manner. There is an integrating codependency among all three areas because systems—no matter how capable—can be limited by the authorities, jurisdictions, and boundaries of policy; furthermore, operations not only require proper guidance but can often be impeded or advanced by the quality of available technology and systems. In summary, this framework offers a basic diagram to understand the strategic context of the study and how to organize the research activity into three simple categories. It also provides a starting point to explain the desired outcome of the study.

HISTORICAL BACKGROUND

By way of historical background, the Homeland Security Act of 2002 created the Department of Homeland Security (DHS) and assigned the new department responsibility for leading and coordinating national *critical infrastructure protection* (CIP). Homeland Security Presidential Directive 7 (HSPD-7) further defined CIP roles for DHS and sector-specific agencies (SSAs)—components within DHS and interagency partners—with supporting responsibilities. CIKR protection issues were also addressed in other presidential directives, including HSPD-5, calling for coordination among all elements of government, as well as between the government and the private sector, to manage domestic incidents.

In 2006, the Critical Infrastructure Task Force of the Homeland Security Advisory Council (HSAC) raised the issue that the government's critical infrastructure policies were focused too much on "protecting assets" and not enough on improving *resilience* against a variety of threats. Task force members advocated resilience as the overarching framework to reduce critical infrastructure risk. In 2008, U.S. Congress held numerous hearings to address resilience, and subsequent policy documents placed greater emphasis on resilience as a broad concept. Programs within the DHS and the Federal Emergency Management Agency (FEMA) have since evolved to bring more qualitative and quantitative focus on preparedness and resilience across the public and private sectors (Congressional Research Service [CRS] 2012). Reducing the potential risks associated with the loss of critical infrastructures resulting from a terrorist attack, a natural hazard, or a technological disaster is now a key part of the homeland security strategy and a topic of continued interest in Congress (GAO 2010).

In February 2013, the White House promulgated Presidential Policy Directive 21 (PPD-21): Critical Infrastructure Security and Resilience, a formative policy—issued only three months after Superstorm Sandy—revoking Homeland Security Presidential Directive 7 (HSPD-7). In addition to reducing the number of critical infrastructure sectors from 18 to 16, it directed the establishment of two National Critical Infrastructure Centers under the DHS to improve situational awareness in the areas of physical security and cyber security. It further asserted three strategic imperatives to advance the federal government's focus on critical infrastructure security and resilience:

- Refine and clarify functional relationships across the government to advance the national *unity-of-effort.*
- Enable effective *information exchange* by identifying baseline data and systems requirements for government.
- Implement an *integration and analysis function* to inform planning and operations decisions.

This policy directive places a timely focus on the issue of national preparedness and provides the fundamental guidance and first steps to establish a national framework that helps operationalize functional resilience. The focus on roles and responsibilities of federal departments, expanded engagement by SSAs, and promoting research and development are noteworthy, yet questions remain:

1. Will this PPD close the existing gap between volumes of national-level policy guidance and the local/regional stakeholders who frequently don't see the impact or relevance of top-down guidance?
2. How will these broadly worded tasks be put into use by agencies and departments that are already competing for scarce resources and often lack the ability to add new responsibilities to their current portfolio?

Other strategies and policies that inform this study, some previously mentioned, include the *National Security Strategy (NSS)*; Presidential Policy Directive 8 (PPD-8): National Preparedness; the Department of Homeland Security Strategic Plan for Fiscal Years (FY) 2012–2016; the DHS *National Response Framework (NRF)*; the DHS *National Infrastructure Protection Plan (NIPP)*; Homeland Security Presidential Directive 8 (HSPD-8): National Preparedness Goal (NPG); the DHS annual *National Preparedness Report (NPR)*; DHS/FEMA *Crisis Response and Disaster Resilience 2030*; and the White House's *National Strategy for Physical Protection of CIKR* and *National Strategy for Global Supply Chain Security* (GSCS). Additionally, there are other CIKR-related presidential directives of significance to this study:

- HSPD-3: Homeland Security Advisory System (HSAS)
- HSPD-9: Defense of United States Agriculture and Food
- HSPD-10: Biodefense for the 21st Century
- HSPD-19: Combating Terrorist Use of Explosives in the United States
- HSPD-20: National Continuity Policy
- HSPD-22: Domestic Chemical Defense

The DHS's National Protection and Programs Directorate (NPPD), Office of Infrastructure Protection (OIP) is responsible for working with public- and private-sector CIKR partners in the 16 infrastructure sectors and leads the coordinated national effort to mitigate risk to the nation's CIKR. Its Partnership and Outreach Division works with sector representatives, including asset owners and operators, to develop and sustain strategic relationships and information sharing. Through the Protective Security Coordination Division (PSCD), the NPPD provides all-hazards support to local and state counterparts to:

1. assess vulnerabilities, interdependencies, capabilities, and incident consequences;
2. develop, implement, and provide national coordination for protective programs; and
3. facilitate CIKR response to and recovery from events. PSCD has deployed nearly 100 protective security advisors (PSAs) across the states and territories to serve as links between state, local, tribal, and territorial organizations and DHS/NPPD infrastructure mission partners.

PSAs are also responsible for promoting the Enhanced Critical Infrastructure Protection (ECIP) initiative. Launched in 2007, the ECIP is a voluntary program designed to maintain partnerships between DHS and CIKR owners in high-priority sectors. One of the elements of the ECIP effort is a security survey designed to gather information on the current security posture and awareness of critical assets. In 2010, the vulnerability assessment methodology was revised to enhance standardized data collection and analytical capabilities. DHS has also developed the Regional Resiliency Assessment Program (RRAP) to assess the risks associated with resiliency. An examination of infrastructure "clusters," regions, and systems in major metropolitan areas, RRAP uses security surveys and vulnerability assessments in its analysis (GAO 2012).

The National Infrastructure Simulation and Analysis Center (NISAC) is a modeling, simulation, and analysis program within DHS, comprised of personnel in Washington, D.C., as well as at Sandia National Laboratories (SNL) and Los Alamos National Laboratory (LANL). Congress mandated that NISAC serve as a "source of national expertise to address critical infrastructure protection" research and analysis. NISAC prepares and shares analyses of critical infrastructure sectors, including their interdependencies, vulnerabilities, consequences, and other complexities, under the direction of the Office of Infrastructure Protection.

Across the nation, state fusion centers provide a location for cross-agency representatives to build all-hazards resilience functions at a local and regional level. Where the culture among government councils and policy working groups is more political in nature and more likely to focus on issues of governance and funding, fusion centers have a functional focus that aligns with building resilience through horizontal coordination and organizational relationships. Fusion centers also have the potential of becoming a regional hub of functional resilience because of their information-sharing capabilities across networks, leveraging the advantages of local and regional cooperation (NIAC 2009; DomPrep 2012, 23–24; GAO 2012).

Figure 3.2 Resilience "Tree"

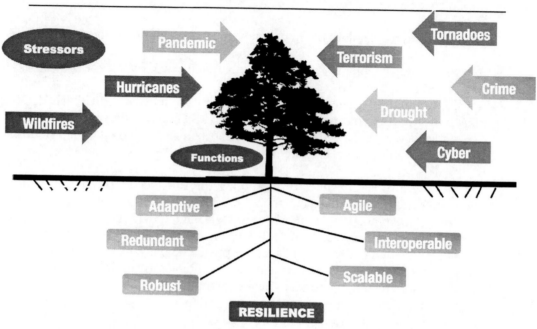

Functional Resilience Forces

Source: Egli 2013.

RESILIENCE

The trees that stand the longest and strongest are those with the deepest roots firmly set in a solid foundation. The critical functions that our society depends so heavily upon are like a tree with essential "functions" to perform, blown side to side and battered by an array of stressors: pandemics, hurricanes, fires, flooding, tornadoes, terrorist attacks, droughts, and cyber crises.

In the past, many of our infrastructure trees have been quickly uprooted by these stressors. Different industrial branches, critical parts of our infrastructure, have been broken off in these storms, slow to regrow and to return to their critical functions. However, if the tree is firmly rooted in resilience it is able to bend, withstand external disasters, and flex, but not break, under the pressures of external stressors.

Resilience, and its supporting offshoots—adaptive, redundant, robust, rapid, interoperable, and scalable systems—provide the necessary support to ensure that the tree can face the impact of various storms. Yet, if the winds are strong enough, roots can still be torn out of even the most fertile ground. That is why it is vital that the roots have a strong, durable underpinning to cling to and draws strength from the roots of adjacent trees with collective support to face disasters. The bedrock for resilience is the pillars of national preparedness: prevent, protect, mitigate, respond, and recover. These principle themes focus on national preparedness beyond reactionary responses. A root of resilience that finds its strength in the soil of national preparedness allows the tree (and its critical functions) to withstand the impact of unpredictable and complex storms (Figure 3.2).

Resilience is defined by the DHS as "the ability to resist, absorb, recover from, or successfully adapt to adversity or a change in conditions" (DHS 2009). The traditional approach to securing CIP networks focuses on protecting physical systems; however, the reality is that we can only reduce vulnerabilities rather than completely eliminate them. So, given the inevitability of natural disasters and terrorist attacks, this study makes the case for improved risk management long-term mitigation, and deeper examination of critical infrastructure resilience.

When physical infrastructures are damaged by any disaster, the goal is to minimize the disruption and resume operations as soon as possible, striving to maintain continuity of critical services. A strategy of community resilience seeks to manage risks by building the skills and capabilities to do three things:

1. maintain continuity of function in the face of chronic disturbances;
2. develop the means for gradual degradation of function when placed under severe stress; and
3. sustain the ability to "quickly recover to a desired level of functionality when extreme events overwhelm mitigation measures."

In this way, the ultimate goal of resilience is to maintain the greatest amount of normalcy in critical sectors and services despite one or more threats or incidents (Flynn and Burke 2012).

Resilience requires mobilizing of human potential, especially at the level of the individual citizen, community, and local government. Success is measured by incentivizing the participation of the private sector, creating collaborative relationships, and leveraging the role of *regional* organizations. Community resilience involves *local* capacity-building and shortening the time period of response and recovery to disasters. Conferences, workshops, and surveys highlight that *state* governments and local jurisdictions can best leverage increasingly scarce resources for disaster management through horizontal collaboration networks at the *intrastate* and regional levels. While national policy guidance is an important source of strategic direction that informs regional efforts, it usually offers mandates with a top-down approach that may or may not be accompanied by funding resources.[3] Recent national-level research indicates that community resilience can be achieved best through bottom-up efforts by local and regional agencies, informed and resourced appropriately by national programs (DomPrep 2012). Private nonprofit organizations such as the All-Hazards Consortium on the Mid-Atlantic East Coast offer an example of successful regional efforts that have emerged across the country.

This study attempts to distill the lessons learned and the major CIKR themes that have emerged since 2001. It is meant to serve as a catalyst to change how we think about preparedness and disaster management by shifting from a rigid focus on physical protection and continuity to a continuum of options that fits the unique requirements of the sector through functional resilience. Many traditional engineers, environmentalists, bureaucratic planners, and public policy experts may feel uneasy because this approach is a change that cannot be scripted or mandated for every situation; rather, it must be adapted through a more inclusive style with interagency coordination and public-private unions—"rolling with the waves, instead of trying to stop the ocean" (Zolli 2012).

Another objective of this study is to forge a consensus among students, practitioners, planners, and decision makers at local, state, regional, and national levels to transform our thinking from "guarding the fortress" of critical infrastructure protection to a strategic posture of functional resilience. In a post-9/11 world, with its asymmetric threat environment and stressful disasters (including Hurricanes Katrina, Irene, and Sandy, as well as unprecedented seasons of tornadoes, flash floods, wildfires, and domestic killings), society is already vulnerable, and people are deeply affected by disruptions—physically, environmentally, financially, and technologically. The nation needs economical, practical, and near-term, if imperfect, innovations that provide a tolerance for uncertainty and experimentation: testing, failing, adapting, training, learning, and growing; reminding ourselves that disruptions are to be expected and things will go wrong, often when we least expect it. This involves living in a culture of preparedness that integrates resilient thinking into all activities—an active virtue that informs everything we do (Homeland Security Council 2007; NIAC 2009, 2010; Zolli and Healy 2012).

Resilience does not envision a homogeneous, well-defined future; rather, it takes the realistic view that change and complexity are a given. Informed by history and humbled by the post–Cold War reality of dispersed and uncertain threats, it assumes we cannot divine exactly how things will unfold; it accepts that we *will* be surprised. And risk is less an equation to be calculated numerically, and more the recognition that mistakes *will* be made, and we should devote more energy and resources to learning how best to respond to and recover from those inevitable failures—"falling forward"[4] to learn the lessons of resilient thinking (National Academies 2012; NIAC 2012b; Zolli 2012).

The study reveals both fragmented policy implementation and the existence of natural tensions among resilience stakeholders (local, regional, state, and federal levels), which further aggravate the challenge of coordinating efforts across the homeland security enterprise. Against the backdrop of this reality and growing security imperatives, the following sections offer the most significant outcomes through research findings (Chapter 7) and recommendations (Chapter 8) to improve resilience across facility-level (Brashear and Jones 2010), organizational-level (Crichton, Ramsay, and Kelly 2009), and community-level (Norris et al. 2008; Stewart, Kolluru, and Smith 2009; NRC 2011) constructs.

This is not solely an academic study to investigate the various origins of resilience, nor does it an attempt to fully analyze the wider body of literature. Disaster management and emergency response seldom conform to the orderly constructs of business continuity, mission assurance, and physical security. While it is important to understand the existing views of resilience as outlined in these chapters and where this effort falls within the public policy literature, the thesis of the text is that we, as a society, must look *beyond*

Figure 3.3 Sixteen Critical Infrastructure Sectors

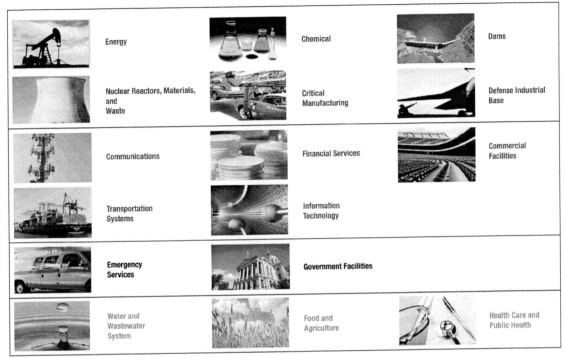

Source: Images from the U.S. Dept. of Homeland Security, http://www.dhs.gov/critical-infrastructure.

the constructs offered to date. There is an urgent need to transform our policies and plans to match the complex and uncertain nature of the future crises—crossing the traditional preparedness boundaries with a flexible, adaptive, holistic approach. Furthermore, the hypothesis of this study—and the supporting exploratory research—is that collective action approaches have the potential to build personal-, facility-, organizational-, and systems-level preparedness in a cumulative manner. Increased levels of community resilience can be achieved if we view resilience as a public good in the broader national and homeland security context.

CRITICAL INFRASTRUCTURE PROTECTION

Critical infrastructure comprises the key resources—structures, facilities, and systems—required for the basic services and functions to sustain daily life across all domains. The government defines critical infrastructure sectors (Figure 3.3), each governed and supported independently and each at different life cycle stages or levels of maintenance.[5] Some systems are mature legacy systems (power, water, transportation); others are continuously emerging and transforming (information technology, banking, and financial). There are five sectors often viewed as "lifeline infrastructures" because of their enabling role with all human and physical activity in society: energy, communications, transportation, finances and water—all in need of modernization to support the changing needs of our growing population[6] (Gerencser 2011).

The traditional approach to infrastructure protection and reducing risks to essential services—especially following the attacks of 9/11—has emphasized countering the threats of attack by attempting to predict the greatest risks and assembling a layered network, a defense-in-depth, to identify, deter, and defeat that threat as early and as far from American borders as possible (The White House 2005, 2006). While this is an important role for the intelligence community and security/defense forces to continue, especially when it comes to protecting the most vital national assets, such an approach has its limitations in achieving overall national preparedness.

We need a transformation in CIP and sustainment of services that integrates resilience, as an active virtue, into all services and functions; thus, we need to be *moving beyond physical protection to an increased focus on flexibility, agility, and dynamic preparedness*. Research indicates that the majority of national infrastructure and key resources are owned and operated by the private sector; therefore, any comprehensive framework for a national solution must involve a principal focus on sharing of non-classified information in the context of public-private partnerships in order to foster a whole-community approach.

Moving beyond the *protection* of critical infrastructures, we propose the *systemic investment* in infrastructure based upon resilience criteria. While infrastructure protection must continue with a focus on acute vulnerabilities in order to anticipate future disasters and attacks, complete protection or perfect security can never be achieved; it is impossible to anticipate all hazards and economically impractical to protect all infrastructures. Innovations needed to overcome deeply entrenched habits (including congressional spending on members' pork barrel projects through the authorization and appropriations process) will require strong leadership that places a new focus on the state of homeland security and community resilience.

Critical infrastructures must be further studied and understood as an interconnected and interdependent system-of-systems architecture. We must examine the future implications of demographics, global supply chains, climate change, and homeland security imperatives so that we can expand on current methods. Trying to defend ourselves against every possible disaster—using intelligence-based predictions to protect our infrastructures—is physically impossible and economically exhausting (Cooper-Ramo 2009).

While the nation hardens and protects vital assets to ensure national defense and continuity of government, it would benefit from an expanded commitment to investments in aging and eroding infrastructure through functional resilience and preparedness. Placing CIP as a subset under a broad resilience umbrella will require a new emphasis that unifies Americans in a collective effort that is part of a global economy, yet driven by local realities. In the end, government alone cannot make the nation fully resilient. It is a collective process that must include—and ideally start with—each individual and family at home.

ALL-HAZARDS APPROACH

According to PPD-21: Critical Infrastructure Security and Resilience, the term *all-hazards* means "a threat or an incident, natural or manmade, that warrants action to protect life, property, the environment, public health or safety; and to minimize disruptions of government, social, or economic activities. It includes natural disasters, cyber incidents, industrial accidents, pandemics, acts of terrorism, sabotage, and destructive criminal activity targeting critical infrastructure" (The White House [PPD-21] 2013b).

Beyond the policy definition, an all-hazards approach informs all aspects of prevention, protection, mitigation, response, and recovery activities because it addresses the full range of threats and hazards, including domestic terrorist attacks, natural and human-made disasters, accidental disruptions, and other emergencies. An all-hazards perspective to preparedness also provides homeland security planners and disaster managers at the national, regional, state, tribal, and local levels with a comprehensive taxonomy that considers all possible risks.

The guiding documents promulgated by the Department of Homeland Security and agencies within the department (FEMA, TSA, USCG, CBP, etc.) incorporate an all-hazards approach that crosses all threat domains (physical, human, and cyber) and geographic domains (air, land, maritime, and space) to ensure a comprehensive approach to planning and execution of national-level strategies. All-hazards disaster management and emergency preparedness efforts ambitiously seek to prepare all sectors of American society—business, industry and nonprofit; state, territorial, local, and tribal governments; and the general public—for all disasters the nation might face.

Long before the events of September 11, 2001, terrorism preparedness was included in FEMA's planning efforts. Since the 9/11 attacks, the increased focus and funding for national security has emphasized preparedness for terrorist attacks and infrastructure protection. However, the nation's recent experience with large-scale natural disasters, including wildfires, droughts, tornadoes, hurricanes, and flash floods—underscores the importance of taking an all-hazards approach that considers the risks of natural and accidental disasters, as well as terrorism.

Consistent with this approach, two Homeland Security Presidential Directives (HSPDs) issued in 2003 required DHS to take an all-hazards focus in implementing the directives. HSPD-5 tasked DHS to establish a single, comprehensive approach to the management of emergency events, whether the result of terrorist attacks or large-scale natural disasters. In addition, HSPD-8 required DHS to coordinate the development of a national domestic all-hazards preparedness goal, establishing measurable readiness priorities that balance the potential threat of terrorist attacks and large-scale natural disasters with the resources required to prevent, respond to, and recover from them. The directive also designated the Secretary of Homeland Security as the principal federal official for coordinating the implementation of "all-hazards preparedness" in the United States.

Whole-of-Nation Theme

A whole-of-nation theme reflects the post-9/11 reality that in order to prevent, protect, mitigate, respond, and recover in an asymmetric threat environment, the community must draw upon the collective actions of all levels of the public and private sectors. An effective whole-of-nation approach requires significant cooperation among a diverse set of sometimes-reluctant government bureaucracies. Furthermore, it involves cooperation from the defense community and civilian agencies sharing information from the intelligence community and domestic law enforcement agencies as permitted by law. It also requires close coordination among federal, state, and local governments and relies greatly upon the private and commercial sector.[7]

The Presidential Policy Directives on National Preparedness (PPD-8) and Critical Infrastructure Security and Resilience (PPD-21) require more than mere administrative action by the federal government to facilitate "an integrated, all-of-nation, capabilities-based approach to preparedness" (The White House 2011, 2013b). To achieve this goal, DHS and FEMA are incorporating a "whole community approach to build and sustain preparedness nationwide." FEMA defined it as "a means by which residents, emergency management practitioners, organizational and community leaders, and government officials can collectively understand and assess the needs of their respective communities and determine the best ways to organize and strengthen their assets, capacities, and interests" (FEMA 2011, 3–5).

FEMA has promulgated three guiding principles:

- Understand and meet the actual needs of the whole community.
- Engage and empower all parts of the community.
- Strengthen what works well in communities on a daily basis.

And from these broad principles, FEMA offers six strategic themes in pursuing a whole community approach:

- Understand community complexity.
- Recognize community capabilities and needs.
- Foster relationships with community leaders.
- Build and maintain partnerships.
- Empower local action.
- Leverage and strengthen social infrastructure, networks, and assets.

As FEMA Administrator Craig Fugate testified, "Government can and will continue to serve disaster survivors. However, we fully recognize that a government-centric approach to disaster management will not be enough to meet the challenges posed by a catastrophic incident. That is why we must fully engage our entire societal capacity." To this end, the current "whole community approach attempts to engage the full capacity of the private and nonprofit sectors . . . in an effort to improve the ability of local residents to prevent, protect against, mitigate, respond to, and recover from any type of threat or hazard" (FEMA 2011, 2–3).

In 2012, policymakers expanded this concept to a more inclusive "whole-of-nation" approach, building on "whole community" to include all members of the public and private sectors. Beyond merely engaging other elements of the interagency in the mission of infrastructure protection, a whole-of-nation approach maximizes the potential of all private citizens and organizations to advance the preparedness process.

CROSS-DOMAIN SOLUTIONS

Cross-domain solutions may relate to enterprise services or research in the systems engineering world, but it is also an important theme in homeland security because strategies in the public and private sectors must be integrated across air, land, maritime, space, and cyber domains. And within critical infrastructure resilience, strategies span across the physical, human, and cyber domains, making it a serious cross-domain challenge. Therefore, homeland security planners at the strategic, operational, or tactical levels must approach policy formulation and execution with a cross-domain mind-set that recognizes all sectors and missions, as well as all security classification levels (nonclassified to highly classified).

Homeland security policies and doctrine require a cross-domain approach as policymakers and operational agencies attempt to respond to an asymmetric threat environment with limited resources and capacity to fulfill their missions. As homeland security leaders attempt to reconcile the requirements of the maritime domain, aviation security imperatives, border security gaps, national transportation systems, and global supply chains, it is clear—especially looking through the lens of transnational criminal and terrorist threats—that All-Domain Awareness (ADA) is needed across all operating agencies. Threats, disasters, and cyber attacks are not limited to, nor do they respect, any particular domain or budget category; therefore, interagency planners must take a cross-domain, as well as a whole-of-nation, all-hazards approach. Furthermore, cross-domain strategies require the integration and collaboration of actors across geographic, physical, political, and economic boundaries, and underscore the importance of coordinated efforts within joint, interagency, multinational, academic and private sectors.

Real-world examples of cross-domain challenges exist within the homeland security enterprise; some examples include counterterrorism, counter-narcotics, counter-weapons of mass destruction (WMD), terrorist financing, transnational crime, identity management, maritime transportation security, emergency response, and disaster management. These threats or challenges emerge against the backdrop of an asymmetric, interconnected, and interdependent environment and are best addressed with a similar interconnected approach, which requires collective action, interagency coordination, and cross-domain strategies. For example, America's southwest border with Mexico, including land, air, cyber, and maritime challenges, as well as a complex mix of diplomatic, economic, safety, and security, issues, provides a poignant example of a region—and a significant homeland security challenge—that requires a whole-of-nation, all-hazards, multi-threat approach enabled by cross-domain solutions.

GLOBALIZED ECONOMY AND SUPPLY CHAINS

As we progress in the twenty-first century, the world is growing "smaller" while the potential for global disruptions caused by local failures or incidents is expanding. The scale of economic impacts from natural disasters, attacks, and failure of critical infrastructure has broadened as global markets become more interdependent and less localized. This reality places increased importance on the task of improving critical infrastructure resilience in the face of uncertainty to mitigate the adverse impact of disruptive events on global supply chains.

The collapse of critical infrastructure in the wake of Japan's earthquake and tsunami in 2011 highlights the potential impact on global markets due to supply-chain disruptions after a disaster occurs within a nation that distributes critical technologies. Widespread power outages and damage in Japan resulted in disruptions to factory production around the world, including automotive manufacturers and computer firms in the United States. With the potential ripple effect from local disasters growing indefinitely as the economy becomes more globalized and interdependent, we must think and plan more resiliently than ever.

The consequences of supply-chain disruptions are amplified by the interconnected globalized economy and the rapid spread of technology. For example, expanded use of broadband networks, fiber optics, and digital technologies has accelerated the growth of Internet users who can access social media and web-based markets, allowing international participation in the global economy to grow rapidly.

As reflected in the supporting research—particularly the case studies in Appendix A—it is important to understand the interconnected, simultaneously operating, and interdependent nature of the system-of-systems architectures that operate inside the global supply chain. In order to fully understand the cascading impact that a single event can trigger and the cross-modal operational and economic ripple effect that can be imposed by an isolated disaster, one must recognize the extent to which the infrastructure sectors are dependent on one another. As pointed out throughout this study, the interconnected nature of global supply chains, as well as physical and cyber infrastructures—while yielding greater speed and efficiencies—results in more acute vulnerabilities and single points of failure that can cause equally rapid and interconnected catastrophic failures.

The modern supply chain is uniquely vulnerable because "the very characteristics that strengthen the supply chain in most situations expose it to greater risk of catastrophic collapse" (Regional Catastrophic Preparedness Grant Program [RCPGP] 2012). According to supply-chain experts, "A supply chain is both a network and a system." It is clear that asymmetric forces have an impact on supply chains, requiring constant change and adaptation to function, but disruptive events can "throw the system off balance." The attributes of critical infrastructure resilience that might enable the supply chain to adjust and dynamically respond to meet the challenges when shaken by internal or external factors are examined in this study. (Skjøtt-Larsen et al. 2007; RCPGP 2012).

As described in the upcoming "Cyber Security" section, events that cause business slowdowns are often difficult to detect and can have an adverse impact on domestic or global supply chains; other more public and well-publicized events can also have a crippling impact on the same supply-chain systems. For example, the union worker strikes in the Ports of Los Angeles/Long Beach (White 2012) had a major economic impact because when containers stopped moving, it caused a cascading ripple effect across the domestic supply chain (also refer to Appendix A, Figure A.3). No physical infrastructure was destroyed; no cyber attack took place; no terrorist attack or natural disaster occurred. It was union dockworkers who refused to cross picket lines during the clerical workers' strike that stopped the flow of vessel traffic and shipping containers. This example, like other commercial trade or transportation incidents—airline industry labor strikes, regional snowstorms causing trucking congestion, or a dirty-bomb exploding in an urban area—disrupted public transportation and the flow of commerce for days, even weeks, and caused a supply-chain problem that affected the flow of people and commodities (Orosz 2012).

Similarly, in the aftermath of Hurricane Sandy, the closure of airports servicing New York City (John F. Kennedy, LaGuardia, and Newark International airports) and the northeastern United States caused a global disruption in transportation for thousands of people who were stranded in airports all over the world. Flight cancellations and closures caused rerouting of passenger traffic that had an impact on international activity such as business meetings, professional conferences, and aviation cargo transport. The Port Authority of New York and New Jersey (PANYNJ) rebounded quickly from the winds, rain, floods, and storm surge due to their rapid response, significant external assistance, and a resilient approach that had been reinforced by years of training and exercises. PANYNJ reopened five days after the storm made landfall. In lieu of grand strategies and supply-chain master plans, these examples point to the need to "enable greater self-reliance, cooperation, and creativity before, during, and after a crisis" (Zolli 2012).

During the research phase of this study—especially the expert interviews and case studies—it became clear that students, policymakers, and even senior decision makers are often unaware of the degree to which domestic and global supply chains are vital ligaments of the U.S. economy and are highly interdependent. These fragile connections are due to an overdependence upon advanced technologies and networks such as global positioning systems (GPS), internationally supplied medical resources (special vaccines), and just-in-time delivery of critical equipment and hardware (i.e., electric power transformers) (Orosz 2012). The case studies in Appendix A support this study and future research by students, planners, and policymakers seeking to understand preparedness and resilience, particularly supply chains and the cascading economic impact caused by disasters.

CYBER SECURITY

Research and interviews conducted throughout this project revealed the major importance of cyber security as an integral part of maximizing critical infrastructure resilience. Cyber challenges appear in the major findings (Chapter 7, Section 7.16) and recommendations (Chapter 8) of the text. Recent events confirm that, due to the proliferation of technology and Internet access, issues of vulnerability in the cyber domain impact all 16 infrastructure sectors. The rapid growth of information technology over the past two decades has resulted in capability gaps in our cyber-physical security infrastructure, leaving public and private networks exposed to attacks, even by amateur hackers. Policy, legislation, and congressional budgets also reflect the importance of cyber security because it touches all infrastructures in an interconnected and complex environment that is widely misunderstood. While acknowledging the important role cyber security—and its designation as one of the security domains along with land, air, maritime, and space—plays in national preparedness, this report focuses primarily upon requirements to advance national-level policies in support of critical infrastructure resilience and will address cyber-security issues as they intersect this broader imperative.

President Obama (2012) has declared that the "cyber threat is one of the most serious economic and national security challenges we face as a nation" and "America's economic prosperity in the 21st century will depend on cyber security." He published an opinion piece in the *Wall Street Journal* emphasizing the importance of "taking the cyber-attack threat seriously" and pursuing best practices to harden the networks of vital business, manufacturing, and critical infrastructure networks. "In a future conflict," the President writes, "an adversary unable to match our military supremacy on the battlefield might seek to exploit our computer vulnerabilities here at home" and target critical infrastructures and national capabilities (Obama 2012). The *Washington Post* also reported on vulnerabilities to industrial control systems given that computers controlling critical infrastructures (including water, power, banking, transportation, nuclear reactors, and dams) are even more exposed than previously realized (O'Harrow 2012a). Furthermore, Executive Order 13636: Improving Critical Infrastructure Cybersecurity, was issued in February 2013 in response to repeated cyber intrusions into critical infrastructure systems; the primary goal was to expand information sharing with the private sector (White House 2013a).

National infrastructures such as the power grid, telecommunications systems, water sources, and transportation networks, with various levels of redundancies and backup capabilities, provide critical services and increasingly depend upon interconnected computer systems. Components fail, accidents occur, and sabotage can happen, leading to significant degradation of the physical and economic security. From a cyber-security perspective, several factors compound the problem (Lukasik, Goodman, and Longhurst 2003):

- While the probability of random events can be calculated, nefarious acts are not random because they are the result of analysis and planning by hackers to target system vulnerabilities, and are therefore more difficult to predict.
- Integrating infrastructure sectors to improve efficiency yields greater vulnerability to cyber attacks by providing potential access points where attackers can more easily trigger large-scale damage. While interdependencies can make a system more robust and efficient, that same complexity can also allow attackers to inflict cascading casualties across that same interconnected system.
- Market pressures to streamline costs and improve supply-chain management have created greater interfaces and access points for intruders to enter; the cumulative effect of specialization, outsourcing, and regulation have complicated the ability to protect infrastructures, thereby exposing computer networks.

Our daily life, economic vitality, and homeland security rely upon a stable, safe, and resilient cyberspace, and we depend on a wide range of networks to support government activities, communicate and travel, power our homes, run our banking systems, and provide vital military services. Yet cyber attacks and disruptions have increased significantly over the last decade, exposing sensitive personal, business, and security information; disrupting critical market and supply-chain operations; and imposing high costs on a struggling economy (DHS 2012a). In response to this growing threat, cyber-security standards have been developed to safeguard computer activities, databases, and critical information in Supervisory Control and Data Acquisition (SCADA) systems and to prevent identity theft. Sensitive data are now frequently stored on computers connected to the Internet, and many tasks that were once accomplished manually are now carried out by computer; therefore, the need for information assurance (IA) and cyber security are growing. While using SCADA systems resulted in greater efficiencies, the associated interdependencies and technologies have had the cumulative impact of eroding, not supporting, functional resilience (Zolli 2012).

Cyber security is involved in all of the elements of critical infrastructure resilience. Cyber security is also a common thread running through all the case studies and policy analysis because it is the backbone of the networks that support functional resilience. During this study, it was also surprising to observe the degree to which policymakers, planners, and decision makers failed to realize how dependent their personal and organizational activities, are upon cyber command and control, SCADA system protection, and fundamental information assurance. The case studies cover domestic and international scenarios going back to 2011, and they highlight the ubiquitous nature of cyber security because it supports physical and virtual infrastructure worlds. Events such as power outages, WikiLeaks scandals, financial market disruptions, regional cellular phone outages, and corruption of GPS signals reveal that cyber issues can be the genesis of what eventually becomes—and manifests itself in different systems and capabilities as—a physical infrastructure problem. Cyber security and CIKR resiliency are inextricably linked—for better or for worse (Orosz 2012).

Private-sector businesses require cyber security in order to protect their trade secrets, proprietary information, and personally identifiable information of their customers or employees. Cyber-security standards enable organizations to practice safe security practices to minimize the frequency and impact of cyber-security attacks. These protocols provide general guidance as well as specific methods to implement cyber security. For certain standards, cyber-security certification by an accredited body is available, and there are many advantages to obtaining certification, including the ability to obtain cyber-security insurance (Pfleeger and Pfleeger 2006).

Creating more resilient infrastructures and supply chains will require a deeper understanding of *nonphysical* and *off-premise* cyber factors among security personnel, business leaders, policy planners, and senior decision makers: Cyber vulnerabilities are embedded inside the virtual and invisible layers of our command and control systems and information networks, and anyone with the right device, basic knowledge of computer systems, and the time to explore vulnerabilities can find multiple methods to exploit or disrupt unsuspecting networks. Sobering reports routinely surface in the media, which should be a wake-up call to all computer or SCADA system users, including those on botnets.[8] Another example appeared in an article describing what all amateur computer hackers can do through iPhone PowerPoint software: by simply inserting corrupted data in a photo's code to disrupt the software, a computer can subsequently crash, opening the way for it to be hijacked (O'Harrow 2012a).

Computer hackers can cause intentional or unintentional disruptions to homeland security systems with a cascading impact across civil society through low-cost actions. The civil GPS case study (Figure A.8) highlights one such cyber vulnerability. This particular weakness represents an acute point of failure because all infrastructures rely directly or indirectly upon an accurate and reliable GPS signal, which includes position, navigation, and timing inputs. There are other scenarios in which GPS service continues with a strong signal strength—although being spoofed—and users in sectors such as power, transportation, communications, utilities, financial, agriculture, and water supply continue to use the GPS information, unaware that it is providing erroneous outputs with potentially dangerous impact.

Similarly, cyber hackers can cause business slowdowns that are difficult to detect, report, or mitigate. A *slowdown* differs from other disasters because the system continues to operate at a degraded level. The discrepancy may go unreported for a significant period of time, unlike shutdowns or termination of services that trigger rapid corrective action by alternative resources to pick up the slack in output or productivity through redundant. Much harm could be done to the domestic supply chain and regional economy by simply causing a business slowdown that goes undetected in a major maritime shipping port. For example, if a computer hacker accessed the scheduling system at one or two shipping terminals at the Ports of Los Angeles/Long Beach (POLALB) and introduced a bug that caused every tenth container to be routed to the wrong destination, it would cause an immediate regional commerce slowdown. And with current business practices, it might take weeks before the problem could be diagnosed and the source of the discrepancy discovered and remedied. In the meantime, misdirected containers must be rerouted and destinations of all containers moving through the port (past and present) would be double-checked—requiring additional personnel, time, and expenses (Orosz 2012).

U.S. planners have learned much from the efforts of international partners in developing cyber-security solutions. For example, the Australian Defence Signals Directorate (DSD) won the 2011 U.S. National Cybersecurity Innovation Award for its accomplishment in instituting four fundamental security controls that stop the spread of infection from targeted cyber intrusions (SANS Institute 2011). These controls

- use application whitelisting to help prevent malicious software and other unapproved programs from running;
- patch applications such as PDF readers, Microsoft Office, Java, Flash Player and web browsers;
- patch operating system vulnerabilities; and
- minimize the number of users with administrative privileges.

With limited budgets and shortages of skilled workers, the Australians conducted a comprehensive study of all known targeted intrusions against government systems—both military and civilian—to determine what would have stopped the cyber infections from spreading. They found that 35 controls would be valuable and additional risk reduction may be gained by taking all 35 measures; however, the aforementioned four controls must be done *first*—across all organizations—in order to leverage the benefit of other actions to defend against targeted intrusions. At least 85 percent of the intrusions that DSD responded to in 2011 involved adversaries using unsophisticated techniques that would have been mitigated by these four strategies as a package. Although such controls will not stop the most sophisticated attackers, they have proven highly effective against the majority of information loss across government agencies that have instituted the measures systematically. As U.S. cyber-security officials have emphasized, no single strategy can prevent malicious activity, but the effectiveness of implementing these strategies in concert with other best practices remains very high (SANS Institute 2011).

These examples are prescient reminders for all planners and policymakers that we must improve our understanding of cyber-security issues in the modern digital world if we intend to strengthen homeland security and preparedness through smart resiliency.

INCIDENT PUBLIC-PREPAREDNESS SCALE

The incident public-preparedness scale offers a disaster management graphic to show the interconnected nature of larger scale events (as they escalate from local to national), and how coordination complexity varies by type of event (ranging from minor local incidents, to regional natural disasters, state-level emergencies, and major national-level homeland security events). Figure 3.4 lists different types of emergency management

Figure 3.4 Incident Public-Prepardness Scale

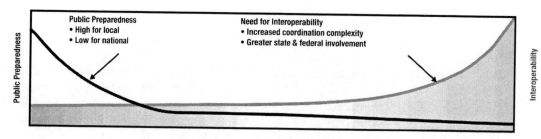

Coordination Level	Local	Regional	State		National
Examples	• Minor traffic incidents • Vehicle fires • Minor train/bus accidents • Accidents with injuries but no fatalities	• Train derailment • Major bus/rail transit accidents • Major truck accidents • Multi-vehicle crashes • Hazmat spills • Injuries & fatalities	• Train crashes • Airplane crashes • Hazmat incidents • Multi-vehicle • Tunnel fires • Multiple injuries & fatalities	• Port/airport incidents • Large building fire explosion • Industrial incidents • Major tunnel/ bridge closure	• Terrorist attack/WMD • Floods, blizzards, tornadoes • Transportation infrastructure collapse • Extended power/water outage • Riots • Mass casualties
Expected Time Duration	0–2 Hours	2–24 Hours	Days		Weeks

Source: Contestabile, *Concepts on Information Sharing and Interoperability,* 2011.

Notes: The Incident Public-Preparedness Scale graphic and concept was developed in conjunction with a DHS/ FEMA Urban Area Security Initiative (UASI) grant to the National Capital Region (NCR). Points of view or opinions expressed in this graphic are those of the author and do not necessarily represent the official position or policies of DHS or FEMA. In addition, this graphic was presented at the Institute of Electrical and Electronics Engineers (IEEE) Conference on Homeland Security Technology, 2011, as "Information Sharing for Situational Understanding and Command Coordination in Emergency Management and Disaster Response" by Robert I. Desourdis, Jr., and John M. Contestabile and is copyrighted to IEEE.

events and the increasing complexity that can emerge from each. Another variable along the continuum is *time,* as the incident scale can escalate with the duration of the event. Viewing incidents at local, regional, state, and national levels recognizes that the complexities—and the resulting degree of coordination across various agencies/ jurisdictions—increase when moving from left to right (local to national). These players must come together, coordinate, and adapt quickly as events occur, escalate, and impose cascading impacts across infrastructure sectors.

There is also a vertical scale that points to the level of public preparedness normally in place. For example, the number of first responders involved and the percentage of the public affected by a *local* incident is relatively small, while the preparedness level is high because these are incidents that are routinely encountered. The scene of the incident is usually cleared in less than two hours, the disruption to the public and to systems is minimal, and only rarely is there a cascading impact on adjacent infrastructure sectors.

Some events can rapidly grow into something more significant than initially expected. For example, if an accident involved a vehicle that was carrying illegal narcotics, or if another vehicle involved in the accident were transporting hazardous waste that was spilled, it would require the involvement of more units and agencies. This would cause the scale to become a *regional* incident and take a longer period of time to resolve (2 to 24 hours). And if this event occurred during a high-traffic period and caused roadway congestion, motorists would likely seek alternative routes via surrounding highways, thereby having an impact on local transportation.

Some events expand into a *statewide* span of control while others start immediately as a state concern. The threat of a hurricane or tornado would normally start as a statewide threat, take place over a period of days, impact overlapping local, regional, and state systems, and require activation of Emergency Operations Centers (EOCs). More agencies are involved as the complexity increases, requiring greater coordination, information sharing, and perhaps the state governor to activate the National Guard to supplement local and regional resources.

Finally, some events are classified as *national incidents* because they grow into a national disaster (disease epidemics, pandemics, wildfires, major flooding) or are so catastrophic—as 9/11 was—that the president immediately declares it a national disaster or homeland defense event. The impact of this type of event extends across multiple infrastructure sectors and may touch multiple domains (air, land, sea, and cyber). Hurricane Katrina was considered a national-level event because it affected interstate commerce and the entire nation absorbed refugee populations from the Gulf Coast region.

Supply-chain interruptions associated with large-scale events can extend for months and spread into geographic areas far beyond those states immediately involved. Events of this magnitude may require a federal disaster declaration, triggering FEMA participation, activation of the Stafford Act, and potential support from the National Guard Bureau (NGB) or Title-10 military forces coordinated through the combatant commander for the homeland (USNORTHCOM). If the disaster has a terrorism nexus, the Federal Bureau of Investigations (FBI), elements of the Department of Homeland Security (DHS), and the intelligence community would also be involved.

An important lesson from this section is that catastrophic events require a multi-jurisdictional, multidiscipline, interagency, cooperative response. While this increases coordination complexity and the need for more information sharing and joint planning, it is essential to mission success (Contestabile 2011).

Parallels to Unrestricted Warfare

We must take an asymmetric approach to homeland security that includes an innovative attitude toward disaster management and community resilience. In the Vietnam conflict, U.S. military planners had conceptual problems adjusting their understanding of warfare to the realities of combat in Southeast Asia (Petraeus 1987). The well-documented dichotomy between the unconventional tactics of our enemies and America's top-down propensity to conduct conventional large-scale operations cannot be repeated in the execution of twenty-first-century missions of homeland defense and homeland security.

As highlighted by recent disasters—among them the destruction brought about by Superstorm Sandy in the fall of 2012, or the horrific school shooting that same year in Newtown, Connecticut, or incidents of domestic terrorism such as the 2013 Boston Marathon bombings—disaster management and national preparedness do not lend themselves to binary risk calculations; rather, they are part of a complex and ambiguous process that evokes the *joint* action of local, state, and federal actors across the public and private sectors. This alliance should result in a new approach to preparedness with a focus on response and recovery that aggregates the collective action of politicians, emergency planners, and local and regional leaders, yet still reflects the diverse goals of each stakeholder. This section attempts to link the lessons of modern irregular or unrestricted warfare (UW) with the imperatives of critical infrastructure resilience, suggesting an ontology that can help close policy gaps and operationalize preparedness strategies in the homeland.

In 2007, the Johns Hopkins University Applied Physics Laboratory hosted a symposium on UW that examined the unconventional, asymmetric, and irregular nature of the twenty-first-century security environment, drawing from a wide range of experience in the academic, military, intelligence, and commercial worlds. The findings of this event offer a useful comparison to the innovative thinking that must be applied to the complex and uncertain field of infrastructure protection as well as the broader areas of national preparedness and resilience. The following observations from these deliberations provide further background for this study, because the future of resiliency efforts (strategy, policy, analysis, technology) can benefit from those who have studied conflict and faced the same operational challenges and asymmetric environment in which we study resilience (Luman 2007).

- National preparedness, like UW, requires a unique ability to deal with complexity and uncertainty.

When considering the adversarial nature of UW, it employs small, well-organized units that draw from unity-of-effort more than unity-of-command and a hierarchical military force. The enemy is integrated within society, operates globally, and broadens its reach with technology. This unconventional area extends across the spectrum of political, social, economic, and military networks, blurring the distinctions between previous constructs. Since the Vietnam War, America has increasingly faced the need for special forces that can innovate against a creative and intelligent adversary, drawing capabilities from a multidisciplinary community. Solutions in this environment require integrated courses of action (COAs), scalable science and technology (S&T), and innovative research development technology and engineering (RDT&E).

- Disaster management, like irregular warfare, requires closing gaps and seams in an environment of diverse threats.

The agility and flexibility of crisis planning requires leveraging the existing capabilities in an intergovernmental (not just interagency) manner, because the contribution of all governments (including local, state, regional, and tribal) are required in a whole-of-nation approach. Just as UW requires a shift from conventional to unconventional mind-sets within the military, a new focus on individual and community resilience will require a cultural transformation in how our society views current vulnerabilities, risk assessments, functional processes (vs. physical infrastructures), investments in preparedness, attitudes toward government services, and the types of threats we face.

- Resilient thinking, like unconventional warfare, requires expanding the talents and capabilities of our team.

The formation of public-private partnerships is highlighted in all the strategies and policies, including the *National Security Strategy (NSS)*; Presidential Policy Directive 8 (PPD-8): National Preparedness; Presidential Policy Directive 21 (PPD-21): Critical Infrastructure Security and Resilience; and the *National Response Framework (NRF)*, but it will take more than promulgating written doctrine to mobilize and integrate groups of people. Informed and empowered leaders must assert the importance of these changes and forge a consensus at the highest levels of national leadership. Active working relationships with the commercial industry, labor unions, private owners and operators, not-for-profit organizations, and academia are often lacking or missing altogether. As integral players in the analyses, risk assessments, and resilience planning, we will need all players at the table to understand the full range of capabilities, authorities, jurisdictions, and financial costs and sustain public interest.

- Risk assessments, like conventional warfare, need to be modified to reflect lessons learned from recent history.

Since the 9/11 attacks, Hurricane Katrina, Japan's earthquake/tsunami/nuclear disaster, Haiti's earthquake, the Deepwater Horizon oil spill in the Gulf of Mexico, and Superstorm Sandy, we as a nation have matured in our recognition that the traditional approach toward evaluating risks—like conventional warfare—needs to be expanded so that it captures the true nature of the threat environment. The traditional rubric of risk assessments as a function of threats, vulnerabilities, and consequences is insufficient to capture the range of natural disasters, cyber and terrorist attacks, and pandemic health risks we face. For those events for which we can collect quantitative data and conduct predictive analytics (natural disasters), there is a degree of predictability that will allow for risk metrics, but for other deliberate events (terrorist attacks), there is little data and less confidence in predictability because they involve too many uncertainties. We must recognize the asymmetric nature of modern threats and establish a functional resilience approach that focuses more on how to prioritize hazard mitigation, respond to disasters, and recover services than trying to prevent an irregular threat that is unavoidable and unpredictable.

NOTES

1. Heuristics are experience-based techniques for problem solving, learning, and discovery. Where the exhaustive search is impractical, heuristic methods are used to speed up the process of finding a satisfactory solution, and also to provide mental shortcuts to ease the cognitive load of making a decision (Pearl 1984).

2. There are other frameworks being used effectively among local, regional, state, and federal planners, and this model is just one way many have found useful to conceptualize the complex variables in the homeland security enterprise. Within each category (governance, operations, systems) are formal and informal enablers that must be considered by any first responder, regional planner, or policymaker.

3. As of early FY13, DHS funding had become scarce—after investing $34 billion in federal funds through the Urban Area Security Initiative (UASI) since 9/11—and the regions are now faced with sustaining homeland security programs through innovation, collaboration, and resilience efforts (DomPrep 2012).

4. "Falling forward" taken from *Carry a Big Stick—Famous Quotes from Theodore Roosevelt*, compiled by George Grant (1996).

5. On February 12, 2013, the White House issued Presidential Policy Directive 21 (PPD-21): Critical Infrastructure Security and Resilience, which reduced the number of sectors from 18 to 16 by eliminating separate categories for "postal and shipping" and "national monuments and icons."

6. According to a December 14, 2012, report by Pew Research Social and Demographic Trends, the Census Bureau's new projected U.S. population for 2050 is 399.8 million. See http://www.pewsocialtrends.org/2012/12/14/census-bureau-lowers-u-s-growth-forecast-mainly-due-to-reduced-immigration-and-births/.

7. Statistics since 2001 indicate that some 80 percent of initial reports of security threats (e.g., New York City's Times Square bomber) have come from private citizens or local law enforcement officers on routine patrols (National Fusion Center Association). See www.nfcausa.org.

8. A *botnet* is a collection of Internet-connected computers whose security defenses have been breached and control ceded to a third party. Each compromised device, known as a "bot," is created when a computer is penetrated by malicious software (malware). These compromised devices, and subsequent networks, allow criminals to more easily attack servers, and commit cybercrimes (Microsoft).

4 | Threats and Challenges

Figure 4.1 Disaster-Impact Scale

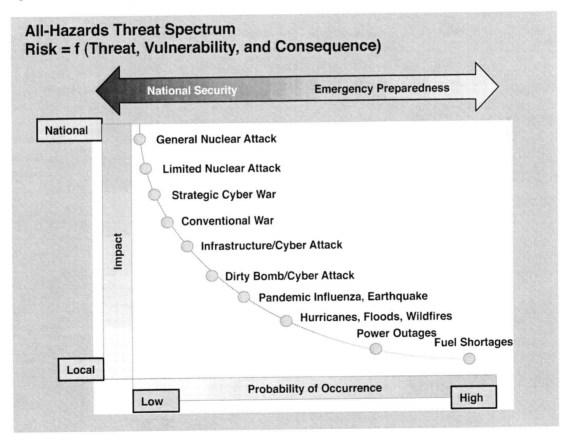

THREATS PICTURE

Destabilizing threats to critical infrastructure and key resources (CIKR) are normally categorized into natural, human-made, or health disasters. Figure 4.1 offers a graphic of the threat environment for national security and emergency preparedness showing a spectrum of natural and human-made events. This is a conceptual diagram that places disaster events along a continuum of low-to-high *probability of occurrence* with levels of relative *impact on society* on the vertical scale. Although the locations of events on the graph are rough estimates and subject to many independent variables, this diagram—albeit oversimplified—is often used as a tool for general discussions about the nature of threats. While useful, it fails to capture the complex mixture of threat-impact scenarios that can start at any point on the probability continuum, yielding an impact that is eventually local, regional, national, and even international in scope (i.e., Katrina, Sandy, Fukushima).

The "new normal" appears to be a more regular occurrence of natural and human-made disasters that involve disaster management and federal emergency response; clearly, they require us to become a more resilient society. Consider events such as the H1N1 pandemic (2009), the earthquake in Haiti (2010), the Deepwater Horizon oil spill (2010), the earthquake-tsunami-nuclear disaster in Japan (2011), the earthquake in Israel (2011), the Tuscaloosa, Alabama, tornado (2011), the Joplin, Missouri, multiple-vortex tornado (2011), record flooding of the Missouri and Mississippi Rivers (2011), Superstorm Sandy (2012), and the Moore, Oklahoma, tornado (2013).

The number of international and domestic terrorist attacks over the last decade underscores the persistence of global terrorist threats. Because of the dispersed nature of terrorist organizations and the variety of threats, terrorist attacks on the United States and our interests do not have to be as sophisticated as the 9/11 attacks to be catastrophic. And there are troubling trends that indicate recruiting and radicalization by extremists continue—including "virtual jihad" on the Internet, as evidenced by the Boston Marathon bombers—despite the elimination of many senior Al Qaeda leaders. Furthermore, there have been increased numbers of incidents involving homegrown extremists or isolated attacks as seen at Fort Hood (2009), Times Square in New York City (2010), the Tucson, Arizona, shopping center gunman attack (2011), the Aurora, Colorado, movie massacre (2012), and the Newtown, Connecticut, elementary school shooting (2012).

It is also important to recognize that a global economy, integrated supply chains, technology advancements, and complex systems with interdependencies—a strength and source of efficiencies when supporting commerce, trade, and communications—are also a potential source of weakness to our nation. These highly interconnected networks rely upon the services of multiple infrastructure sectors, making them more vulnerable, because failures in one sector can rapidly cascade to others and prevent the entire system from functioning properly. For the same reasons, these interdependent assets and capabilities may present an attractive collection of targets to terrorists and magnify the potential impact of a single attack or natural disaster. It also means that relatively small and unsophisticated attacks, and even near-miss events, can generate a significant impact for a small investment on the part of the attacker, potentially triggering a chain of political, economic, and security reactions that are highly disruptive and very expensive (Flynn and Burke 2012).

After 9/11, the national focus shifted to counterterrorism, military action, and protecting the homeland with increased attention on security requirements by U.S. Congress, the White House, and emergency management professionals at the local, state, regional, and federal levels. As time passed and the nation started healing from the painful terrorist attacks of 2001—and as other domestic events such as Hurricane Katrina (2005) occurred—planners expanded their analyses beyond a narrow focus on security to a broader *all-hazards* posture.

For example, there are several unique threats that deserve special consideration because of their potential impact on emergency response and disaster management capabilities. These threats—pandemics, solar weather, and electromagnetic pulses—have received increased attention from policymakers, researchers, and analysts, yet they remain a serious concern among homeland security leaders.

PANDEMIC

As a nation, we are not prepared to handle a severe outbreak of pandemic influenza that would introduce previously unknown levels of disruptions. The infamous 2009 outbreak of the H1N1 "swine flu" virus demonstrated the need for a more resilient pandemic response plan. The threat of a H5N1 pandemic has been looming since 1987, a threat that has been highlighted since the 2013 outbreak of the H7N9 strand in China. These strands of avian influenza have mobilized the public and private sector, while drawing a sharp reaction from the commercial industry and health providers. Studies of flu outbreaks stretch back to the 1918 influenza pandemic, which triggered a major focus on medical research within the scientific community and sparked the interest of commercial industry when employers realized they could rapidly lose over 40 percent of their workforce in a modern-day outbreak.

More specifically, during the 2009 H1N1 pandemic our disaster management framework was informed by the existing National Strategy for Pandemic Influenza, but that particular response plan was developed at the time of the crisis. Public health officials and policymakers immediately observed that the virus "did not cooperate," because it failed to follow the plan outlined in the national strategy:

1. It was a new virus, so we did not have the vaccine. This resulted in a public health emergency for the Department of Health and Human Services (HHS). The situation involved national policies, including Homeland Security Presidential Directive 5 (HSPD-5).
2. There were specific demographic threats (i.e., pregnant women and young children).
3. The virus originated in Texas and Southern California rather than where the plan anticipated, in Asia.
4. There was no national framework that enabled PPPs, whole-of-government, and international collaboration to specifically address this threat scenario, so a four-part interagency action plan was developed at the time to target this particular disaster. The plan included:

a. Global Surveillance: Provided situational awareness through the World Health Organization to understand the nature of the threat and where it was most severe; required a national-level response led by HHS with all public health hands "on deck."

b. Mitigation: Allowed rapid determination of how to minimize the impact of H1N1; served as a catalyst for changing cultural health norms through simple measures, such as washing hands and coughing techniques (inside elbow vs. inside cupped hands).

c. Vaccinate: Recognized that sources of the vaccine were outside the country and established a plan for distribution of 30 million vaccines and voluntary participation protocols, including rapid identification of young children and pregnant women; required PPP engagement across HHS, Centers for Disease Control and Prevention (CDC), public schools, and retail stores such as Walmart.

d. Strategic Communications: Required innovative ways of messaging across all sectors of society; one of the greatest challenges was to maximize passing of information through social and public media without inciting widespread panic (Reed 2012).

SOLAR WEATHER

The solar storm of 1859, also known as the 1859 Solar Superstorm or the Carrington Event, was a powerful solar flare, which was observed and recorded by the nineteenth-century English astronomer Richard Carrington. There was also severe solar activity in 1921 and 1988 for which there were no warnings or predictions. These events could trigger a cascading power blackout more devastating than the Northeast blackout of 2003, terminating critical services across all sectors. There appears to be a lack of planning efforts underway for this threat, but it is one that should receive greater attention, including within the private sector. As with the Y2K threat, this is a situation where the government must promote a range of public policy efforts across society in order to have a process in place to instill critical infrastructure resilience.

ELECTROMAGNETIC PULSE

An electromagnetic pulse (EMP) is a burst of electromagnetic radiation, typically generated by certain types of high-energy explosions, nuclear weapons, solar storms, radio frequency weapons, or a suddenly fluctuating magnetic field. The resulting rapidly changing electric fields and magnetic fields may affect electrical/electronic systems, producing damaging current and voltage surges. An EMP attack on the electronic infrastructure of the United States caused by the detonation of a nuclear bomb over the country would be crippling. "And once you confuse the enemy communication network," according to a 1998 article in a foreign military journal, "you can also disrupt the work of their command and control network." Furthermore, the article stated, "when you disable a country's military high command through disruption of communications, you will, in effect, disrupt all the affairs of that country" and its ability to ensure continuity of government (quoted in Maloof 2012).

In 2008 testimony, a senior Pentagon official told the House Armed Services Committee that China was working on advanced EMP weapons designed to knock out electronic systems using energy bursts. "The consequence of EMP is that you destroy the communications network," he said. "[The United States is] heavily dependent on sophisticated communications, satellite communications, in the conduct of our forces. And so, whether it's from an EMP or it's some kind of a coordinated anti-satellite effort, we could be in a very bad place if the Chinese enhanced their capability in this area" (quoted in Maloof 2012).

The EMP Commission made its first report to Congress in July 2004, stating that a nuclear-generated EMP is "one of a small number of threats that has the potential to hold our society seriously at risk and might result in the defeat of our military forces." The commission was to look at potential EMP threats for the next 15 years and assess the vulnerability of the U.S. military and especially the civilian infrastructure in terms of emergency preparedness. The goal of the examination was to determine how quickly the United States could recover from damages to military and civilian systems. In addition, the commission was charged with establishing the feasibility and cost of hardening critical military and civilian systems against such an attack (Miller 2005; Electromagnetic Pulse [EMP] Commission 2008).

The executive report indicated that an "EMP will cover a wide geographic region within line of sight to the nuclear weapons. It has the capability to produce . . . significant damage to critical infrastructures and thus to the very fabric of U.S. society, as well as to the ability of the United States and Western nations to project influence and military power." The report also pointed out that the impact to critical infrastructures will stem primarily from interference with and subsequent malfunctioning of electronics. The U.S.A. Patriot Act of 2001 defines critical infrastructure as "assets and systems—whether physical or virtual—so vital to the United States that their destruction or incapacity would have a debilitating impact on national security, economic welfare, national public health, or any combination of those factors (Section 1016e). These critical infrastructure facilities include electric power, oil refineries, water treatment plants, banking systems, pipelines, transportation systems, and communications. They all depend on electrical and electronic systems to operate and therefore can be very vulnerable to the EMP effects of a nuclear weapon or radio-frequency weapons (Radasky 2007; EMP Commission 2008; Maloof 2012).

"The primary avenues for catastrophic damage to the nation are through our electric power infrastructure and thence into our telecommunications, energy and other infrastructures," the 2008 EMP Commission report said. "These in turn can seriously impact other important aspects of our nation's life, including the financial system; means of getting food, water, and medical care to the citizenry; trade; and production of goods and services." Electric power is a lifeline service underlying U.S. society and all other critical infrastructures. The 2004 executive report recommended that

Figure 4.2 Hazard Categories

Terrorist Hazards

Biological Threat	Chemical Threats	Cyber Attack	Explosions	Nuclear Blast	Radiological Dispersion Device

Technological & Accidental Hazards

Blackouts	Hazardous Materials	Household Chemicals	Nuclear Plants	Home Fires

Natural Disasters

Drought	Earthquakes	Extreme Heat	Floods	Hurricanes	Landslides & Debris Flow

Severe Weather	Space Weather	Thunder & Lightning	Tornadoes	Tsunamis	Volcanoes

Wildfires	Winter Storms & Extreme Cold

Health Hazards

Pandemic Influenza	Infectious Disease Epidemic

Source: Images from the Federal Emergency Management Agency, http://www.fema.gov.

the U.S. government spend up to $200 billion over 20 years to "harden" U.S. critical infrastructure (Radasky 2007).

National-level policies categorize incidents in an all-hazards context of human-made, natural, and health disasters (see Figure 4.2). The next section summarizes the range of emergencies listed in the *National Response Framework (NRF)* and the *National Infrastructure Protection Plan (NIPP)*, as well as in other DHS, FEMA, and HHS documents.

Exemplars for the Future

The initial research for this study was conducted during the summer of 2012—a particularly active season for disasters and attacks—and the following section is a snapshot of open source reports summarizing the types of hazards that may occur in the homeland. These current events provide an exemplar for public- and private-sector planners and first responders who contend with the complexities of the modern threat environment. Is this level of activity representative of the normal flow of events? Does this represent a spike in hazardous activity, or are there simply more systems in place to better detect, report, and monitor these threats? Either way, these events illuminate the clear need to refocus the nation on preparedness and critical infrastructure resilience.

- The economic recession that started in December 2007 continues to adversely affect government budgets and private markets, both of which have considerable bearing on security and infrastructure investments. Private capital is slow to fill the infrastructure gap as commercial industry investors are avoiding debt and long-term financing—two key requirements for infrastructure projects. Investors seek long-term projects with stable cash flow, which means many projects will continue to fall at the feet of government.
- West Nile virus spread nationally with 5,674 cases in 2012, including 286 deaths—the highest number of cases since the virus was first found in 1999, according to the Centers for Disease Control and Prevention (CDC). More than 62 percent of the cases were reported in seven states, with the highest percentage in Texas.[1]
- *Clostridium difficile (C. diff)*, a potentially fatal infection that attacks the intestines, caused serious medical concerns across America's hospitals, nursing homes, and other medical facilities. According to a special media report, the medical community has reduced rates for nearly all other infections in recent years, but *C. diff* remains at all-time highs and may be more prevalent than federal reports indicate (McKinney 2012).
- On June 29, 2012, a powerful regional thunderstorm called a *derecho*, with hurricane-force winds, formed rapidly in the Midwest and hit the mid-Atlantic region with a force that left residents in the Washington, DC–area without power for up to two weeks due to infrastructure damage and utility outages.

- In Colorado Springs, Colorado, a dry summer forest fire in 2012 quickly turned into an urban blaze due to high winds, resulting in loss of life and the burning to the ground of nearly 350 residential homes, as Waldo Canyon (at the foot of Pikes Peak) became the site of an uncontainable wildfire. Again, in June 2013, the worst fire in Colorado history broke out in the Black Forest area, resulting in the loss of over 400 homes.

- In an Aurora, Colorado, movie theater on the opening night of the 2012 Batman film *The Dark Knight Rises,* a "lone wolf" gunman—formerly a doctoral student in neuroscience at the University of Colorado—opened fire, killing 12 and wounding 58 other moviegoers.

- Also in 2012, the worst drought in over 50 years—along with the single hottest month in recorded American history—plunged more than half the country into a state of emergency and caused problems on several fronts: American farmers struggled as crop yields fell and costs rose. The Mississippi River was closed for several days due to low water levels, vessels ran aground, and nearly 100 ships/barges were stranded along an 11-mile section of the river. The heat wave extended across the eastern seaboard and was powerful enough to melt the tarmac below jetliners in Washington, DC.

- In August 2012, Knight Capital Group, an American equity broker operating on Wall Street, started using a new software program to execute its trades. Within an hour it caused major disruptions to the entire market, sending errant trading orders that cost the company over $400 million. Shares in the company plunged that day, and within the week, shareholders were forced to accept a suboptimal financial rescue.

- America faces major infrastructure challenges to improve processing, transportation, pumping, and pricing of hydrocarbons, having become the third largest oil-producer,[2] and single largest NG supplier in the world.

- During the 2012 London Olympics, the demand for electronic bandwidth was seven times greater than it was four years earlier (2008). The non disaster demand for cellular services and burgeoning dependencies on internet, civil GPS, and wireless voice services portend the type of telecommunications problems that can emerge during a natural or human-made disaster. These systems can be individually jammed, disrupted, or overwhelmed—as cellular phone users experienced during the 9/11 attacks and Hurricane Katrina.

- Technology and globalization are accelerating the trading of fake identity cards. Identity management is a significant all-domain, cross-agency challenge that can lead to the compromise of physical, cyber, and human systems. With today's advanced software and printers, high-quality fake IDs are easier to make, and orders are taken over the web, enabling producers to remain further hidden from the public eye.

- In Milwaukee, Wisconsin, in August 2012, a sole gunman shot six worshipers and wounded three others in a Sikh temple. Outside the temple, the gunman—a known white supremacist—also ambushed, shot, and wounded a police officer who had responded to the 911 calls. The gunman then fatally shot himself in the head after being wounded by another officer.

- In October 2012, Hurricane Sandy, one of the strongest storms in U.S. history, battered the northeastern United States. Millions of people in New Jersey and New York were isolated due to damaging winds, rainfall, and storm surge; eight days after the storm's landing, a strong nor'easter brought low temperatures and snow to the same communities that were already struggling for survival without heat or electricity.
- In Newtown, Connecticut, a mentally unstable youth entered an elementary school—having taken assault weapons from the home where he lived with his mother—and killed 26 people (20 children under the age of seven and six teachers) before fatally shooting himself.
- In late January 2012, it was reported that computer hackers took control of a federal website and threatened "war" on the U.S. government. The site for the U.S. Department of Justice's Sentencing Commission was penetrated by a group that claimed they would release sensitive information and attack other government sites.
- Two bombs were detonated near the finish line of the Boston Marathon on April 15, 2013. The explosions immediately caused three deaths and over 200 injuries. A three-day manhunt for the perpetrators followed and led to a lockdown of Watertown, Massachusetts and the surrounding areas (including Boston).
- On May 20, 2013, the city of Moore, Oklahoma, and other nearby areas of central Oklahoma were devastated by a tornado. The highly destructive tornado took 24 lives, including 10 children.

In review, the current threat environment presents an asymmetric and uncertain flow of *black swan* events[3]—ones we don't expect and cannot predict based on existing data—and *wicked problems*—known challenges that are overwhelming to current emergency planners—and this trend appears to be growing (Allen 2012). Based on this informal threat summary, there is a need for comprehensive all-hazards policies that account for these natural and human-made disasters through focused preparedness efforts and critical infrastructure resilience.

NOTES

1. See http://www.ourcoloradonews.com/tellercounty/news/west-nile-virus-cases-deaths-jumped-in-cdc-says-stay/article_f147d616-c0c1-11e2-af77-001a4bcf887a.html, updated May 19, 2013. See also www.cdc.gov/westnile.

2. The two countries ahead of the United States are Russia and Saudi Arabia.

3. The *black swan* metaphor was developed by Nassim Taleb to explain the disproportionate role of high-impact, hard to predict, and rare events that are beyond the realm of normal expectations in history, science, finance, and technology.

5 Policy and Literature Review

Figure 5.1 Collective Action

Collective Action
Provides the Organizing Principle & Economic Case

- Independent action is being taken across highly interdependent sectors

- Homeland security and resilience are public goods—people expect them to be provided (like clean air, clean water, weather forecasts, and national defense)

- Uncoordinated efforts by self-interested parties and free riders put services at risk: therefore, a collective approach is needed

- Collective action incentives can provide the rationale for public-private-academic investments

Sources: Oil Spill: DVIDSHUB (Flickr username), March 13, 2013, Coast Guard continues response to oil spill south of New Orleans, http://www.flickr.com/photos/dvids/8554330825. Blue Sky: Geograph, Green energy, brown fields and a blue sky, http://www.geograph.org.uk/photo/3108441. Smoke Stacks (crop down to size): Wikimedia Commons, Smoke plume from chimney of power plant, https://commons.wikimedia.org/wiki/File:Smoke_plume_from_chimney_of_power_plant.jpg. Soldier with Radio: Wikimedia Commons, The U.S. Army-Radio report, http://commons.wikimedia.org/wiki/File:Flickr_-_The_U.S._Army_-_Radio_report.jpg. Shrimp Net Dump: Wikimedia Commons, Northern shrimp on shrimp boat, http://commons.wikimedia.org/wiki/File:Northern_shrimp_on_shrimp_boat.jpg. OR Crab Sorting: Wikimedia Commons, Sorting Crabs Ffionphort, http://commons.wikimedia.org/wiki/File:Sorting_Crabs_Ffionphort.jpg.

COLLECTIVE ACTION

In order to operationalize resilience and disaster management imperatives, this study turns to *collective action* (Appendix A, Figure A.14) to address national preparedness through expanded interagency coordination and private-sector participation. Resilience is a public good (like clean air, clean water, and national defense), requiring public-private partnerships and greater investments to account for positive and negative externalities across the infrastructure sectors. In a rapidly changing and uncertain environment, we as a nation cannot continue to make independent decisions in a highly interdependent world. The interdependencies across these complex systems have made us more efficient and transparent, but, at the same time, more vulnerable to disruptions and less resilient (Ostrom 2007; Cooper-Ramo 2009). Consequently, we can no longer make budgetary or risk-related decisions in isolation of the collective good of society. Such decisions must be evaluated through the lens of security and functional resilience imperatives.

This is a collective action problem involving public and private groups operating in a shared domain. The critical infrastructure system of systems is a complex network in which many operational and policy actors with different goals, resources, and mandates participate to achieve their own organizational and political goals. The diverse policy environment and regulated private industry—including physical structures, budgetary constraints, economic realities, and organizational cultures—have a significant impact on the national and homeland security fields (Flynn 2004; DOT 2006; The White House 2010).

National preparedness and resilience as public services are enabled, in part, by interagency policy execution. Each of these services is considered a *public good*. Public goods are goods that are hard (or impossible) to produce for private profit because the market fails to account for their large positive externalities. National security and homeland security are viewed as public goods because they are "nonrivalrous, nonexcludable public services where consumption of goods by one member does not reduce availability for others, and no one (agency or person) can be excluded from using the goods" (Samuelson 1954). Collective action suggests that groups "share intentions" regarding public goods through shared activity—activity that requires "common knowledge" to support the provision of public services (Gilbert 1989).

Following this argument, infrastructure protection and resilience are *public goods* that, if not addressed in a coordinated manner, will suffer the potential shortfalls raised by collective action themes such as tragedy of the commons, prisoners' dilemma, free riders, the principal-agent problem, bounded rationality, and common pool resources (Olsen 1965; G. Hardin 1968; Dawes 1980; R. Hardin 1982; Ostrom et al. 1999; Ostrom 2000; Ostrom et al. 2002; Schlager 2002). Furthermore, while collective action literature often targets issues such as "people problems," there are many examples in which collective security involves agencies and organizations because collective behavior is rooted in *relationships* among individuals and institutions (Ostrom 1990; Ostrom et al. 1999; Ostrom 2000; Ostrom et al. 2002).

Interagency Coordination

Along with the review of collective action theory, it is important to examine relevant references regarding interagency coordination among federal agencies, offices, and departments supporting resilience. The literature reveals that the lack of multi-agency cooperation as it relates to implementation of national-level policy—particularly in the security field—represents a continued vulnerability of the national transportation system and supply chains (Flynn 2006).

We know that security analysts struggle to forecast security risks—especially when faced with ill-defined and asymmetric threats across all domains—because conducting threat assessments is a highly uncertain process (Andreas 2003; The White House 2005, 2010). Major security challenges such as preventing an attack, expanding interagency cooperation, or deterring a breach in transportation systems make preparedness and resilience a very complex enterprise.

There is a significant body of literature addressing the criticality of whole-of-government or interagency coordination in a broader context, and the findings from this literature can be applied to national preparedness. Within this context, the goal of interagency coordination is to improve the effectiveness of cooperation, planning, and partnerships among federal, state, regional, tribal, and local government agencies, organizations, and departments (DHS 2008, 2009; The White House 2010). The challenge is reflected in the complex labyrinth of policies, legislation, departments, and authorities that influence critical infrastructure protection, along with the fact that the 16 infrastructure sectors are regulated, operated, and managed by an interdependent collection of mostly private actors, which is largely uncoordinated in assigned roles and missions.

For example, when Congress and the administration of President George W. Bush were considering formation of the Department of Homeland Security (DHS) in the wake of 9/11 terror attacks, they found that the responsibilities for homeland security functions were widely dispersed across the government. The number of federal departments, agencies, and offices involved in homeland-related tasks was nearly impossible to quantify (Daalder and Destler 2001; Kettl 2004). And according to the Office of Management and Budget (OMB), "Nearly seventy agencies spend funds on counterterrorist activities—and that excludes the Defense and State Departments as well as the intelligence community" (OMB 2001). The organizational and political scope of the interagency process[1] can be overwhelming to those inside or outside government.

Christensen and Laegreid (2007) discuss "whole-of-government" initiatives as a reaction to the negative effects of New Public Management (NPM) reforms such as structural devolution, "single-purpose organizations," and performance management, but also as a reaction to a more uncertain twenty-first-century security environment. Despite widespread support for a whole-of-government approach, several issues require careful consideration. Areas of potential difficulty include "ensuring accountability for publicly funded activities, overcoming the silos created by departmentalism or vertical styles of management," and balancing interagency participation with "the unwelcome effect of '[too] many hands'" involved—the latter often yielding "fragmentation and lack of coordination" (Hunt 2005). Furthermore, and largely missing from much of the public administration literature, is attention to "the role of interpersonal relationships and individual behavior as they impact [the] organizational values, ethics, and culture" of the interagency process (Hunt 2005; see also Osborne and Gaebler 1993).

Within the U.S. government, the National Security Council (NSC) plays the central coordinating role for the interagency process and cross-governmental policy formulation. Overcoming the obstacles that hinder greater interagency coordination remains a challenge as revealed in case studies and national security policymaking throughout U.S. history. For example, the annual budget formulation process by departments, agencies, and components often discourages interagency coordination and, by its competitive nature, contributes to organizational and infrastructure stratification (Allison 1971; The White House 2005; National Research Council [NRC] 2008). To further understand the criticality of multi-agency coordination and cross-governmental efforts to confront the complexities in government with unity-of-effort, one must identify the overlapping connection between collective action and interagency coordination themes.

INTERSECTION OF COLLECTIVE ACTION AND INTERAGENCY COORDINATION

Collective action variables incentivize public and private organizations to achieve the highest possible levels of cooperation and unity-of-effort. Certain actions or inactions identified in case studies and expert interviews affect the achievement of key operational goals and policy objectives in the critical infrastructure protection (CIP), resilience policy, disaster management, and preparedness communities.

When faced with the challenges and complexities of interagency coordination in the support of critical infrastructure resilience, the realities of the incident scale (refer back to Figure 3.3), and the nature of the threats we face, new operational and policy remedies are needed to leverage the benefits of collective action. Events such as the 9/11 terrorist attacks as well as the aftermaths of Hurricane Katrina and Superstorm Sandy underscore that public policymakers "struggle with the same large-scale puzzles of years past, and our government structures remain ill-matched for the problems they face" (Kettl 2006).

The interface of collective action and interagency coordination highlights the need to overcome three broad tendencies within resilience policy in general, and public-private partnerships, in particular:

1. ad-hoc approaches to policy formulation and analysis (Viteritti 1982; deLeon 1988);
2. the inability to identify the complexity of joint actions (Pressman and Wildavsky 1973; Kettl 2002); and

3. complex governance chains that strain accountability systems (Romzek and Dubnick 1987; Ingraham 2005).

These realities serve as a reference point in the further linkage of collective decisions and interagency coordination imperatives.

While not necessarily explained by existing theories, the elements of collective action—in large measure—support the justification for the form of governance we observe in the United States. Every day, people engage in collective action for mutual defense, child rearing, environmental protection, and many large-scale activities where individuals or agencies do not have strong relationships with each other. Engagement of this sort suggests that:

1. incentives can make it worthwhile to contribute jointly to a group;
2. motivations that reach beyond utilitarian self-interests are involved; and
3. interagency players in seemingly collective action events often fail to understand their own interests (Buchanan 1972; Hardin 1982; Donley 2005). All of these scenarios reflect parallel structures that exist in the interagency and collective action domains.

When common pool resources or collective goods such as CIP and homeland security can be supplied by government elements within the interagency, policy stakeholders—both public and private—observe decisions being made that reflect *social dilemmas*. Social dilemmas occur whenever agencies or individuals in interdependent situations face choices in which the maximum benefit of short-term self-interests yields outcomes that leave all participants worse off than feasible alternatives; that is, if everyone follows the status quo, the public good (preparedness) is not provided or is underprovided, and everyone would be better off (more resilient) if all elements of the interagency were to contribute (Ostrom 1990; Ostrom et al. 2002). Based on the findings of this study, one can view preparedness and resilience factors as "public goods" in the homeland and global commons.

Drawing from environmental studies, we recognize that "everything is connected to everything else," and the world of critical infrastructure resilience (CIR) is a study in interconnections. Similar to the Internet, cyber security, and medical sciences, resilience is marked by connections and convergences across disparate groups that make the enterprise stronger, yet more vulnerable to cascading disruptions. Collective action behavior in the "resilience commons" can be cast in economic terms—connected back to Garrett Hardin's insightful "Tragedy of the Commons" essay published in *Science* (1968)—because (1) critical infrastructures are "common properties" being overexploited, (2) the benefits (i.e., externalities) of the exploitation are enjoyed by those using the infrastructures, and (3) the costs should therefore fall on all equally. In order to share the ownership costs proportionately among the users, we need to ensure that free riders are included in the accounting and, where necessary, restructure the way we think about and manage CIR in the twenty-first century (*Economist* 2013a, 18; Frischmann 2013).

Applying collective action principles in the global commons, polluters should pay more heavily for their environmental impact (i.e., negative externalities); likewise, the costs of national preparedness and CIR (positive externalities) should be covered not just by the public sector or those currently paying but by all those benefiting from or free riding on the critical infrastructures. CIR is an example of a collective issue because it involves common pool resources that everyone can access under the same conditions—the very definition of a *public good.* Interconnected infrastructure sectors are used by many interests for different activities in a "nonrivalrous" and "nonexclusionary" manner, such that one person's use does not diminish another's (Samuelson 1954). To get the most benefit, the public and private sectors must share the obligation to maintain infrastructure resources in an open manner—recognizing that while there are often single-interest owners, we all benefit from the public good. As with environmental resources, "social norms and non-market mechanisms can keep commons from becoming tragic under a wide range of circumstances," but we may need to coerce or (better yet) incentivize expanded private-sector participation (Frischmann 2013).

To clarify the nexus of collective action, interagency coordination, and public- and private-sector collaboration, there are 12 overlapping themes and indispensable attributes needed to operationalize CIR policies: (1) transparency, (2) rationality, (3) reciprocity, (4) cooperation, (5) communications, (6) culture, (7) investments, (8) research, (9) field experience, (10) trust, (11) institutions, and (12) policy implications (see Table 5.1).

Table 5.1 Overlapping Collective Action and Interagency Coordination Themes

Transparency	Rationality	Reciprocity
Cooperation	Communications	Culture
Investments	Research	Field Experience
Trust	Institutions	Policy Implications

TRANSPARENCY

To enable cross-domain organizational integrity and confidence in interagency coordination, there must be a systemic commitment to policy disclosures and collaboration internally and externally (Gilbert 1989; Kettl 2008). Solving interagency collective action problems facing different kinds of citizen, agency, or institutional activity across various domains is no easy feat. Thus, we must institute monitoring mechanisms and risk-reduction practices based upon appropriate control and organization transparency. (Micheletti 2003). All participants expect common knowledge of the situation and of payoffs to be received by individuals under various combinations of strategies, and no external actor or central authority is normally present to enforce agreements among participants about their choices (Ostrom 1998).

RATIONALITY

Agencies will not act voluntarily and rationally to achieve common interests unless incentives or external influences compel their action (Ostrom 1990, 2007; Sandler 2004). Theorists using rational choice theory assume real uncertainty about the duration of a situation, or that some players are 'irrational' in their commitment to reciprocal cooperation. Agencies often want to change the rules and bring about structural change when they observe that public goods or common pool resources are being depleted. But much like individual decision makers, agencies are limited by the constraints of bounded rationality and expect other similar elements to follow a diversity of heuristics, norms, and strategies rather than adopt a single rational strategy (Simon 1957; Ostrom 1998).

RECIPROCITY

Agencies and organizations must decide how prepared they are to support the collective enterprise, working across operational domains and budgetary boundaries in response to disasters and emergencies (Carney 1987; Smith 2010). When assessing the likelihood that members of a society will cooperate, the basic norm is that groups tend to react to positive or negative actions of others in-kind. There is strong evidence that reciprocity is a core behavior of many individuals in collective action and social dilemma situations. Humans, agencies, and organizations alike have a strong capacity to learn reciprocity norms and social rules that enhance the opportunities to gain benefits in coping with a multitude of crises and social dilemmas. In general, researchers observe a tit-for-tat pattern where one party cooperates first and another party correspondingly does whatever the original party did in the first round (Axelrod 1984; Ostrom et al. 1999).

COOPERATION

Dramatic improvements are needed in interagency coordination and collective action to bridge across national, regional, and local policy imperatives (Ostrom 2007; Paganelli 2012). In any particular population facing repeated social dilemmas, one of the following collective behavior choices will be selected:

1. Always cooperate first, and stop cooperating if others do not reciprocate; punish non-cooperators if feasible.
2. Cooperate immediately only if one judges others to be trustworthy; stop cooperating if others do not reciprocate; punish non-cooperators if feasible.
3. Once cooperation is established by others, cooperate oneself; stop cooperating if others do not reciprocate; punish non-cooperators if feasible.
4. Never cooperate.
5. Mimic actions 1 or 2, but stop cooperating if one can successfully free ride on others.
6. Always cooperate—which is very rare in all cultures and communities of interest. (Olson 1965; Ostrom 1990, 280–285)

COMMUNICATIONS

Open lines of communication are essential to bridge barriers and catalyze information sharing at all levels of public policy development and implementation (Relyea 2004; Kettl 2008). Communication facilitates coordination and cooperation because parties engage in the transferring of information from those who know an optimal strategy to those who do not fully understand what actions would be optimal. Furthermore, communication fosters ownership and mutual commitment as well as increased trust by adding value to the subjective payoff structure. It also reinforces organizational values by developing group identity. Good communications allow individuals or organizations to increase their trust in the reliability of others (Smith 2010).

CULTURE

Government interagency and private-sector agencies possess a unique organizational ethos based upon their tradition, history, and established norms (Gilbert 1989; Flynn 2007). Particular rules adopted by participants within the system or relationships under consideration vary significantly to reflect local circumstances, cultural ethos, and history. Cultural analyses must include an effort to understand how institutions, coalitions, and international agreements are vulnerable to corruption, manipulation, legislative irregularities, extortion, or nefarious activity. Democracies are fragile institutions that are inherently subject to manipulation if citizens and officials are not vigilant. According to Olson (1971), the size and culture of a group is critical in determining whether group-oriented behavior can grow out of voluntary, rational pursuit of individual interests. Too often within disaster management, "regional councils are focused only on transportation, sanitation, and water issues, and they are missing the whole-of-community approach and convincing the leadership that resilience is a win-win for everyone" (DomPrep 2012, 45).[2]

INVESTMENTS

Public and private stakeholders seek to achieve maximum collaborative benefit of collective action while minimizing costs in time, effort, and resources (Hardin 1982; Sandler 2004). Research indicates that organizations temporarily caught in a social dilemma are more likely to invest resources to innovate and change the agency structure itself in order to improve joint outcomes or collective action. The solutions to collective action problems often revolve around transaction costs (Ostrom 1990; Ostrom, Gardner, and Walker 1992). The more organizational and community investments there are, the lower the costs of acquiring information, bargaining, monitoring, and enforcement; additionally, people and agencies are more likely to communicate with each other about coordination problems thereby reducing free rider tendencies among parties (Olson 1971; Wilson and McCay 1998; Ostrom 2007).

Research

More qualitative and quantitative research is necessary to develop a reliable theory of why cooperation levels vary so much and why specific configurations (independent variables) of situational conditions increase or decrease cooperation (dependent variable) in first- or second-level dilemmas. Also, we cannot assume "that only one type of institution exists for all social dilemmas, such as a competitive market, in which individuals pursuing their own preferences are led to produce mutually productive outcomes" (Ostrom 1998, 16; see also Gilbert 2006).

Field Experience

The views and experience of practitioners—especially among local, state, and regional actors—must be considered by scholars, researchers, and policymakers to ensure policy is actionable and enforceable (Gilbert 1989; Ostrom et al. 2002). The ability to cooperate in collective action problems, such as those relating to the use of common pool resources or the provision of public goods, is a key determinant of economic and operational performance. Practical field experience has a significant impact on influencing institutions to encourage opportunistic behavior and promote cooperation; such experience helps shape the characteristics of the individuals or agencies involved and the degree to which they cooperate. Practitioners tend to use reliable heuristics—rules of thumb—that have been learned over time and consistently yield good outcomes and reliable results in particular situations. Also, with frequently encountered, repetitive situations, individuals and agencies tend to learn better methods that are tailored to particular situations (Ostrom 1990; Ostrom et al. 1999; Smith 2010).

Trust

Trust is the essential ingredient needed to galvanize intergovernmental coordination and forge consensus across the public and private sectors (Searle 1990; Goertz 2006). Trust plays a fundamental role in solving social dilemmas where the experience of one agency has an impact on another agency's choice and decisions must be made before the actions of others are known. In collective decisions, trust affects whether an agency or individual is willing to initiate cooperation with the expectation that it will be reciprocated. At the core of individual reason and organizational behavior are links between trust, the investment others make in trustworthy relationships, and the probability that agencies will follow consistent rules and cooperative norms. Trust, as a mutually reinforcing principle, is also influenced by structural variables, personal relationships, and the past experiences of participants (Rainey 1997; Scharpf 1997).

INSTITUTIONS

Institutions are the structural and bureaucratic ligaments that connect patterns of interagency coordination and collective action behavior (Olson 1971, Ostrom 2007). It is necessary to understand how different types of institutions support or undermine norms of reciprocity within hierarchies and among members of groups facing collective choices. Policies that provide alternative opportunities for institutions caught in dysfunctional networks are as important as those that stimulate positive networks and institutions (North 1990). Successful institutions create a positive environment when they utilize nonviolent techniques of conflict resolution to address differences constructively and form new rules to deal with disputes more effectively (Yamagishi 1986).

POLICY IMPLICATIONS

Policy implementation requires interagency consensus and cross-governmental coordination, which often falls short due to a lack of funding or recognized framework for action (Gilbert 2006; Medina 2007). If individuals or agencies are ineffective collective action contributors, then the state is an essential external authority that must resolve social dilemmas. And if agencies or individuals can draw from positive heuristics and norms to solve existing problems and create new structural arrangements to solve others, then the image of what a national government might do is very different. Collective action implies a considerable role for government: including national defense, monetary policy, foreign affairs, global trade, international diplomacy, economic stability, and strategic communications. In general, national governments are too small to govern global commons and too big to handle small-scale policy problems, pointing to the need for right-sized public-private partnerships (Hardin 1982; Searle 1990; Gilbert 2006).

Consider the challenge issued in the *National Strategy for Homeland Security*: to focus on the resilience of infrastructure systems as a whole, identifying "investments that make the nation better able to absorb the impact of an event without losing the capacity to function" (Homeland Security Council 2007).

The challenge is that this study—and the national-level policies under review—must be actionable at the local, state, regional, and federal levels in order to be useful. Perhaps the most valuable outcome of this literature review is the practical utility of the list of themes at the *intersection* of collective action theory and interagency coordination. These holistic themes are important factors when attempting to influence public-private multiagency actors.

As the nation attempts to implement existing homeland security, preparedness, and resilience policies (and introduce new ones), our efforts must be informed by these fundamental themes. This is particularly true when trying to forge consensus across a group of independent cross-sector leaders regarding *the most* important elements of critical infrastructure systems, and *where* to invest limited resources for the best impact. Addressing this comprehensive whole-of-nation issue, with the benefit of these proven themes, increases the probability of unity-of-effort and policy implementation where it is needed most.

Notes

1. The interagency process refers to the decision making and coordination methods designed to support the Executive Office of the President in developing national and homeland security strategies by synchronizing the cross-governmental efforts of all departments and agencies.

2. During regional preparedness workshops across the country in 2012, *culture* was considered by many participants as the primary obstacle to collaboration at all levels of the homeland security enterprise: local vs. state, regional vs. federal, paid vs. volunteer, urban vs. rural (DomPrep 2012, 44–45).

6 | Methodology

PROBLEM DEFINITION

The dynamic variables of preparedness and disaster management require public and private actors to navigate a labyrinth of public policy and operational systems in a globalized and political environment. How, then, does one begin to understand the nature of the problem and distill the most significant themes from disasters and crises that have occurred in the past dozen years since the 9/11 attacks? Understanding preparedness policy performance in networks is difficult because the allocation of managerial resources in network structures is fluid while managerial action varies widely across time and space within a given program or system (Agranoff 2006).

Given the complex, uncertain, and changing conditions of the disaster management landscape, this study draws upon a combination of research mixed methods: a hybrid approach of qualitative and quantitative approaches utilizing historical surveys, collecting descriptive data from case studies, and interviewing experienced practitioners across the country. The sources include preparedness leaders from the public and private sectors and from international centers of excellence. The goal was to obtain general information and empirical data to identify the most significant issues surrounding national preparedness and critical infrastructure resilience.

With this background, the problem statement for this study is, "Highly complex and interdependent systems, along with inadequate policies and legislation that support critical infrastructures, impede the ability to adequately strengthen national preparedness and functional resilience." The hypothesis is, "Effective policy execution requires increased collective action and interagency coordination across the homeland security enterprise to promote functional resilience." Public policy variables—drawing from McGuire (2006)—represent the independent variables such as activation (integrating persons and resources to achieve goals), framing (arranging rules and values within networks), mobilizing (developing commitment for processes from internal and external players), and synthesizing (creating an environment of ownership and teamwork among actors). Therefore, the dependent variable—desired systemic outcome—is the "sustainment of preparedness and resilience within the whole-of-nation homeland security enterprise."

Disaster-related case studies, strategic document reviews, and interviews with subject matter experts were employed to provide historical context, document interagency experience, develop research questions, and test the findings (Marshall and Rossman 2006; Creswell 2007). As previously mentioned, the problem definition frames the challenge of this qualitative study in the context of homeland security policy, public-private planning, and interagency coordination. It bears repeating:

> Highly complex and interdependent systems, along with inadequate policies and legislation that support critical infrastructures, impede the ability to adequately strengthen national preparedness and functional resilience.

DATA COLLECTION AND ANALYSIS

We examine the role of multi-agency efforts in improving community resilience and preparedness within the context of all-hazards and whole-of-nation variables. More specifically, we draw upon disaster case studies and expert interviews to answer research questions and make major findings and recommendations, asserting a fundamental link between collective action principles and interagency coordination, laying the foundation for research findings and suggested remedies. Additionally, this provides the basis for the development of an implementation process that will help operationalize resilience policies.

The research for this report draws upon multiple case studies, expert interviews, and a review of documents to support the findings and recommendations. The advantage of a multiple-case design and the range of interviewees is that increased sources of data strengthen the validity of the research and expand the analytic benefit (Yin 2009). Furthermore, the selected all-hazard cases support future generalization—representative of a broader population of cases—and offer several "most likely" cases because they are considered predictors of future outcomes (George and Bennett 2005; Gerring 2007). The cases selected involve a cross-section of disaster events and preparedness themes that highlight the challenges of responding to incidents that differ in geography, duration, severity, and response requirements. These cases—taken individually and together—offer the comparative analysis needed to study homeland security, resilience, and preparedness requirements within the whole-of-nation context. Although all the cases point to preparedness and homeland security policy, each one uncovers different causal factors relative to collective action requirements and therefore contributes to answering the fundamental research questions regarding the need for critical infrastructure resilience. The 13 case studies selected do not include the 9/11 terrorist attacks or Hurricane Katrina because they have been analyzed extensively elsewhere.

This data collection and analysis approach relied heavily upon access to (1) credible interviewees from across the interagency, (2) open-source public documents, and (3) organizations and agencies within the public and private sector. Because the research focused on local-, state-, and national-level intergovernmental and private-sector coordination of resilience-related policies, most of the subject matter experts interviewed for the study were (1) members of the planning and operational staffs of government agencies and departments, (2) representatives from private industry, and (3) members of the academic community.

7 | **Major Findings**

The major findings were derived inductively[1] from a combination of case studies (Appendix A), subject matter expert (SME) interviews (Appendix C), relevant external documents (Appendix F), and strategic policies and references by distilling the themes that emerged during comparative analysis and consolidation of common terms of reference. Further amplification and discussions are provided for each category within the appendices, especially within SME interviews (Appendix C).

STRATEGIC CONTEXT

7.1   The events of 9/11 caused an expensive surge in security, emphasizing intelligence gathering, prevention, and physical protection measures; more recently, there has been an increased focus on preparedness, including mitigation, response, and recovery.

7.2   The greatest challenge is facing the impact of increased complexity and uncertainty in an environment that is interconnected and interdependent. A disaster in another part of the world can have a serious secondary impact on regional economies, which is difficult to predict and model.

7.3   The speed with which data sources and information are growing often exceeds the ability of government to process it. In an era when we need more public-private partnerships (PPPs), the gap between government and private business seems to be growing; furthermore, private companies tend to want their privacy protected during any activity, yet if a crisis occurs, they want government to respond to support their interests.

7.4   Academia is often missing as a strategic partner in studying preparedness, resilience and infrastructure protection.

7.5   There is currently no strategic intergovernmental preparedness or resilience action plan. Our current approach to transportation and infrastructure spending relies too heavily on political influence and "fixing things" around the country.

CULTURAL FACTORS

7.6   While attempting to build *whole-of-nation resilience*, one faces significant cultural differences between local, state, and federal governments; local planners are focused on frequently occurring scenarios (for which they are funded), and the national focus is on lower probability, high-impact scenarios.

7.7   There is a culture of denial that says, "This won't happen to me," or "If it does, I'll just deal with it when the time comes." During difficult economic times, people are often unwilling to invest in resiliency and infrastructure protection because they view it as spending money they don't have for something they can't see.

7.8   There is overconfidence and a misconception that government will "be there" to provide immediate relief, which results in overdependence on government agencies (FEMA, USCG, and so on).

7.9   Many interagency bureaucracies are unwilling to make—or are highly resistant to—policy changes. This can lead to a failure to recognize risk levels or an inability to think critically about the threat environment. Therefore, absent a catastrophic event, there is likely to be little change because of a culture of maintaining the status quo.

NATIONAL FRAMEWORK

7.10   A national framework is needed that cultivates a *culture of preparedness* and integrates *resilience* in all areas. Currently, there is no organizing principle that provides rewards to keep people engaged. While it is worthwhile, we need more than a "See Something—Say Something" slogan. (Refer to Appendix D.)

7.11   By systematically mapping infrastructure dependencies and interdependencies nationwide, one can better understand the unique resilience factors by geographic region, including policies, statutes, operations, systems, organizations, funding, incentives, and people—identifying the mixture of interconnected relationships.

7.12   The U.S. Department of Homeland Security (DHS)–sponsored Sector Coordinating Committees (SCCs) organized the private sector at the national level, but the concept was never replicated at the local level. A similar program needs to be formed regionally to keep communities engaged.

7.13   *Resilience* should be part of everything we do. Increased emphasis on community resilience is best achieved by leveraging existing interests and priorities of the general public—not necessarily adding a new program or budgetary requirement. Consider building a program around traditional priorities such as crime reduction, improved health, better education, economical housing, food quality, etc.

7.14   There is a great need for a *framework for action* that governs preparedness. For example, during World War II, there was a campaign to galvanize the nation with five words: "Defeat Germany—Hold Against Japan." What is the equivalent call-to-action in today's society?

7.15   The key to preparedness success is *unity-of-effort*; in a community sense, we must *unify the tribe*. Although there are different cultures, agencies, and governance, we are essentially a tribal society that must pull together under a national framework to create and sustain resilience.

7.16   Identifying and prioritizing essential functions (at the personal or organizational level) is a prerequisite for resilience planning because internal analysis drives future actions during crisis. When a disruptive event occurs that triggers a *continuity of operations* plan, there is an immediate reduction in staffing, based on that baseline determination of mission-essential tasks.

7.17   For homeland security professional development, the 1986 Goldwater-Nichols Department of Defense Reorganization Act offers a model for local, state, and regional first responders and government officials to enable integration across various intergovernmental organizations. Similar to joint Professional Military Education (PME) requirements for military officers, the expansion of cross-agency training can be implemented by linking participation to promotion and career opportunities.

7.18   Looking at National Preparedness (PPD-8), the first two plans ("prevent, protect") can be viewed as cultural factors in the social sciences that seek deterrence through policies and the political process; the last two plans ("respond, recover") draw from engineering sciences, requiring physical action and emergency services; and the final plan ("mitigate") bridges both groups by offering the means to reduce the impact of disaster by taking preventive and resilient measures.

7.19   Critical Infrastructure Security and Resilience (PPD-21) advances the federal government's focus on security and resilience, offering the policy foundation for operationalizing a national framework with three strategic imperatives: (1) national unity-of-effort, (2) information exchange, and (3) integration and analysis to inform decisions.

Resilience

7.20   Every complex system can fail, but the speed of recovery is the best measure of a healthy system. We need to move beyond a *protection* mind-set that focuses on securing national assets and instead seek *continuity* of function in the face of risk to achieve effective resilience.

7.21   The concept of resilience is not easily introduced into the budget, planning, and policy processes because it is difficult to measure, quantify, and integrate into legislation.

7.22   It is difficult to motivate and incentivize individuals, families, and small businesses to invest in resilience measures that seem like costly investments that do not provide immediate benefit. The value proposition is not always clear to the individual, and should be made clearer.

7.23   Resilience is an active process that should be operationalized across all sectors based on the expectation that disasters will occur; the primary focus should be placed on mitigation, response, and recovery versus prevention and protection—the latter being low-return investments in an uncertain threat environment.

7.24   The DHS wants to incentivize the private sector to invest in community resilience through high-value programs—including voluntary certification and insurance industry partnerships—to explore ways to strengthen security practices.

7.25   Critical infrastructures that integrate functional resilience into their systems and practices tend to be more durable, robust, and disaster-resistant, have longer life expectancies, and are more readily adapted for reuse and repurposing.

7.26   *Functional resilience* involves agility in resolving problems for long-term mission assurance. At the tactical and operational level, managers are concerned with continuity of the business over shorter time periods. Flexible manufacturing facilities and versatile employee skills are examples of functional resilience in supply-chain management.

7.27   While *resilience* is referenced in national- and agency-level strategies with various levels of support, it lacks a clear programmatic mandate. Current policies do not contain performance or assessment standards to achieve resilience, and there are no cohesive interagency programs with legislative support to systematically link *critical infrastructure and key resources (CIKR)* and resilience objectives.

POLICY

7.28   Some 85 percent of all critical infrastructures are owned and operated by the private sector, but the majority of policy guidance is developed and enforced by the public sector. There are few national infrastructures—most are locally, regionally, or internationally owned.

7.29   While there has been a proliferation of national policy guidance in *critical infrastructure protection (CIP)* and preparedness in recent years (*National Response Framework [NRF]*, *National Infrastructure Protection Plan [NIPP]*, and Presidential Policy Directives 8 and 21), there is no comprehensive organizing framework that provides a strategy for action or implementation.

7.30   There are practical lessons that can be learned from international partners who face the same struggles to improve resilience, business continuity, sustainment, and mission assurance.

7.31   The responsibility for execution of current policies is fragmented and uncoordinated; therefore, the gaps within the interagency and private sector may remain unclear until a disaster actually occurs, and then is too late to address.

7.32   Because there have been no major attacks on U.S. critical infrastructure since the 9/11 terrorist attacks, the nation has a reduced sense of urgency and an uneven focus on infrastructure protection, resulting in decreased congressional funding to support CIP.

LEGISLATION

7.33   The authority, jurisdictions, and legislation in effect in some areas of preparedness and emergency response policy are outdated. For example, the 1990 Oil Pollution Act (OPA-90) was one of the applicable statutes when the Deepwater Horizon oil spill occurred in the Gulf of Mexico, but it failed to provide adequate authority and regulatory guidance for the environmental disaster in 2011.

7.34   There is a need for a comprehensive review of all national-level legislation and statutes relative to resilience policy, as well as a need to synchronize post-9/11 and post-Katrina strategies and policies with current legislative statutes and the Code of Federal Regulations (CFRs).

7.35   The Title-5 regulatory process is flawed and in need of reform. Such reform can be achieved by updating the Regulatory Flexibility Act of 1980, which requires federal agencies to analyze the impact of regulatory actions on small businesses.

7.36   The congressional authorization and appropriations process supporting national infrastructure is outdated because the resources too often go to Congress's most senior member for "fixing things." A new legislative approach is needed that incentivizes the private sector to invest in local and state infrastructures.

WHOLE-OF-NATION

7.37   Terms of reference such as *whole-community* and *whole-of-government* have been supplemented in the current policy by *whole-of-nation*.

7.38   The whole-of-nation concept is not widely understood and lacks a common definition across the public and private sectors.

7.39   The term whole-of-nation reflects lessons learned since 9/11, emphasizing all-inclusive participation in CIP and preparedness—no person, community, organization, agency, or departments are excluded.

7.40   Whole-of-nation approaches start at the individual level and extend to family, community, regions, and states, forming the basis for how we plan, organize, and implement resilience policy.

7.41   A cultural change is needed within CIP and disaster planning that places greater emphasis on personal responsibility for crisis preparedness and less dependency on government services. FEMA officials expect individuals to be self-sufficient for the first 72 hours after a disaster.

7.42   Despite its declared goal to enhance collaboration, the DHS/FEMA grant program has been handicapped by the competition for limited Urban Areas Security Initiative funds, often yielding more focus on dollars than on community resilience; this points to the need for a more equitable grant program that achieves measurable results and is regionally coordinated to support strategic resilience and preparedness goals.

PUBLIC-PRIVATE PARTNERSHIPS

7.43   Public-private partnerships (PPPs) are a widely recognized approach that appears in most current federal policy guidance. PPPs are considered the key to addressing future CIP and resilience shortfalls.

7.44   Because the majority of all infrastructures are owned and operated by private entities, coordination with the private sector is essential in order to accomplish homeland security policy and preparedness goals.

7.45   Since budgets are constricted in the current economic climate and infrastructure needs continue to grow, PPPs are an essential part of the way forward for local, state, and regional CIP efforts. They represent potential sources of private equity and venture capital investments for all infrastructure sectors.

7.46   Several examples of operating PPPs are reflected in agency auxiliaries, including the Civil Air Patrol (USAF), InfraGard (FBI), FEMA Corps (FEMA), and the U.S. Coast Guard Auxiliary (USCG), demonstrating the value of PPPs with mature partnerships and standing agreements across government, utility, volunteer, and commercial organizations. (Refer to Appendix D.)

7.47   Leveraging the knowledge and experience of the private sector—particularly owners, operators, and investors—will help forge the kind of relationships needed to expand PPPs in an uncertain post-9/11 threat environment.

CAPABILITIES APPROACH

7.48   A transition built on scenario-based planning is under way in some agencies; it points toward a broader all-hazards approach to achieve flexible preparedness, resiliency, and capabilities against a wide range of complex uncertainties.

7.49   After the 9/11 attacks, the critical infrastructure focus was primarily on hardening facilities against future attacks (i.e., "prevent and protect"), but Hurricanes Katrina (2005), Irene (2011), and Sandy (2012) highlighted the need for increased emphasis on "mitigate, respond, and recover" capabilities.

7.50   Beyond the post-9/11, post-Katrina mind-set of securing critical infrastructure, there is a need for a broader view across all functional areas with a focus on interdependencies that might lead to cascading disruptions. The goal is to ensure *a spectrum of capabilities* to handle all-hazards preparedness.

7.51   When developing preparedness capabilities, it makes more sense to develop generic functional resilience rather than focusing on ways to predict a single security threat. As a nation, we need to develop flexible capabilities that are interchangeable or can be easily shifted to match the nature of the disaster.

7.52   A comprehensive decision support tool is needed to work across organizations and data boundaries. With the current processing tools, sought-after information is eventually found in the system, but the ability to collect, sort, and analyze infrastructure information in a systemic and automated manner is lacking.

7.53   We need a systematic functional resilience framework that is scalable and can be generalized to various operational and geographic areas. Future planning and analysis must be done based upon empirical data, including essential functions, capabilities, and large-scale optimization in a resource-scarce environment.

INFORMATION SHARING

7.54   The force multiplier for information sharing is the trust that must be forged between parties. Although difficult to prescribe, organizational mechanisms must be established that foster a spirit of teamwork, cooperation, and shared perspectives.

7.55   Since 9/11, the Department of Homeland Security has significantly expanded information-sharing efforts nationally through organizations such as the 10 FEMA regions, state fusion centers, and the Protective Security Advisor (PSA) program, providing mechanisms for open dialogue with the public on infrastructure protection issues.

7.56   The private sector often views the flow of information as one way—from them to the government—and it (the private sector) is not motivated to share information due to (1) potential regulatory repercussions, especially if reporting internal discrepancies; and (2) the risk of proprietary information being exposed to market competitors.

7.57   There is a tendency across the interagency to over-classify information based upon so-called need-to-know security restrictions; however, a new approach is needed to significantly expand information sharing through more open "need-to-share" criteria.

7.58   Some highly regulated sectors (telecommunications, energy, aviation, and nuclear power) already have mature information-sharing mechanisms with the federal government, while others are less engaged and must establish more robust information-sharing capabilities.

7.59   The Freedom of Information Act (FOIA) complicates public-private sector collaboration and information sharing because businesses are reluctant to share sensitive or proprietary information if it can be released later to the public or market competitors. Utility companies are sensitive to privacy issues because they protect information regarding business operations, and may mark information "For Official Use Only" to protect the material from future FOIA requests for disclosure.

7.60   Social media has become a primary source of information across society because of extensive digital networks, broadband connectivity, and fiber optics developed to support widespread use of the Internet, Facebook, and Twitter, especially among the younger generation. This technology and social networking sites (SNS) in general are important areas to explore for applications to preparedness and resilience operations. (Refer to Appendix D.)

MITIGATION

7.61   Although it can be expensive and often difficult to quantify the value, mitigation matters. Because of the interconnected nature of infrastructures, mitigation investments actually improve resiliency across all sectors.

7.62   We can learn about mitigation from the commercial industry, especially transit authorities and electric power utilities—organizations that measure performance based on recovery time and continuity of services. The standard should be continuity of functions (in the face of certain risk) and delivery of critical services.

7.63   Because of complex CIKR interdependencies, failure to take effective mitigation measures in local communities (such as trimming trees in the vicinity of electric power lines) can trigger a sequence of cascading regional, state, and national service disruptions or outages.

GLOBAL SUPPLY CHAIN

7.64 Due to the nature of infrastructure interdependencies, coupled with the uncertainties of disaster risk management, global supply-chain resilience has received significant attention in the public and private sectors; and there is a growing source of data available for planners and decision makers.

7.65 Recent disasters, such as earthquakes (Japan), volcanoes (Iceland), and hurricanes (Gulf Coast), reveal that resilience and mitigation of risk in the global supply chain are vital to safeguarding commercial markets from the indirect impact of disasters. As the American automobile and computer industries learned during the Japan's Fukushima, the concentration of key suppliers in a disaster area can have disruptive cascading effects on otherwise unaffected parts of the supply chain.

7.66 Supply-chain risks are increasing, and "black swan" events that were once rare now occur more frequently, not necessarily because triggering events occur more often but because infrastructure interdependencies magnify their impact. Additionally, the push for improved efficiency and cost savings has increased supply-chain risk and reduced margins for error.

7.67 Modern public and private supply chains are dynamic links of interconnected networks. Given the scale and complexity of today's supply chains, it is impossible to predict or prepare for every possible risk scenario, so the best posture is to build resilience into domestic and global supply chains—proactively mitigating critical vulnerabilities and developing the capability to recover quickly from disasters.

7.68 The majority of the nation's oil supply is routed through the Port of Houston, where it is refined and transported to the rest of the country. Assessments and National-Level Exercises (NLEs) that evaluate oil refining and distribution vulnerabilities reveal a lack of resiliency in the delivery systems for refined oil.

INTELLIGENCE

7.69 There is an increased focus by the intelligence community (IC) on building partnerships with the homeland security and law enforcement communities, working through state fusion centers and shaping the "Domestic Architecture for National Intelligence."

7.70 Based on guidance contained in legislation, executive orders, and national strategies, the IC, led by the Office of the Director of National Intelligence (ODNI), is attempting to better support integration of the domestic threats picture and expand partnerships with the private sector.

7.71 A significant challenge in defining intelligence requirements for *critical infrastructure resilience* is coordinating all standing members of the IC along with non-IC domestic organizations and building consensus across the intelligence enterprise.

7.72 Serious threat concerns—such as homegrown extremists, domestic terrorists, foreign operatives inside our borders, and domestic improvised explosive devices (domestic IEDs)—are examples of emerging threats that require all agencies to work together more closely.

RISK ASSESSMENT

7.73   We need new ways to distribute risk across the homeland security enterprise. This goal can be achieved by improving the DHS grant program and working with the insurance industry to gather data and establish market incentives that encourage resilient behavior in society.

7.74   The current computational models for risk assessment and determining critical-ity are inadequate for the types of natural and human-made disasters we face in the twenty-first century; the models lack flexibility and do not account for the threat of unknown and seasonal variables.

7.75   As we raise the focus on resiliency and hazard mitigation across infrastructure sec-tors, we still need to provide robust security and physical protection for certain critical nodes (nuclear power plants, electric grids, key transportation hubs, and the like).

7.76   Some critical risk management lessons may not emerge unless we participate in a realistic simulation or exercise; likewise, some principles are not fully understood until an actual disaster occurs.

7.77   The current approach to risk calculations being used by government and industry is flawed and works only if there are reliable data regarding threats, vulnerabilities, and consequences. Such data is seldom available and in some cases is impossible to acquire therefore, subjective information is often utilized to support decisions and grant proposals.

OPERATIONAL APPLICATION

7.78   The current National Incident Management System (NIMS), as a management model, needs improvement. The system is currently "too brittle and lacks scalability" for very complex disasters. It is too large of an operational model for a local tornado, and too small for a major incident such as Hurricane Katrina or the Deepwater Horizon oil spill.

7.79   An example of a complex business continuity project on the mid-Atlantic corridor is the DHS-funded pilot with the State of New Jersey and the private sector, focused on the NJ Turnpike/Exit 14, where there is a major geographic node at the intersec-tion of oil, shipping, fiber, rail, highway, banking, data processing, cell phone, and power systems.

7.80   During Hurricane Katrina, there was an immediate demand to work across stove-piped organizations that required a common set of values and shared vision within intergovernmental and private-sector teams. When operating in a crisis environment where there is limited legal authority to direct organizations, *unity-of-effort* (vs. *unity-of-command*) is practically the only effective approach.

CYBER SECURITY

7.81 Due to the rapid advancements and globalization of information technology and dependencies on Internet access, cyber security has an impact on all 16 critical infrastructure sectors, creating both greater efficiencies and greater vulnerabilities.

7.82 Cyber-security challenges exist across the interagency and commercial industry because of uncoordinated efforts within cyber and critical infrastructure policy areas, where one community emphasizes physical security (led by the chief security officer) and another community focuses on information assurance (led by the chief information officer).

7.83 U.S. Department of Defense/Cyber Command (DOD/CYBERCOM) is a microcosm of the nation—reflecting the complex nature of executing cyber-security policies at different levels. And while all sectors are unique in their cyber vulnerabilities, the goal—within cyber policy—is to examine each infrastructure area (sector by sector) and apply specific lessons learned.

7.84 From an infrastructure protection view, cyber security cannot be separated from physical security requirements, because cyber is embedded within all infrastructure sectors. And the private sector is wrestling with the same cyber challenges being faced by the public sector.

7.85 In cyber security, DHS studies the lessons learned from NLEs to identify the most crucial legislative, regulatory, and policy gaps that exist and determine what cyber-security requirements might be addressed through CIP efforts.

MARITIME SECURITY

7.86 The nation does not understand how dependent it is—especially economically—upon maritime commerce. Since World War II, the United States has underinvested in maritime transportation infrastructures and is at risk because of safety, security, and economic imperatives.

7.87 Ports represent a cross-modal intersection of overlapping and interconnected systems (shipping, rail, highways, tunnels, etc.) directly supporting regional safety, security, economic, and environmental objectives.

7.88 Ports and port authorities offer a unique security environment to study interdependencies and PPPs because, although each port is different, there are common policy and planning requirements that can be generalized across the country.

7.89 The ports provide an operational laboratory to experiment with whole-of-nation, intergovernmental, all-hazards challenges and could be used to develop an integrated planning model that can touch all challenges at the local, state, regional, and national levels and help define the elements of functional resilience.

Measurements

7.90   There is an increased emphasis on quantitative measures, infrastructure condition, business continuity, and response capabilities across all sectors to better set priorities and inform budget decisions.

7.91   DHS/FEMA is emphasizing metrics, capability-based assessments, and measurable performance by applying *systematic scoring methods* to better quantify response, recovery, and readiness.

7.92   There should be more analytical rigor and quantitative information used in preparedness planning to reduce the amount of guess work. Everyone is surprised by natural disasters, but that shouldn't always be the case. FEMA research indicates that there are disaster cycles and geographic trends that can allow better preparedness decisions at the regional level.

7.93   DHS needs to better define operational requirements across the ten FEMA regions. FEMA regularly provides training and education at the local, state, and regional level, which can also be used as a vehicle to improve practitioner skills in the areas of data collection and defining operational requirements.

Note

1. Inductive reasoning consists of inferring general principles or rules from specific facts collected—the process of moving from generalizations to individual instances or findings (Dictionary.com 2013).

8 Recommendations

STRATEGIC RECOMMENDATIONS

8.1 FACE THE CHALLENGE

Place systemic critical infrastructure and resilience objectives at a higher priority on the national agenda; assert the need for a comprehensive national policy and regulations that support preparedness and critical infrastructure resilience. Promulgate a national strategy for CIR that is informed by PPD-21 and directly supports the emerging preparedness frameworks (prevent, protect, mitigate, respond, recover).

8.2 FORMALIZE FUNCTIONAL RESILIENCE

Federal, state, and local government agencies and departments should incorporate functional resilience as an organizing principle to inform the strategies and policies of government and the programs they support. Operationalize this through a systematic resilience implementation process, based upon risk maps, functional resilience framework, and a prioritized action plan.

8.3 CRAFT A NATIONAL RESILIENCY FRAMEWORK

Expand public- and private-sector awareness by designing and publishing a national-level functional resilience framework—based upon required capabilities—that reflects a continuum of preparedness ranging from physical protection to functional continuity, built upon the national preparedness principles of "prevent, protect, mitigate, respond, and recover."

8.4 BUILD A COMPREHENSIVE ARCHITECTURE

Establish an integrated national-level resource that captures disaster-related data (1) to document lives and property lost, injuries, and economic impacts; and (2) to support academic research, computational modeling, and the basis for expanded resilience incentives within legal frameworks and the insurance industry.

8.5   EXPLORE NEW MARKET SOLUTIONS

Drawing from improved risk data sources, prototype new mechanisms working with major insurance and reinsurance companies to simultaneously share risk and encourage best practices; provide limited immunity for companies that share data; design insurance policies and indemnification programs to incentivize more resilient behavior.

8.6   CONDUCT LEGISLATIVE REVIEW

Examine existing laws, authorities, and statutes to identify barriers to critical infrastructure resilience—especially in the area of public-private sector information sharing—and propose legislation to provide companies with appropriate liability and Freedom of Information Act (FOIA) protection.

8.7   IDENTIFY WHOLE-OF-NATION BARRIERS

Engage behavioral, social, and engineering sciences in the academic and R&D communities to identify high-impact research opportunities that target the source of preparedness and community resilience. Research should focus on individual human factors and changing behaviors at the personal, family, community, and regional level.

8.8   CATALYZE PRIVATE-SECTOR INVESTMENTS

Encourage the expanded investment of private equity and venture capital by working through existing relationships between private investors/business sector and their vital interlocutors: customers, suppliers, insurers, banks, professional organizations, and product distributors.

8.9   IDENTIFY COORDINATION HUBS

Systematically map—nationally, regionally, and locally—the collective groups of emergency managers, private utilities, and infrastructure owners/operators that form communities-of-interest within a geographic region or corridor based on trusted relationships and networking. These maps, sometimes referred to as Regional Emergency Coordination Plans (RECPs), are designed to encourage open communication before, during, and after an emergency.

8.10   REFORM RISK METHODOLOGY

Expand the thrust of risk assessment from attempting to prevent attacks and protect physical property (typically achieved by assessing risks using threat, vulnerability, and consequence calculus) to a risk-intelligent model that builds resilience based on systemic capabilities-based analyses with an increased focus on "mitigation, response, and recovery."

8.11 MAP GLOBAL SUPPLY CHAINS

Conduct a comprehensive review of available resources and modeling tools to map internal and external supply chains across all domains; leverage ongoing studies in the public and private sector to provide situational awareness of resiliency vulnerabilities, critical capabilities, and key intermodal hubs.

8.12 IDENTIFY ALL-HAZARDS NATIONAL-LOCAL GAPS

Close major gaps that exist between national policy guidance and local-regional owners and operators by identifying discrete areas of all-hazards cross-domain disconnects; identify a key geographic intermodal hub to serve as a research exemplar to facilitate this study (ports, mega-community, and so on).

8.13 DEVELOP RISK MAPS

Systematically map (with analytical link analysis and graphic tools) key CIKR relationships based on dependencies and interdependencies in the mega-regions. This effort will identify vital areas of economic commerce, geographic hot spots, single points-of-failure, and acute functional vulnerabilities, revealing the connectedness of major geographic areas and hubs of intermodal activity (PANYNJ, POLALB, the Gulf Coast, and others).

OPERATIONAL RECOMMENDATIONS

8.14 INTEGRATE TECHNOLOGY SYSTEMS

Explore the utility of combining the power of existing technology, leveraging the power of social media (Facebook, Twitter, Google, etc.), social networking sites (SNS), critical incident management systems (CIMS), geographic information systems (GIS), and global positioning system (GPS) to support a new system-of-systems architecture for emergency response and disaster management.

8.15 IMPROVE DATA SHARING

Develop an analytically sound enterprise platform that provides CIKR and preparedness planners with an effective collaborative tool, leveraging data fusion and automated protocols to collect and process disparate time-critical data from homeland security information sources.

8.16 OPERATIONALIZE RESILIENCE FOR BROADER APPLICATION

Develop a resilience implementtion process that can be adapted and generalized regionally, and demonstrate its utility by prototyping and testing at specific geographic locations. Employ sound analytical methods to quantify and visualize risk maps, showing essential functions, dependencies, and interdependencies, providing decision makers with a standardized methodology to set priorities and optimize scarce resources in the face of disasters.

8.17 FORM A HOMELAND SECURITY AUXILIARY

Develop a homeland security–sponsored volunteer auxiliary program and public-private partnership, called National Drive for Unified Resilience (NDUR), pronounced "ENDURE," to inspire participation in resilience at an individual and community level, modeled after USAF's Civil Air Patrol, USCG Auxiliary, and so on (refer to Appendix D).

8.18 EXPAND MARITIME 9/11 STUDIES

Build upon previous studies to incorporate a broader range of maritime threats, including a small-vessel attack (USS *Cole* scenario); a dirty bomb or weapon of mass destruction (WMD) hidden in cargo containers; disruption to maritime commerce posed by attacking port transportation infrastructures (bridges, railways, tunnels); attacks on cruise ships or oil processing terminals; underwater improvised explosive devices (IEDs); and major evacuation from an urban port location as occurred with the 9/11 boatlift from the New York City borough of Manhattan.

8.19 MASTER INDEX FOR RESOURCES AND CAPABILITIES

Develop a master reference of regional- and national-level resources to ensure rapid identification of infrastructure support services and capabilities before disaster strikes. In compiling this reference, focus less on specific locations of physical supplies and more on those critical organizations/agencies that regularly provide those resources and capabilities—and represent key supply chain and distribution contacts during a disaster.

8.20 INSPIRE FIRST RESPONDERS

Prototype a plan—one comparable to the Goldwater-Nichols Department of Defense Reorganization Act—for local, state, and regional first responders and government officials by cross-training and educating practitioners outside their service organization; the plan should be similar to joint military Professional Military Education (PME) requirements and linked to promotion and attractive career opportunities.

9 | Conclusion

"Of all the countries in the world," Alexis de Tocqueville contended in his 1833 *Democracy in America*, "America has taken greatest advantage of association and has applied this powerful means of action to the greatest variety of objectives." He admired the way Americans used voluntary associations to creatively solve problems. Americans, he wrote, "associate for the goals of public security, of commerce and industry . . . there is nothing the human will despairs of attaining by the free action of the collective power of individuals" (Schleifer 2010). In a globalized economy with highly interconnected systems, only this spirit of innovation, sense of personal responsibility, and vision for collective action can make American critical infrastructure more resilient.

Resilience is not something that can simply be assigned to government planners or studied by policymakers. It is a vexing challenge that extends across the boundaries of federal, state, regional, and local communities and transcends public-sector capabilities. Only a whole-of-nation public-private approach can offer an adequate answer. Furthermore, it is not enough to compile lessons learned from recent disasters: lessons learned are really lessons observed until they are operationalized. Functional resilience requires that we systematically distill the major lessons of modern crises *and* formulate a framework for action that can be implemented at all levels of the homeland security enterprise.

Recognizing the major challenges of our era—eroding infrastructure, the growing interconnectedness of the global economy, and an uncertain future marked by climate change, natural disasters, and terrorism—this book provides a holistic approach to prepare for and face the storms of the future. There is a growing consensus that resilience does work and should be embraced with a sense of urgency as public policy.

The unifying threads that weave this document together—strengthening homeland security and disaster management to achieve resilience—are offered to inspire a new generation of leaders. They will help planners systematically prepare for the future by examining infrastructure, studying complex interdependencies, defining functional resilience, and prioritizing action plans. The long-term objective of this study is to mitigate the adverse impact of future disasters through resiliency policies and procedures.

In the process of interviewing subject matter experts (SMEs) across the interagency, within academia, and in the commercial industry for this study, it became evident that *preparedness* and *resilience* are among the most significant challenges facing the national security community and homeland security planners at all levels. While the discussion often started with a critical infrastructure or cyber-security topic, it eventually returned to the broader issue of *resilience*—or an adjacent theme such as continuity or sustainment—because this topic impacts everyone at a personal, family, and community level.

One of the immediate challenges of this study was sorting through the volume and variety of articles, books, reports, stakeholders, and case studies to evaluate where we are currently as a nation, especially in the wake of the 9/11 attacks, hurricanes Irene (2011) and Katrina (2005), Superstorm Sandy (2012), the Boston Marathon bombings (2013), and the Moore, Oklahoma tornado (2013). Drawing from the lessons of recent disasters and building on basic assumptions and expert inputs, we document the current state of critical infrastructure resilience, serving as a catalyst to further research. Specifically, areas of research should be focused sharply on how we—as a nation—can best improve resilience and homeland security, looking for major themes "beyond the storms" of traditional risk assessments and operational threat response.

Like Japan and the United Kingdom, America is an island-nation with economic arteries connected to all domains—air, land, maritime, space, and cyber. The nation produces fewer industrial goods than in the past, and relies heavily upon the global supply chain with just-in-time delivery of goods. This is a fragile system that depends heavily on a strong infrastructure; therefore, a significant increase in preparedness and a better understanding of resilience are essential for success.

Critical infrastructures are interdependent systems and must be studied and understood in that context. And managing infrastructure sectors in an isolated and independent manner—recognizing that virtually all are independently owned—does not contribute to security in a complex and rapidly-changing environment. Public policies, as well as regional safety and security programs, are fragmented because there is no single executive agent to synchronize cross-domain issues, and even if it wanted to, the federal government is unable to exercise control because the majority of infrastructures are privately owned and operated.

Regardless of where we stand on the ideas surrounding preparedness, or how we attempt to transform our methodologies, there is little disagreement that the state of our nation's infrastructure is broken and eroding rapidly—and something must be done at the highest levels of government (locally, regionally, and nationally) to address the problem in a systematic, integrated, and coordinated manner. According to a senior executive within the commercial maritime industry, the single greatest threat to our national economy is the "neglect and depreciation" of maritime transportation infrastructure due to a failure to invest in the overall national system (Carmel 2012). This comment was not unique to the maritime domain; it was a clear theme across all sectors and domains as stakeholders expressed similar concerns about the current state of critical infrastructure resilience.

There is a need for a dedicated communications campaign that defines the infrastructure vulnerabilities and associated security challenges more clearly so the general public understands the nature and severity of the problem. A strategic communications plan can help market infrastructure security challenges through a combination of government initiatives, think tanks, congressional studies, commercial industry support, and academic research. Furthermore, the interconnected nature of the global supply chain and the potential adverse impact of attacks (or disasters) on the U.S. economy argues for the establishment of a national homeland security volunteer auxiliary organization along with a national framework which expands the level of awareness and public commitment within the American public.

Another challenge is the assessment of risk (upon which decisions related to critical infrastructure protection [CIP] are anchored), because precise threat estimates are elusive. Consequently, one of the recommendations from this study is to expand the current method of risk assessment—from a *threat, vulnerability, and consequence* calculus to a capabilities-based assessment of essential *functions*—which will inform decisions concerning appropriate safeguards to maintain or recover continuity of operations. Evidence from this study indicates that further research and analysis is needed to identify models and tools that can be leveraged for a resilience-based approach toward CIP and preparedness (Flynn 2007; National Research Council [NRC] 2008; Allen 2012).

Another barrier to critical infrastructure resilience—impeding vital information sharing between the public and private sectors—is in the area of rules and authorities based on legislation and judicial testing. Laws and statutes are needed to provide liability protection for private companies that conduct risk assessments and supply information on vulnerabilities with government entities. Without appropriate legal and regulatory protection, companies risk exposure to antitrust sanctions stemming from sharing information, or they risk lawsuits from customers over the disclosure of the companies' vulnerabilities. Without the necessary protection from liability and Freedom of Information Act (FOIA) requests, as well as the government's willingness to guard proprietary business information, the private sector will be a missing partner in securing the nation's infrastructure.

Finally, this study synthesizes large amounts of information and struggles to simplify the complexities of resilience and preparedness—topics that resist simplification. The best outcome would be that this report helps forge a consensus—among public- and private-sector decision makers and staff elements—regarding the need to expand our national focus from expensive physical protection to more economical functional resilience. This objective is within reach if we commit to unity-of-effort across intergovernmental actors, build new levels of trust that enable robust public-private partnerships, and offer stakeholders a national framework for action. These are historic and consequential times that demand strong leadership in the public and private sectors, if we intend to move—and inspire—our nation *"Beyond the Storms"* of homeland security, resilience, and disaster management.

Appendix A
Case Studies

Table A.1 Summary of Case Studies

Case Study	General Description
Hurricane Sandy	Worst storm in history in terms of impact to the Northeast United States
Port Authority of New York and New Jersey	Major hub of intermodal resilience challenges
Ports of Los Angeles/Long Beach	Strategic crossroads of commerce and security provide key lessons
Japan Earthquake	Earthquake triggered a tsunami and nuclear disasters on island
Hurricane Irene	Only hurricane to make landfall in 2011, revealing systemic failures
North American Derecho	Powerful storm system uncovered fragile utilities sector
India Power Outage	Largest blackout in history, affecting one-tenth of the world's population
Civil GPS Vulnerabilities	Position, navigation, timing signals have an impact on all sectors
Chemical Sector	National and global supply chains have fragile points-of-failure
Norris Dam	Pre–World War II infrastructure was first major TVA project
Western Rivers Flooding	Missouri and Mississippi rivers experienced record flooding in 2011
Northeast Blackout of 2003	Local failures triggered cascading regional disruption of power
Collective Action Theory	Introduces work of Nobel Prize–winning economist Elinor Ostrom

The case studies are helpful for policy formulation and public policy instruction because they not only organize facts about each event within its historical context but also frame the situation for the reader within relevant fields of study: preparedness, disaster management, emergency response, resilience, public-private partnerships (PPPs), collective action, etc.

The case studies illuminate the challenges of preparedness and critical infrastructure resilience under the most strenuous conditions. And they provide examples in which organizations successfully overcame collective action hurdles, as well as scenarios in which the lack of PPPs caused disaster planning to fall short in the face of overwhelming crises. The following cases also underscore the interconnected nature of the 16 infrastructure sectors, revealing both strengths and weaknesses in interdependent systems, global supply chains, and the current state of resilience.

These 13 case studies provide real-world lessons in critical infrastructure resilience, offering examples that:

1. occurred during and after the promulgation of major national-level policies;
2 reflect a cross-section of preparedness scenarios; and
3. provide a wide variety of operational missions, geographic locations, and public-private and interagency coordination challenges.

Figure A.1 Superstorm Sandy

Superstorm Sandy
Major Disaster Triggers Local, Regional, Global Disruptions"

- Largest Atlantic hurricane on record, over 1,000 miles in diameter, impacted 24 states

- Second only to Katrina in damage costs and economic interruptions (loss estimate $66B), 10 million customers lost power

- 253 deaths across a seven-country path from Caribbean to Northeast U.S.

- Major inflection point for preparedness and resilience planners:

  - U.S. most densely populated region
  - Impacted global supply chains
  - NYSE closed for two days
  - Travelers stranded across the globe
  - 14-foot storm surge flooded facilities
  - Power, communications, housing deficits

Source: NOAA, Weather, http://www.noaa.gov/wx.html.

Hurricane Sandy came ashore near Atlantic City, New Jersey, on October 29, 2012, in the final days of the annual "hurricane season," obviously no respecter of calendars or the most densely populated region of the country.[1] The location of landfall was particularly concerning because its trajectory put New York City—the largest city in the United States—on the north side of the storm's path, referred to as the "dangerous semicircle" of the hurricane because of the most powerful forces and highest winds. The storm—over 1,000 miles across, with winds over 90 miles per hour and double the size of Hurricane Irene (2011)—was a monster storm because it hit the most densely populated part of the United States, threatening 60 million people along the Mid-Atlantic and New England coasts. It was the largest hurricane ever recorded in the Atlantic, with its clouds extending some 2,000 miles from Florida to Canada, at one point covering one-fifth of the contiguous United States. Like Japan's tsunami in 2011, Sandy placed large modern industrialized cities at the mercy of nature's fury (Welch 2012).

The timing of this rare late-October storm was particularly lethal because it converged with cold weather systems from the north and west to form a *superstorm*, with high winds felt as far inland as Chicago and the Great Lakes (700 miles from the New Jersey shore) and over 30 inches of snowfall reported as far away as West Virginia. The hurricane was also energized by surrounding weather systems. High winds extended over 500 miles from Sandy's center, forcing authorities to order evacuations of coastal areas from Maryland to Connecticut, including 375,000 residents evacuated from New York City. The New York Stock Exchange canceled trading for two days and nearly 7,000 flights were canceled when New York airports (LaGuardia and John F. Kennedy International) were closed—stranding passengers at airports all over the world. New York's subway, which handles over 8 million passengers daily, faced record flooding when the East River overflowed its banks, flooding large sections of Lower Manhattan. Battery Park had a water surge of nearly 14 feet, and seven subway tunnels under the East River were flooded. The Metropolitan Transportation Authority said that the destruction caused by the storm was the worst disaster in the 108-year history of the New York City subway system. Seawater even flooded the Holland Tunnel and Ground Zero construction site (McCoy and Strauss 2012).

This storm was a wakeup call, raising questions about extreme weather patterns possibly becoming the new reality for emergency managers and disaster planners who had not seen a major hurricane make a direct impact in many years. Storm surge, rising waters caused by high winds, heavy rains, and an untimely full-moon high tide prompted many coastal cities to evacuate across the Northeast region. Storm surges damaged water pipes, leaving fire hydrants with little or no water pressure. There was a record 32-foot wave measured at the offshore harbor entrance to New York City. Power plants were flooded, and 8 million people in the New York City region (nearly the entire population of the city) were without electricity. There were major neighborhood fires in Queens and Breezy Point, Long Island (burning 111 houses), caused by transformers that exploded when the storm surge hit near oceanfront properties. The storm caused 253 deaths and left thousands homeless. Staten Island alone saw 23 fatalities, the highest number of storm-related deaths in any of the New York City boroughs (Sharp 2012; Frazier 2013).

Based on lessons learned from disasters such as Hurricanes Katrina, Irene, and Sandy, national and state leaders leveraged partnerships with many entities inside and outside of government. In addition to expediting assistance to the impacted states through the rapid turnaround of 12 pre-disaster Emergency Declarations and three Major Disaster Declarations under the Stafford Act, the White House (working through DHS/FEMA) initiated new applications of the act for cost-share adjustments and debris-removal programs. For example, a 100 percent federal cost-share is an option available to the U.S. president in the implementation of the Stafford Act, but it is rarely authorized. In this case, a 100 percent cost-share option was exercised, limited to 10 days, for emergency power restoration and emergency public transportation assistance, including direct federal aid for certain areas in New Jersey, New York, and Connecticut. This allowed accelerated efforts to restore critical power and transportation systems as a matter of public safety.

Sandy also revived debates over climate change and rising sea levels, as questions emerged from weather forecasters and disaster management experts. Does Sandy portend more severe weather events due to climate change? Are we witnessing a new age of superstorms with more frequent occurrences of extreme weather? If the sea level is rising, what is the resulting impact on storm surge damage? Are natural forces increasingly causing more damage to populated areas? Should large cities like New York build seawalls—similar to London, Rotterdam, and Venice—to create barriers from any future storm surge? We cannot ignore the fact that extreme weather events are increasing in frequency and power. And regardless of the cause, we must be better prepared for future storms while we rebuild our coastlines, infrastructure, and communities from Sandy, but we must do so in a resilient-smart and risk-intelligent manner (Kerry, Lautenberg, and Gillibrand 2012; National Academies 2012).

According to the *New York Times,* for nearly a decade, scientists told New York city and state officials that New York "faced certain peril due to rising sea levels, more frequent flooding, and extreme weather patterns" (quoted by Chen and Navarro 2012). The warnings increased after Hurricane Irene in 2011, when the city shut down its subway system and water rushed into the Rockaways and Lower Manhattan. After Sandy, officials discussed major infrastructure changes that could protect the city's fragile shores and more than 8 million residents. Many argue for a levee system or seawalls to improve on existing protections, but these systems could cost as much as $10 billion, making it a daunting challenge during times of financial hardship. Furthermore, a state report on rising sea levels suggested erecting structural barriers to restrain floodwaters as part of a broader approach, along with relocating buildings and people farther from the coasts (Chen and Navarro 2012).

The problem with this approach (installing more physical structures) is that, in addition to affordability, we cannot build enough barriers to protect ourselves from all major threats and vulnerabilities—especially given that 23 of the 25 most densely populated counties in the nation are located in coastal areas. Building physical seawalls as a reaction to a recent disaster is tempting, but thinking more resiliently points us to more innovative ways to respond to and recover from what will be inevitable storms of a different scope, scale, location, and impact. We simply cannot spend enough money or build enough walls to protect ourselves from disasters and attacks; rather, we must actively integrate resilience principles in our communities with an all-hazards multidisciplinary approach that incrementally raises our level of preparedness.

Among the observations from Superstorm Sandy, the following items comprise a growing list of lessons learned for those studying preparedness and resilience or responsible for disaster management and emergency response. Each of these items was derived from personal observations in the storm region days after the event or from interviews with local authorities involved with the crisis firsthand.

Although general in nature, these items contain many of the specific planning variables needed to shape a regional framework for action and understand functional resilience imperatives:

- A hurricane in late October impacting highly populated urban areas did not fit the regional planning scenarios, and despite the weather forecasts that preceded Sandy, the region was not prepared; extreme weather—and the accompanying disaster management/emergency response demands—imposed unexpected levels of damage; available resources (physical, human, transportation, safety equipment) were insufficient for the level of demand.
- Money, governance structures, and published strategies are insufficient to prepare for a disaster of this magnitude; it requires a culture of resilient thinking and innovative approaches that are embedded into everyday functions, systems, and processes.
- In the Northeast region of the United States—especially since the 9/11 crisis—

intelligence analysts and disaster management planners were "planning for the last crisis" by focusing more on the terrorist security threat than on the potential impact of extreme weather.

- The Incident Command System (ICS) should enable a coordinated response among various jurisdictions and functional agencies, both public and private; after Sandy, however, senior officials in the New York/New Jersey region expressed concern that ICS failed to provide a disciplined framework that all players understood, and struggled to address cross-state and regional issues.

- Electric power is the lifeline that enables all other critical infrastructure sectors to work; wireless service, gas station pumps, water and sewage treatment, roadway stoplights and basic commerce stop if energy is unavailable or disrupted.

- Wireless carriers restored cell services within days, and the abundance of diesel fuel allowed FEMA to position generators in the hardest-hit communities, so people could at least charge phones and continue texting and emailing family and friends.

- Community engagement and information sharing during and after the disaster were significantly enhanced by social networking tools that helped bridge public-private barriers; local trust networks emerged in formal and informal settings.

- Grassroots organizations formed rapidly in the disaster recovery environment due to a culture of innovation, problem solving, and rapid coordination across dissimilar agencies; small teams of volunteers, NGOs, and FEMA Innovation leaders leveraged the unstructured environment to pass information and foster whole- community coordination.

- Nonprofit PPPs supporting homeland security, emergency management, and business continuity (the All-Hazards Consortium in the Mid-Atlantic Region, for instance) demonstrated the vital role of integrated planning and coordination among private-sector owner/operators of critical infrastructure and the local/state/federal government.

- Although no disaster or geographic location is the same, as with previous extreme weather cases (Hurricanes Katrina, Irene, Isaac, etc.), the New Jersey/New York region provides an exemplar for the rest of the country in how to prepare for and respond to a natural disaster with complex weather systems in a cross-modal, all-hazards environment.

- Interviews with emergency planners and first responders in the region indicated that communities listened to public safety announcements and knew what was on the emergency checklists, but in general, few people thought subways would actually be flooded, tunnels would be compromised, ports and airports would be closed, because it didn't seem possible; actually, the best preparation for Superstorm Sandy was the most recent major storm to impact the region—Hurricane Irene that came up the East Coast in late August 2011—approximately one year before Sandy.

- For the authorities in the New York/New Jersey region, resilience was reflected in simple terms: how quickly they could recover. They consider resiliency from a *systems approach* rather than a numerical risk calculation—"a way of thinking" where everyday working people make decisions based on previously agreed-upon operating principles.

- The level of information sharing was improved after 9/11 and Hurricane Irene due to advanced digital technology and skillful leveraging of social networks through tech tools provided by companies like Ushahidi, a nonprofit that specializes in the collection and dissemination of vital information. FEMA staff also established a "base camp" site for planners and innovation team members to accelerate sharing of ideas at a common web location.
- FEMA Corps—a new partnership between FEMA and the Corporation for National and Community Service (CNCS) with over 1,000 members within AmeriCorps National Civilian Community Corps (NCCC)—was deployed to augment federal disaster response and recovery capabilities while providing an avenue of public service for young Americans.
- Accelerated assistance can be provided to storm-impacted areas through expedited pre-disaster Emergency Declarations and innovative measures such as cost-share adjustments and debris-removal programs via the Stafford Act.
- The experiences of locations such as Staten Island and the barrier islands of Long Island and New Jersey provide a reminder that dune fields and beaches provide a natural barrier against water and should be built up to provide an improved "shock absorber" against future storms and flooding.
- The most exposed flood zone areas may need to be rezoned, converting some low-lying waterfront housing areas into parkland to expand the buffer against flooding. Educating people is crucial; they need to know the elevation of their homes and clearly understand the risk of flooding and storm surge based on the nearest body of water.

Finally, to highlight the range of issues that surfaced during and after Sandy, consider the Department of Homeland Security (DHS) Daily Open Source Infrastructure Reports. These reports chronicle the flow of events by sector categories and the challenges faced by local, state, and regional officials attempting to coordinate disaster response and recovery in a chaotic post-storm environment. The primary areas that were reported by open sources during and after Sandy reflect the simultaneous and disruptive emergencies faced by first responders, local, state, regional, and national leaders as they converged on the disaster areas and attempted to restore services to the affected people as rapidly as possible. This chronological summary of reports underscores (1) the criticality of the *lifeline* sectors (energy, communications, transportation, financial and water), (2) the interconnected nature of the critical infrastructure in a densely populated region of the country, and (3) the types of issues that must be addressed in building community resilience (U.S. DHS 2012b). The following critical infrastructures were most heavily impacted:

Energy	Financial	Transportation	Communications
Water	Sewage	Environmental	Medical
Emergency Services	Cyber Security	Dams	Commercial Facilities

October 30, 2012

Energy	The supply of gasoline, diesel, and jet fuel into the East Coast nearly stopped on October 29, as Sandy forced the closure of two-thirds of the region's refineries, its largest pipeline, and most major seaports.
Financial	At least two major nuclear power plants in New Jersey shut down and others operated at reduced power as the storm triggered precautionary safety measures. Those plants accounted for about 19 percent of New Jersey's total electricity capacity.
Financial	For the first time since the Great Blizzard of 1888, U.S. stock markets were closed for two consecutive days due to weather; and it was the first unplanned shutdown since the 9/11 terrorist attacks.
Transportation	Airline and ground transportation systems in three major metropolitan areas shut down as Sandy moved closer to the East Coast. More than 10 million public transit commuters were without service.
Transportation	The nation's third-busiest cargo container port was evacuated and closed because of Sandy, according to the Port Authority of New York and New Jersey (PANYNJ) officials. The NYNJ port is a vital economic engine that handled over 5.5 million cargo containers in 2011.

October 31, 2012

Energy	Millions of people from Maine to the Carolinas awoke October 30 without electricity, and New York City was all but closed off by automobile, train, and air as Sandy moved inland, bringing heavy winds and rain. The U.S. death toll climbed to 39.
Transportation	High winds and heavy rain prompted closing of the New Jersey Turnpike's Hudson County Extension, and speed restrictions were imposed.
Transportation	Sandy affected New York City transportation activity, including subway systems, by flooding tunnels, garages, and rail yards and threatening to paralyze the area's mass transit system for days. All seven subway tunnels running under the East River from Manhattan to Queens and Brooklyn took in water, and resulting saltwater damage to the system's electrical hardware had to be cleaned, in some cases off site, before the system could be restored.
Communications	Verizon Communications reported that its wireless service was suffering as flooding in its central offices in lower Manhattan adversely impacted its backup generators and batteries.
Communications	Sandy-caused power outages knocked many of the East Coast's data centers and websites offline affecting networks around the world. As a precautionary measure, large portions of the power grid were shut down in lower Manhattan to prevent damage to underground equipment, leaving over a million people without power.
Sewage	Maryland state officials reported that a power outage caused by Sandy at a water reclamation plant resulted in sewage overflow of 2 million gallons per hour into the main stem of the Little Patuxent River. Similar power failures and sewage-related problems occurred in communities around the New York area.
Medical	Six New York City hospitals had no choice but to evacuate hundreds of patients after losing power at the height of the storm. A backup generator failed at a New York City hospital, forcing more than 200 patients, including 20 babies from neonatal intensive care to move. Without power, there were no elevators, so patients had to be carried down staircases, and ambulances came from around the city to help transport patients to other hospitals.
Emergency Services	A large tidal surge sent water overflowing a creek and flooding storm drains in two northern New Jersey towns, filling streets with up to five feet of water and triggering a frantic rescue effort by boats and trucks.
Emergency Services	Emergency response personnel and first responders would not respond to calls due to safety concerns when sustained winds reached 50 mph or wind gusts were over 65 mph.
Cyber Security	With Sandy's extensive impact on the East Coast, cyber criminals stood ready to take advantage of the storm conditions to make money or steal personal information. Natural disasters open doors for cyber criminals because many users want to make donations to victims and can easily be tricked into giving money away to sites that appear to be charities but are false fronts for thieves.
Dams	To help control flooding in New England, the Army Corps of Engineers used 171 satellite monitoring stations to measure river levels and manage flood control dams. Officials in Cherry Hill, New Jersey, ordered a mandatory evacuation of residents because of rising water levels at a dam, fearing that flood conditions could cause a failure.

November 1, 2012

Energy	Utility crews were by this time assessing damages and working to restore service to over 2 million homes and businesses in New Jersey. The state's largest utility (PSE&G) said it had restored power to 30 percent of its 1.4 million customers who lost services.
Energy	Sandy left large numbers of homes without power in Michigan, across the Mid-Atlantic, and among homes and businesses in New Jersey. Utility companies reported 1.9 million customers without power in New York State. Pennsylvania officials initially reported that 1 million customers were without power and large numbers could remain without electricity for up to one week.
Transportation	Two of the largest airports serving New York—John F. Kennedy International and Newark Liberty International—reopened on a limited operational schedule after losing power during the storm.
Transportation	The U.S. Coast Guard reported that New York harbor would not reopen until damage assessments from Sandy's impact could be completed.
Communications	Telecommunications companies told federal regulators that Sandy knocked out 25 percent of wireless cell towers and cable services in 10 states. A small number of 911 call centers were also affected.
Water	Two cities in New Jersey and one county were under boil water advisories following the storm, but authorities cautioned the number could rise because damage assessments had not yet been completed. Environmental officials were concerned water treatment companies across the state might be without power for a significant period of time, which would drain their backups and limit their ability to pump and treat water.
Sewage	New York City environmental officials reported that untreated sewage flowed into waterways around each of the city's five boroughs. The city's wastewater system handles combined sewage waste and stormwater and directly discharges an estimated 25 billion gallons annually when heavy rain or flooding overwhelms treatment plants.
Commercial Facilities	Breezy Point, Long Island, a beachfront neighborhood ordered to evacuate before Sandy, burned down as it was flooded with storm surge water. More than 190 firefighters were sent to the blaze, still fighting fires more than nine hours after it erupted.

NOVEMBER 2, 2012

Energy	Utility companies in Connecticut started to offer repair estimates to customers who lost power as a result of Sandy, indicating power would be restored to 95 percent of their customers by November 5.
Transportation	Three days after Sandy, New York City's subway system began to restore services, though the morning commute was plagued by long delays and massive gridlock on the main highways and bridges leading into the city. More than 1,000 people waiting for buses packed the sidewalks in Brooklyn. Many gas stations in and around the city had closed due to gasoline supply shortages, while stations that remained open drew long lines of cars that spilled onto the roadways. Teams of police directed customer lines at local gasoline stations to ensure order during the rationing process.
Sewage	Twenty-nine Connecticut sewage treatment plants were running on backup power. State environmental and health officials warned that floodwaters from Sandy in several towns might be contaminated because of raw sewage discharges from treatment plants and pumping stations. Officials in the Bridgeport area advised citizens to stay away from floodwaters and assume they were contaminated.
Environmental	An unknown amount of fuel spilled from a northern New Jersey oil facility that had been closed due to Sandy, contaminating waterways between New Jersey and Staten Island.
Commercial Facilities	Retailers kept stores closed in hard-hit New York and New Jersey while reopening in some other East Coast locations as they worked to assess the damage to their shops and sales.

NOVEMBER 5–9, 2012

Energy	Widespread gas shortages stirred fears among residents and disrupted some rescue and emergency services in New York and New Jersey.
Energy	In the area's second major leak since Sandy, some 7,700 gallons of fuel spilled from a refinery in New Jersey.
Energy	About 21,000 West Virginia homes and businesses remained without power as utility crews continued restoring service that had been knocked out by Sandy; however, officials in some places reported a full recovery would take months.
Energy	Snow and wind caused over 100,000 new power outages in the Mid-Atlantic and Northeast, prompting new calls for evacuation.
Energy	A gasoline rationing plan that let motorists fill up every other day went into effect in New York on November 9, while utility crews made progress restoring power to thousands of homes and businesses in the region still recovering from Sandy.
Financial	Banks in New Jersey coastal cities were stocking up on cash; six area banks suffered complete closures while seven others could not be reached by regulators.
Transportation	The Port Authority Trans-Hudson (PATH) train resumed service under the Hudson River from Jersey City to Midtown Manhattan. A fleet of 350 buses was expected to begin arriving in New Jersey to help ease commuter traffic.
Transportation	Some airlines suspended most flights to and from the New York area as a winter storm approached the northeastern United States.
Communications	Analysts predicted that Sandy would likely cost telephone and cable service providers hundreds of millions of dollars, with companies such as Verizon Communications and Cablevision Systems hit hardest.
Emergency Services	As of November 4, more than 182,000 individuals in Connecticut, New York, and New Jersey had registered for assistance, and FEMA approved more than $158 million for individuals to assist with housing and other disaster-related needs.

Figure A.2 Port Authority of New York and New Jersey

Port Authority of New York and New Jersey (PANYNJ)
International Crossroads of Intermodal Commerce

- Complex hub of interconnected, interdependent global supply chains
- Most densely populated region in the United States
- Nation's #2 port based on volume of container traffic
- Three major airports provide domestic and international services

- Major critical infrastructure challenges
- Over 2,000 maritime waterways
- 12 Foreign Trade Zone (FTZ) sites
- Over 3,500 longshoremen represents major workforce
- 80 tenants span more than 100 different business sectors

Source: Wikimedia Commons, New York City skyline after a stormy afternoon from Port Imperial, NY Waterway in Weehawken, New Jersey, http://commons.wikimedia.org/wiki/File:The_New_York_City_skyline_after_a_stormy_afternoon_from_Port_Imperial,_NY_Waterway_in_Weehawken_New_Jersey.jpg.

This geographic region of multi-agency, intermodal activity represents one of the most complex nodes of activity across all critical infrastructure sectors because it is the intersection of domestic and global supply chains and international commerce. Due to those factors, as well as the relevant operational lessons from the recent Superstorm Sandy, the Ports of New York and New Jersey provide a particularly useful research laboratory to study and analyze the mission-essential elements and critical advancements needed in disaster management and critical infrastructure resilience.

The Port Authority of New York and New Jersey (PANYNJ) is an intermodal hub of aviation, land, and maritime transportation. Its daily container/freight shipments support global supply chains and highlight the problems that can occur because of mass transit challenges with 100-year-old bridges, tunnels, highways, waterways, railways, and pipelines. Furthermore, PANYNJ calls attention to the interconnectedness of financial institutions, telecommunications, and international trade markets.

In facing the stress of Superstorm Sandy, PANYNJ provides an example for other populated industrial regions, drawing lessons from the most densely populated region in the country in how to respond to and recover from a major natural disaster.

PANYNJ—formed in 1921—operates and maintains America's busiest airport system, marine terminals and ports, the Port Authority Trans-Hudson (PATH) rail transit system, six tunnels and bridges between New York and New Jersey, the Port Authority Bus Terminal in Manhattan, and the World Trade Center. The Port Authority provides services for 17 million people who live and work in New York and New Jersey, a region that supports 8.6 million jobs with an estimated gross regional product of more than $929 billion. Their strategic objectives are to enhance regional capacity and transportation; increase the number and proportion of commuters who travel by mass transit; foster a streamlined supply-chain network; maintain and modernize facilities to ensure safety, security, economic, and environmental standards; and engage regional partners in the creation of plans, policies, and investments that provide a robust transportation services for regional residents, businesses, and visitors (PANYNJ 2013).

To achieve these objectives, PANYNJ partners with many federal and state agencies to ensure the safety and security of the ports. Many civil and military agencies, from the U.S. Coast Guard to the U.S. Department of Agriculture to the Port Authority's own police force, coordinate efforts to protect the ports and the surrounding region. PANYNJ handles a wide spectrum of domestic and international cargo, including containers, roll on–roll off automobiles (Ro-Ro), liquid and dry bulk, break-bulk, and specialized project cargo. They maintain 54 container cranes and have three port companies that offer floating derricks, including the 1,000-ton capacity Chesapeake 1000, the largest on the East Coast. Within the region, there is a wide selection of freight forwarders, brokers, financial firms, and port services. The port services not only the 80 million consumers in the New York/New Jersey metropolitan area but also the growing markets of the Midwest, New England, and Eastern Canada by providing a selection of cross-modal transportation systems (PANYNJ 2013).

PANYNJ also has 12 sites that are Foreign Trade Zones (FTZs), secure geographical areas located within or near U.S. ports that U.S. Customs treats as properties outside national borders for trade purposes. Manufacturers have traditionally used FTZs to lower import duties and taxes because the merchandise they receive at an FTZ is still considered international commerce (PANYNJ 2013).

In the days following Superstorm Sandy, local officials said, "In some ways, Sandy made 9/11 look easy"—certainly not in terms of loss of life or threat to national security, but because of the widespread nature of the damage: The planes that hit the Twin Towers caused serious damage to a defined location that could receive a focused response with well-defined boundaries, whereas Sandy's impact spread over a multistate region with unbounded and chaotic implications that required centralized and decentralized action by all stakeholders and local communities.

The PANYNJ and New York City Office of Emergency Management (OEM) conduct exercises to prepare the labyrinth of public safety organizations, integrate the vast response resources available in the region, and ensure the effective functioning of the Citywide Incident Management System (CIMS). Prior to Superstorm Sandy, the published objectives of these cross-agency exercises were evaluated based on the following criteria (PANYNJ 2009):

- implementation of a command structure in accordance with the CIMS;
- establishment and management of multi-agency tactical communications;
- formulation of an Assessment Task Force to conduct a thorough scene assessment and form a Rescue Task Force to perform victim rescue and extrication operations;
- triage, treatment, and transport of patients from the incident site;
- execution of a multi-agency security perimeter; and
- management, coordination, and direction of investigations and intelligence operations.

Major exercises can enlist the participation of over 1,000 personnel—drawing from 800 first responders, 150 New York City OEM members of the Community Emergency Response Teams (CERTs), and support staff and evaluators. These types of comprehensive exercises, along with over $10 billion invested over the last 10 years to secure structures, facilities, and critical infrastructures, were designed to prevent disasters and protect lives and property from harm (PANYNJ 2009); yet Superstorm Sandy revealed systemic shortfalls in disaster management systems and emergency response capabilities. Hazard Mitigation Teams have been established to better understand the greatest vulnerabilities and prioritize the necessary steps to strengthen security and resilience in the future. These strategic steps are intended to build upon the strengths of existing capabilities—reinforcing those things that worked well—and improve the ability to mitigate, respond to, and recover from future disasters.

Figure A.3 Ports of Los Angeles/Long Beach

Ports of Los Angeles/Long Beach (POLALB)
Major Intermodal Hub Critical to National Economy

- The combined port complex is the fifth busiest port in the world, shipping over 40% of the nation's containerized cargo and over 50% of the oil used in California.

- Coordination and security challenges are compounded by 88 separate municipalities and the location of commercial marinas inside the port complex.

- POLA is the busiest container port in the nation, operating 270 berths and over 70 high-capacity cargo cranes; LA's trade accounts for 20% of the cargo moving through U.S. ports.

- POLB is the second busiest seaport in the nation, operating 80 berths and over 70 high-capacity cargo cranes; LB's trade accounts for 13% of the cargo moving through U.S. ports.

Source: Wikimedia Commons, Port of Long Beach, California, http://commons.wikimedia.org/wiki/File:Port_of_Long_Beach,_California.jpg.

The Ports of Los Angeles/Long Beach (POLALB), California, are vital to the economic prosperity and security of our nation because of the variety and volume of international freight, cargo, supplies, produce, technology, chemicals, and fuel that flow through their port facilities. Like Seattle, San Francisco, the Gulf Coast, Tidewater Virginia, the Ports of New Jersey and New York, and other strategic ports, these facilities are complex domestic and international hubs of interdependent infrastructures that support a robust and sometimes fragile global supply chain.

These ports represent a major maritime transportation intersection of intermodal activity and are subject to a unique set of threats that must be a constant focus of the broad cross-section of law enforcement, maritime security, and harbor police personnel. Possible scenarios include:

1. a small-vessel attack (similar to USS *Cole*), especially because private and commercial marinas are located inside the port complex;
2. cargo containers used as a conveyance for a WMD or a dirty bomb;

3. bombing attacks against port bridges (highway or rail);
4. disruption of fuel-oil terminal operations;
5. a cruise ship attack; or
6. an underwater mining or subsurface attack.

After 9/11, domestic aviation transportation was grounded for three full days as a security precaution, and the maritime ports, with the exception of the POLALB, were closed by the Department of Homeland Security, disrupting vital maritime transportation, commerce, and trade. Actions by the POLALB—before, during, and after the 9/11 attacks—provide an example for other ports and hubs of major intermodal activity and complex interdependencies during future disasters, where advanced planning and robust communications among emergency management, law enforcement, the port authority, regulators, labor unions, and congressional leaders allowed increased security and sustained port operations to occur simultaneously.

In 2012, POLALB—which together make up one of Southern California's most important job engines—handled slightly more cargo than they moved in 2011, despite an eight-day strike that shut down most of the Los Angeles port and half of the cargo terminals in neighboring Long Beach. Los Angeles is the only U.S. port to top 8 million containers in a year and is the sixteenth-busiest port worldwide. The neighboring Port of Long Beach sustained steep declines over much of 2012, but had its strongest showing in the latter stages of the year, surpassing 6 million containers (White 2013).

International trade grew slightly in 2012, with the 10 biggest U.S. ports handling 34.2 million cargo containers, or about 800,000 more than they did in 2011, an increase of 2.4 percent. Some ports posted strong gains, including those in Savannah, Georgia, the nation's fourth-largest port, which rose an estimated 9 percent; Hampton Roads, Virginia, number seven, up an estimated 10.4 percent; and Tacoma, Washington, number nine, up an estimated 12.7 percent. Overall, Los Angeles and Long Beach captured nearly 41 percent of the volume of container cargo moving through the nation's 10 biggest ports in 2012, down slightly from the 41.9 percent share they held in 2011 (White 2013).

POLALB together moved 14.1 million containers in 2012, slightly more than they did in 2011, but there were positive signs for both ports. That is good news for the Southern California economy because the two ports are directly responsible for about 595,000 jobs in Southern California and indirectly support an additional 648,500 jobs. For Los Angeles, which handled 8.12 million containers, it was the best post-recession year to date and its third-busiest ever (Sahagun 2012).

The productivity of these ports stimulates local, regional, state, and national economies, representing a major artery for commodities to flow to the entire country. Even though the December 2012 cargo-processing numbers were down 9.4 percent compared with the same month in 2011, dockworkers still handled more than 8 million containers in a year. Those containers carried imports, mostly from Asia, and U.S. exports headed overseas along with empties that were also headed back across the Pacific. The mark was reached despite an eight-day strike in late 2012 by the International Longshore and Warehouse Union Clerical Office, which shut down seven of the port's eight cargo terminals. The two ports also dodged a potential blow to their reputations for reliability that could have haunted them well into 2013 and beyond because of that strike, trade experts said.

From a critical infrastructure resilience perspective, the POLALB emphasize their strategic role in moving cargo through their ports-of-entry to transportation connections on the West Coast for further distribution across the country. The supply chain— LALB trade gateway—is considered an efficient option for moving cargo through the most heavily populated regions and on to other parts of the nation, providing the highest frequency of intermodal access to 14 major freight hubs across the United States. Given the transportation systems available from LALB to other parts of the country, and considering the transit distances through the Panama Canal, a container shipped from anywhere in Asia will arrive at a Gulf or East Coast destination nearly one week sooner if shipped through LALB rather than through the Panama Canal.

The POLALB place their economic survival and sustained prosperity on cross-modal shipping traffic in general and container flow in particular. During a natural or human-made disaster, these ports—and their market investors and customers—will go to great lengths to avoid closure and the rerouting of cargo trade to other West Coast ports, because that represents not only lost revenue in the near term but also the potential loss of market shares in the long term if those shipping companies choose not to return after the incident. These market forces highlight the dynamic nature of supply-chain variables, the sharp impact of disasters on commercial shipping across domestic ports, and the increased challenges for those attempting to forge broader application of public-private partnerships (Orosz 2012). The POLALB are vital national security interests and commercial centers-of-gravity due to their economic importance to the nation, and the lessons of this case study point to the need for a deeper understanding of three key elements: (1) market forces, (2) barriers to public-private collaboration, and (3) utility of collective action in strengthening functional resilience.

Figure A.4 Japan Earthquake

Japan Earthquake
Earthquake, Tsunami, Fukushima Nuclear Disaster

- 9.0 magnitude earthquake off Japan's eastern coast in 2011

- Triggered 133-foot tsunami waves, flooding, erosion, and ground saturation; disrupted global supply chains

- Major nuclear disaster with national and regional impacts; second only to Chernobyl, Ukraine, in 1986

- Significant disaster lessons for international community:

  - National culture of preparedness
  - Society embraced unity-of-effort
  - National leadership caused confusion
  - Digital networks enabled communications
  - Leveraged high-tech social media
  - Submarine cables were highly vulnerable

Source: Wikimedia Commons, SH-60B helicopter flies over Sendai, https://commons.wikimedia.org/wiki/File:SH-60B_helicopter_flies_over_Sendai.jpg.

The Japan earthquake occurred on March 11, 2011, with a magnitude of 9.0 and an epicenter near the eastern coast of Japan, north of Tokyo. It was followed by massive tsunami waves of over 130 feet that breached barriers and devastated coastal communities. The combined impact of both disasters resulted in multiple nuclear accidents, the greatest being at the Fukushima Daiichi Nuclear Power Plant, where hydrogen gas explosions resulted in cooling systems failure and meltdowns in three reactors, prompting massive evacuations of the surrounding areas. The cores of three nuclear reactors melted down in the world's second-worst nuclear disaster (after the 1986 Chernobyl explosion in Ukraine). In total, the disaster resulted in 15,853 deaths, 6,023 injured, and 3,282 missing (BBC News 2012).

This is one of the most significant disasters in history, especially given the proximity of the crisis to interconnected systems that support global economic commerce. As the most powerful earthquake ever experienced by Japan, the event is a valuable case study due to its size and the magnitude of its destructive forces as well as the cascading string of events that created the perfect storm against national preparedness. The Japan earthquake and tsunami of 2011 raised important questions for high-risk regions and communities worldwide. How do current operational protocols and all-hazards capabilities withstand multiple, vastly different disasters occurring in tandem? For instance, while a nation or region may have plans in place for a nuclear disaster, are they executable in the face of sequential natural disasters?

A riveting book titled *Lessons from the Disaster* (Funabashi and Takenaka 2011) traces failures of both natural and human origin that triggered a deadly series of events at the Fukushima Nuclear Power Plant. While the reactors shut down automatically when the earthquake occurred, "the equipment needed to cool them was destroyed by the tsunami, as well as all backup power sources." This led to the following series of cascading impacts:

- confusion at the power plants caused by tactical guidance given by national leadership regarding the handling of the nuclear disaster;
- plant problems resulting in power shortages in eastern Japan, including in the greater Tokyo metropolitan area;
- the shutdown of other nuclear power plants due to decreased public trust;
- nationwide power shortages due to fewer power plants;
- decreased power supply slowing or disrupting key nodes of the economy;
- companies moving from Japan due to unstable economic and infrastructure conditions; and
- the weakening of government bonds and foreign exchange markets due to economic uncertainties.

Overall, "these developments must be viewed as a challenge to Japan's nationhood," amounting to a threat upon their sovereign existence (Funabashi and Takenaka 2011, 5–6).

The nuclear aspect of the disaster also revealed a need for whole-of-nation collaborative strategies in preparing for such emergencies. Because the entire nation of Japan is vulnerable to the threat of radioactive material released by a power plant accident, "it is a matter of urgency that the central government collaborate with local governments at every level (prefectures, cities, towns, and villages) to draft and distribute emergency response manuals in preparation for such accidents" (Funabashi and Takenaka 2011, 9). In an essay concerning the Fukushima Nuclear Power Plant incident, Japanese officials concluded that the first lesson learned from the disaster is that "full public information disclosure and the preparation of contingency manuals are vital" (Funabashi and Takenaka 2011, 71).

Rebuilding cities with a strategy of preparedness and mitigation strengthens infrastructure resilience within a community (Funabashi and Takenaka 2011, 73–75; Lovett 2011). Based on lessons learned, Japanese authorities have implemented the following reconstruction plans to mitigate future damage by:

- "Moving to higher ground:" Rebuild downtowns at higher elevations.
- "Rising up:" Increase heights of buildings with human-made elevated foundation platforms.
- "Multilayered protection:" Develop residential areas behind multiple erected barriers and embankments utilizing tree cover and farmland to mitigate tsunamis.

The earthquake also revealed acute vulnerabilities in the global supply chain, as concentrated and sole-source production of components in Japan resulted in widespread shutdowns and shortages, forcing companies to seek alternative suppliers. Due to widespread power outages and damage to producers of key components, some companies that were unharmed by the disaster were still forced to halt operations (Kachi and Takahashi 2011). The impact of these disruptions expanded globally because automobile and technology manufacturers needed critical parts from Japan. Take, for example, the case of Shin-Etsu Chemical Co., the world's largest producer of advanced silicon wafers found in semiconductors used in nearly all modern technology. They produce 20 percent of the global supply at a factory 40 miles away from the Fukushima Nuclear Power Plant. Shin-Etsu was shut down by the disaster, causing concern in global markets (Lee and Pierson 2011). Another example of global supply-chain challenges was a pigment called Xirallic, used to make car paint sparkle. One hundred percent of the global supply of this pigment is produced by Merck in northeastern Japan—an area hit hard by the earthquake—where operations were stopped for two months, resulting in global shortages for automakers (Dawson 2011).

These examples revealed some fragile and easily disrupted supply chains. "Many automakers [were] surprised to find their standard two-supplier rule for critical parts had been circumvented further down the supply chain. As a result, 'traceability' of lower-tier suppliers has become an industry watchword following the earthquake, according to a senior Toyota executive" (Dawson 2011).

The private sector offers many examples of functional resilience through rapid recovery of operations. After Renesas Electronics hired 2,000 additional support personnel, the Tokyo-based semiconductor manufacturer was able to reopen a major plant a month ahead of schedule (Funabashi and Takenaka 2011, 129). A survey of Japanese companies three and a half months after the disaster indicated that 80 percent had "regained or surpassed their pre-earthquake production levels," with a majority of the remaining 20 percent predicting full restoration by the end of that year. The data further revealed that manufacturing companies recovered more quickly than expected due to the establishment of alternative supply sources (Funabashi and Takenaka 2011, 156).

The disaster also underscores the ubiquitous nature of technology and growing dependence on the Internet and social networking sites (SNS) for communications and situational awareness. Use of Twitter, Facebook, YouTube, blogs, texting, and instant messaging increased dramatically during the disaster, enabling the dissemination of critical information faster than ever before in Japan's history. For example, there were

5,530 tweets per second during the disaster, which, combined with other SNS, were employed to quickly locate family members as cell phone services were overloaded. Videos of the earthquake and its effects appeared on YouTube minutes after it began, offering rapid global awareness in near real time, as Google search volume on the subject skyrocketed. Many have referred to the Japan earthquake as "the most documented event in history" due to the amount of published material (Blackburn 2011; Anderson 2012; Sreenivasan 2012).

The U.S. Geological Survey (USGS) reported that spikes in regional Twitter traffic from affected populations occurred within seconds of the earthquake, while traditional scientific alerts typically take two to 20 minutes to be issued (Lobb 2011). In Japan, populations in harm's way used social media to acquire safety notices and information. Since most government agencies and press maintained Facebook and Twitter accounts, those without access to traditional media (television, radio, etc.) used social media for information. "The surge in traffic . . . to government websites prompted private-sector Internet firms, universities, and other entities to address the problem" (Funabashi and Takenaka 2011) and redistribute Internet traffic to restore normalcy to overwhelmed sites. This highlighted the need for more resiliency and broadband connectivity in the future as people seek emergency information almost exclusively from SNS during and after a disaster (Stephens 2011).

In review, Japan's earthquake helps inform this study and provides timely lessons, including the need to:

- mitigate the cascading impacts of disasters on an interconnected and global economy;
- integrate whole-of-nation collaborative strategies in preparing for and responding to complex disasters;
- conduct effective planning, training, and exercises to prepare for worst-case scenarios;
- map geographic communities of interest with the most likely regional threats in mind;
- understand cascading vulnerabilities to the global supply chain due to the centralized sourcing of vital manufacturing components;
- embed resilience within business continuity plans and all aspects of behavioral and engineering sciences;
- leverage social media in producing individual situational awareness and enabling rapid dissemination of crucial information;
- establish broadband connectivity and digital vs. analog telecommunications networks across the country;
- protect and build redundancies into transoceanic submarine cables;
- provide widespread Internet access at public Internet cafes, evacuation sites, and shelters; and
- establish standard data formats for computer systems, government records, and collaborative tools.

The global supply chain was not the only segment of the economy to be impacted by the disaster; the food chain was also adversely affected by the nuclear event. In January 2013 (nearly two years after the incident), a report from Japan indicated that fish contaminated in waters off the nation's crippled Fukushima Nuclear Power Plant were found to have levels of radiation over 2,500 times the legal limit for safe seafood. Scientists from Tokyo Electric Power indicated that massive nets were being installed 15 miles offshore in attempts to prevent contaminated fish from migrating. The radioactive contamination released from the reactor meltdowns is expected to linger for decades to come (Newman 2013).

Figure A.5 Hurricane Irene

Hurricane Irene
2011 Stress Test of CIKR Resilience

- In 2011, the only hurricane to make landfall in the U.S.

- Came ashore in North Carolina and impacted 12 states and one-eighth of the U.S. population

- East Coast displayed fragile infrastructure that lacked flexible resilience

- Revealed major capability gaps in CIKR system:

  - Region went weeks without power
  - Trees damaged power lines
  - State MAAs not established
  - Systems lacked redundancy
  - EM transportation barriers

Source: NOAA, Weather. http://www.noaa.gov/wx.html.

Hurricane Irene was an intense storm that crossed the Caribbean basin, Puerto Rico, Hispaniola, and the Bahamas before making landfall in North Carolina and moving up the East Coast of the United States in August 2011. The only hurricane to make landfall that year, it caused widespread destruction across 12 states, nearly 60 deaths, and losses totaling over $18 billion. In addition, it tested all elements of the emergency management system. This disaster highlighted the capability gaps in national preparedness, the fragmented coordination across the infrastructure sectors, and shortfalls in resiliency that largely still exist among the federal, regional, state, tribal, and local communities.

Almost 10 years after the devastating 9/11 attacks and six years after Hurricane Katrina, Hurricane Irene presented another stress test of regional preparedness and critical infrastructure resilience. The storm provided many lessons for all-hazards coordination and homeland security strategies across the disaster management system. This case study examines the effects of Hurricane Irene on CIKR and provides valuable information for study.

After making landfall in North Carolina, Irene proceeded up the East Coast through southeastern Virginia. It was downgraded to a tropical storm as it hit New Jersey and eventually New York City, finally transitioning to a tropical cyclone over the northern New England states.

Figure A.6 Hurricane Irene Track

Hurricane Irene Track
August 2011

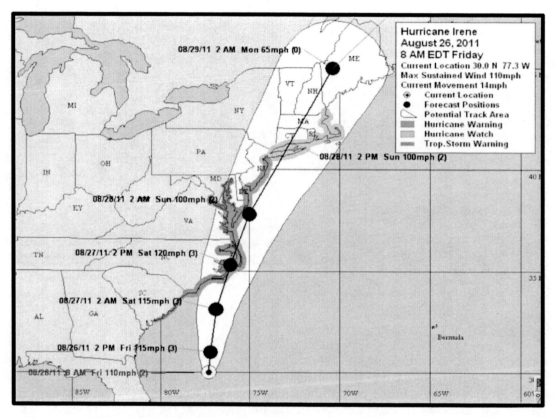

Source: NOAA, Weather. http://www.noaa.gov/wx.html.

The energy sector sustained a considerable amount of damage and lengthy interruptions in service when six million people and businesses all along the East Coast lost power before the storm dissipated. Connecticut suffered the largest power outage in the state's history, with half of Connecticut Light and Power's 1.2 million customers losing utility services. "In Virginia, the hurricane disrupted power to more than 300 critical services, including hospitals, emergency call centers and fire stations" (Kahn 2011). With disruption to services on such a large scale, restoration of electricity was slow; only 57 percent of those without power had utilities restored four days after Irene reached North Carolina, amounting to 3.8 million homes and businesses regaining power out of the total 6.7 million affected. Reports indicated power would be restored to the majority of customers in Virginia and New York by September 2, six days after the hurricane reached the United States (Polson 2011).

The transportation sector suffered significant interruptions and damage during and after the storm had passed. New York City Mayor Michael Bloomberg shut down the Metropolitan Transportation Authority (MTA) system on August 27 in preparation for possible flooding, with New Jersey and Philadelphia quickly following suit and closing down their transit systems (Whitwell and Durante 2011). Nearly all lines in New York City reopened by the Monday morning commute, but the Metro-North Railroad servicing areas of New York and Connecticut remained closed, having sustained heavy damage from flooding, fallen trees, and mudslides (Grynbaum and Haughney 2011). Ground travel was severely interrupted by flooding. Hundreds of roads and highways were washed out, and many bridges were either destroyed or deemed unsafe, isolating certain rural communities from emergency aid and basic services (Associated Press 2011a, 2011b). Air travel stopped along a majority of East Coast hubs during the hurricane, with around 9,000 flights canceled. Planes and crews were stranded around the world due to widespread lack of preparation for the storm, requiring airlines to reposition resources. Normal flight operations did not resume for several days (Katayama 2011).

The telecommunications sector suffered major physical damage from Irene, but wireless providers demonstrated a moderate level of resilience during the harsh weather. Internet and landline service suffered considerable damage, with the Federal Communications Commission (FCC) reporting 210,000 wire lines down and a million cable subscribers losing service (Plumb 2011). The FCC also reported that a total of 6,500 cell sites (or towers) were destroyed by the storm; the state of Vermont alone lost 44 percent of its cell sites—a higher proportional loss than the other affected states. The initial loss would have been greater, but many cell sites were equipped with batteries and generators to mitigate power blackouts, thereby sustaining operations. After a while, however, these backups began to deplete, resulting in increased service interruptions after the storm had passed. Still, providers in North Carolina were able to repair over half of their damaged sites before the storm had dissipated over New England.

The nuclear power industry demonstrated resilient practices throughout the storm, as detailed by the Nuclear Energy Institute (NEI 2011). The majority of sites affected by Hurricane Irene remained at 100 percent capacity, with some slight reductions of power output. Only two of the 24 sites shut down operations. The Oyster Creek Nuclear Generating Station in New Jersey was manually secured as a precaution, and the Calvert Cliffs Nuclear Power Plant near Maryland "automatically and safely shut down, as designed, when a large piece of aluminum siding struck a transformer." The NEI further reported, "Every facility was ready to take the necessary steps to maintain safety, thanks to careful planning and deliberate storm preparations several days in advance of the storm" (NEI 2011).

While U.S. chemical plants did not suffer major physical damage from the storm, their ability to resume operations after Irene passed depended on the condition of external infrastructures that were vulnerable to damage. Fearing a repeat of former disasters, the American Chemistry Council (ACC) recounted that in the past, "extensive damage to the local infrastructure blocked the flow of key supplies like electricity and natural gas necessary to manufacture chemicals, while damaged roads and rail lines prevented the delivery of products to consumers," thus resulting in halted operations and rising natural gas costs. The Society of Chemical Manufacturers and Affiliates (SOCMA) also reported before the storm that they had "a five-day hurricane preparedness program that is implemented each time a hurricane becomes a threat to their general area ... and is reviewed each year before the hurricane season officially starts" (Clark 2011). A chemical waste spill caused by floodwaters was reported at a former chemical site in Bridgewater, New Jersey, after the storm. Although chemical waste was found in the area, the spill did not merit alarm, according to the Environmental Protection Agency (EPA) and local authorities, because "the site's flood control system was built to trap floodwater that spills in, preventing chemicals from escaping the property" (Paik 2011).

The emergency services sector demonstrated areas of improvement in Irene's wake. For example, FEMA was praised for their response and local coordination, with governors along the East Coast recognizing their speed and level of cooperation (Terkel 2011). New York's response illustrated proactive assessments and increased preparedness efforts at the state level, affirming strengths in emergency response while identifying key vulnerabilities to be addressed. New York Governor Andrew Cuomo, after assessing the state and local emergency response during Hurricane Irene and Tropical Storm Lee, found that while their personnel were qualified and well trained, there was a need to provide "a highly coordinated network to support them." Governor Cuomo then proposed that the state create "five Regional Disaster Logistics centers that will stockpile necessary equipment and serve as staging areas for multiple state and local agencies and the National Guard, . . . a state emergency database to coordinate disaster response equipment and personnel, . . . and ten Rapid Response Support Teams that will be deployed in emergencies to coordinate state efforts with local governments" (Homeland Security News Wire 2012).

Other sectors affected by Irene included drinking water, agriculture/food, dams, banking/finance, and health care. In New Jersey, boil water alerts were issued after communities were left with water supplies contaminated by storm runoff and sewage, presenting risks of *E. coli* and other bacteria (WebWire 2011). In agriculture, Virginia estimated losses of over $60 million due to crop damage (Kumar 2011). New York's Gilboa Dam sustained spillway damage from the hurricane, eroded by the large amounts of additional rainwater, and repairs to the dam were not completed until late December of that year (New York City Department of Environmental Protection Communications and Intergovernmental Affairs 2011). However, the New York Stock Exchange and NASDAQ both opened for business as usual the Monday after the hurricane, with only a slightly reduced volume of market activity despite the interruption to public transit systems (Spicer 2011). Multiple hospitals and nursing homes suffered power outages along the East Coast and were forced to relocate patients, raising questions about the best ways to maintain accessibility to those patients' digitized health care records, while other facilities maintained operations by following previously established business continuity plans (Lewis 2011).

In review, Hurricane Irene presented a serious regional challenge to the East Coast that intersected all elements of critical infrastructure and demanded a high degree of local, state, regional, and federal cooperation:

- While some sectors demonstrated a high level of protection and functional resilience, the intensity of the storm revealed vulnerabilities and weaknesses that many thought were corrected after the lessons of Hurricane Katrina.
- The wireless telecommunications, nuclear, and financial sectors all demonstrated varying levels of preparedness and resilience, with limited interruptions to services enabled by redundancies, backup capabilities to reduce external dependencies, and protective measures and precautions.
- Two infrastructure sectors demonstrating significant vulnerabilities and need for greater operational resilience were energy and transportation, due to major interruptions in services, severe physical damage, and delayed restoration of services.

Figure A.7 North American Derecho

North American Derecho
Surprise Storm Reveals Lack of Regional Preparedness

- In June 2012, a rare and fast-moving storm with hurricane-force winds took Mid-Atlantic states by surprise, leaving no time for preparations

- Left 5 million people without power during heat wave; caused 22 deaths

- Delayed power restoration, leaving some without electricity for one to two weeks

- Revealed the need for a posture of resilience in the face of unexpected disasters

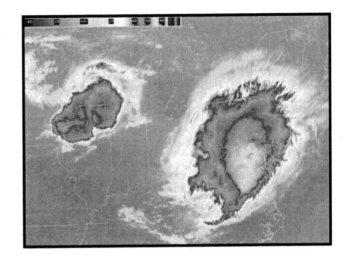

Source: NOAA, Weather. http://www.noaa.gov/wx.html.

During the writing of this report, on June 29, 2012, a fast-moving severe thunderstorm swept through the Midwest and into the Eastern Seaboard, lasting 18 hours and causing unexpected damage and loss of life. The storm was a *derecho,* an uncommon weather pattern defined by a band of complex thunderstorms with long-lived downbursts that are fast and sustain winds at and above hurricane force. The storm had peak wind gusts of 92 miles per hour, left more than 5 million homes without power during a heat wave, and resulted in 22 deaths (Pierobon 2012).

Due to the uncommon nature of such storms in the mid-Atlantic area, governments and utility providers were caught off guard, with some customers not recovering power until a week after the storm. Some of the most severely affected states have derechos as little as once every four years, according to the National Oceanic and Atmospheric Administration (NOAA 2012). Also, given the swift nature of the weather pattern (as opposed to hurricanes and other storm systems), businesses and individuals in the storms' path had little time to prepare for the level of destruction the derecho storm. For this reason, the June 2012 North American derecho is a fitting case study to reveal how various authorities and sectors perform in protecting infrastructure and ensuring functional continuity when there is no time to prepare.

Derechos are uncommon for the East Coast, hard to predict, and arrive with little warning, causing dramatic delays in emergency notifications and upgraded threat levels. Such delays severely limited the situational awareness of first responders, government agencies, private-sector owners, and operators of critical infrastructure immediately prior to the storm, leaving no window for preparatory measures in the face of a storm with the destructive force of a hurricane. A spokesperson for Dominion Virginia Power Company explained, "This was, in our one-hundred year history, the largest non-hurricane storm we've had," and added, "With slow-moving hurricanes there are days to prepare, but by the time you know a derecho is coming, it's too late to do much more than take cover" (Livingston 2012). An executive from Baltimore Gas and Electric (BGE) stated, "In my twenty-four years with BGE . . . no storm has ever combined this magnitude of damage with its suddenness" (Pierobon 2012).

The result of insufficient preparations was mass power outages and severely crippled recovery times. Many customers remained without power for up to a week after the storm—some for over nine days. In West Virginia, Appalachian Power did not restore power to all of their customers until July 15, more than two weeks after the storm had passed (Patton 2012).

In Ohio, the Warren County (population: 212,000) 911 system went down for 90 minutes during the height of the storm, diverting calls to neighboring governments and delaying emergency response in the area. For the majority of the time, calls were processed by adjacent counties, but 911 calls went completely unanswered in Warren County for a 27-minute period (McKibben and Morse 2012).

The 2012 North American derecho offered a sobering glimpse of the state of critical infrastructure resilience in a short-notice scenario, revealing that recovery of services is crippled when governments and utilities are caught by surprise. Emergency planners and first responders typically anticipate the regular hurricane season (June 1–November 1), with forecasts normally providing days of preparation before a slow-moving storm moves into their area of responsibility, but in this case there was little or no warning and the subsequent recovery and restoration of services reflected this capability gap in emergency planning and energy sector procedures.

Figure A.8 India Power Outage

India Power Outage
Largest Blackout in History—One-Tenth of World Population

- In 2012, two major outages in two days impacted 12 states and 650 million people

- Cascading effects caused by grid failure blamed on states overdrawing power

- Additional factors included a growing power deficit, a drought that reduced hydro-power output, electricity theft, and aging infrastructure

- Poor resource management and lack of diversification cited as systemic problems

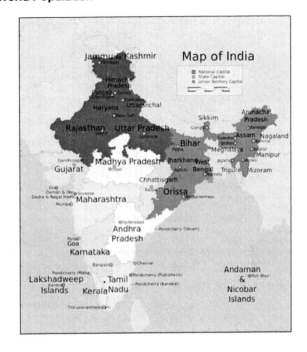

Source: Wikimedia Commons, Indian states affected by July 2012 power cuts, http://commons.wikimedia.org/wiki/File:Indian_states_affected_by_July_2012_power_cuts.svg.

India experienced a major power grid failure due to transmission malfunctions on July 30, 2012. The initial incident affected seven states in northern India, and on July 31 another outage affected 12 more states. After two days, power was restored to most of the region that lost electrical service—an area populated by over 650 million people. At its peak, the massive outage impacted half of India's 1.2 billion people—one-tenth of the world's population. Officials have said the blackout was one of the world's most widespread power failures. The lack of electricity prompted civil unrest and growing frustration among India's population. The government was widely criticized for its "huge failure of management in the power sector." At least 300 trains were held up in the affected regions, while schools and government offices were closed (United Press International 2012).

According to India's central government, the blackouts were caused by states' overdrawing from the strained national power system and widespread individual theft of electrical power, both of which triggered a cascading grid failure across the nation. India is regularly plagued by brief and localized blackouts due to increasing demands on its eroding infrastructure. The rapidly growing economy and a shift toward a larger, urbanized middle class have caused the demand for energy in the nation to outpace the supply. In 2010, India's power deficit at peak load was over 10 percent, signaling the need for more investment in power systems. Since infrastructure changes that might diversify power are not a high government priority, citizens and businesses fend for themselves and adopt alternative strategies to obtain power (Luthra 2011).

India's sources of electricity are comprised of 69 percent coal, 14 percent hydro, 10 percent natural gas, 4 percent oil, 2 percent nuclear, and 1 percent renewable (solar, wind, biofuels, and the like). This lack of diversification is another possible factor contributing to the massive blackouts. India's power infrastructure depends on the country's limited and depleting water supplies for operation, and, much like the United States, the generation of power represents the largest use of water in the country (Luthra 2011). A delayed monsoon season in 2012 left India with decreased power output from hydroelectric sources and diverted more of that water toward irrigation for agriculture that was also endangered by the lack of rain. This led to speculation that decreased total output, combined with increased demand and poor governance of the power grids, all combined to stress the already-fragile power infrastructure to its breaking point, and will likely result in more "widespread outages . . . in coming weeks and months, especially in breadbasket states" (Mukherji, Chaturvedi, and Choudhury 2012).

Regular power shortages due to increased demand on India's aging infrastructure have resulted in a culture of "independent resilience" in the private sector. Businesses and manufacturers in India invest in high-capacity diesel generators and backup fuel supplies to maintain full operational capacity in the likely event of a temporary blackout. The public sector, however, demonstrates far less resilient practices. With the overwhelming majority of Indian power derived from coal, the coal supply is almost completely controlled by a state monopoly "widely considered in shambles." The result has been coal plants maintaining less than seven days of coal stock—a critical level—and many power plants running below capacity (Bandyopadhyay 2012). The tendency toward private self-sufficiency through powerful generators, necessary for business continuity and survival, has allowed the central government to procrastinate and overlook the problems of a degraded infrastructure, states overdrawing energy, and individual power theft by consumers (Associated Press 2012.

India's response to this event offers lessons for the United States and other countries: (1) poor diversification of power sources poses a threat to resilience and continuity of energy supplies;[2] (2) poor management of resources results in failures of a major infrastructure sector; and (3) drought, climate change, and water demand has an enormous impact on power production and can cause cascading vulnerabilities across society.

Finally, a lesson from India can be applied to California, where 75 percent of the state's power supply is generated through hydroelectric energy. The summer of 2012 was one of the driest in U.S. history. California's high dependence on a single-sector resource, with long-term forecasts showing worsening drought conditions in conjunction with a growing demand for power, could result in circumstances similar to India's in the future (Carroll 2012).

Figure A.9 Civil GPS Vulnerabilities

Civil GPS Vulnerabilities
Interconnected System of Systems Impacts All Sectors

- All 16 infrastructure sectors depend directly or indirectly upon a reliable civil GPS signal

- The "timing" element of GPS position, navigation, and timing (PNT) has become the backbone of countless interconnected elements of CIKR systems

- The civil GPS timing signal can be spoofed or corrupted—intentionally or unintentionally—resulting in users employing GPS signals that they may not know are flawed

- A nationwide detection and monitoring capability that can notify, mitigate, and counter the potential corruption of civil GPS timing signal is needed

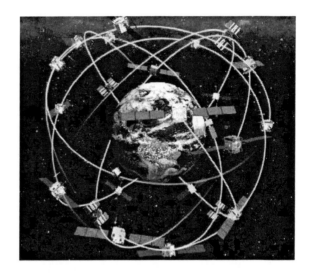

Source: mistergwilson (Flickr username), January 1, 1978, GPS. Retrieved from http://www.flickr.com/photos/56240358@N04/5212225551/.

National reliance upon civil GPS (especially *timing*) reveals a significant point of failure and critical infrastructure vulnerability because of GPS position, navigation, and timing (PNT) services extending across all 16 infrastructure sectors. Government and think tank studies on GPS criticality primarily address outages and are rather limited in scope, lacking a comprehensive examination of signal corruption and broader interconnectivity across networks. According to a National Security Telecommunications Advisory Committee (NSTAC) Report, "to date, few industry or government exercises have sought to replicate the impact of a long-term or permanent GPS outage" (NSTAC 2008). Several critical aspects of GPS dependency that currently lack a strong focus in the interagency and private sector are:

1. the inability of systems to tolerate GPS-like signals that inject corrupted information into the system (i.e., spoofing); and
2. the domestic capability to deny civil GPS services by intended (hostile elements) or unintended actions. There needs to be a coordinated public-private

national capability to address critical infrastructure resilience and national security interests in this critical area.

The impact of even relatively minor local interference of the GPS signal can be large, as the unintentional jamming of GPS in San Diego Harbor in January 2007 showed. It took a considerable amount of time to locate the source of the jamming, but eventually it was found to be related to U.S. Navy ships conducting a scheduled communications jamming training exercise in the port of San Diego. During a two-hour period, the GPS signal was blocked because operators accidentally transmitted signals on GPS frequencies and disrupted civil GPS usage in the local area. The outage affected telephone switches and cellular phone services and shut down the mobile paging system at a local hospital. General aviation GPS navigation equipment outages were reported, and notifications of GPS signal disruptions were made over a four-hour period. The incident highlighted the vulnerability of the low-power GPS signal to intentional or unintentional GPS jamming and interference. It also clearly demonstrated that procedures were not in place—despite determined efforts of co-ordinating agencies—to locate jamming sources in a timely manner and take actions to mitigate them (Carroll and Montgomery 2008).

National-level GPS position, navigation, and timing policy directs the establishment of national systems and capabilities in the civil GPS arena that are not already in place. National Security Presidential Directive (NSPD-39) addresses "capabilities to protect [the] U.S. and allied access to and use of the Global Positioning System for national, homeland, and economic security, and to deny adversaries access to any space-based positioning, navigation, and timings services" (2004). Relevant goals include:

1. improving capabilities to deny hostile use of any space-based PNT services . . . in any area of military operations or homeland security missions; and
2. maintaining GPS as a component of multiple critical infrastructure sectors in accordance with Homeland Security Presidential Directive 7 (HSPD-7): Critical Infrastructure Identification, Prioritization, and Protection (U.S. DHS 2003).

GPS reliance continues to grow across the energy power grid (generation and metering), banking and financial markets (transaction tracking, interbank communications), transportation systems (air traffic control, space launch, and recover, navigation, logistics delivery), and information technology and com-munications (wireless Internet, flood control, Geographic Information Systems). Despite its continued widespread dependency and ubiquitous nature, there is no national capability in place to accomplish the detection, monitoring, notifica-tion, and mitigation of a corrupted GPS signal. Based on GPS disruptions and interferences that have been observed by DHS officials in recent years, including the U.S. Coast Guard's Navigation Center, it is clear that the vulnerabilities and implications to all-domain critical infrastructures have not been fully studied and the risks are not fully understood. Furthermore, the current approach is a reactive system, which depends on users' reports of outages and not the full spectrum of interference scenarios that could exist.

There needs to be a comprehensive system designed and implemented to detect GPS interferences across the continental United States. Such a design should include real-time monitoring, geographic location of threats, and rapid notification and response capabilities. A similar system of systems is needed to (1) deny the nefarious use of PNT signals within the country that would enable a coordinated response, (2) protect friendly users of the GPS system, and (3) (temporarily) deny local exploitation of PNT—resulting in a persistent complementary capability to identify interference and deny hostile use of GPS services. This national capability would benefit from a monitoring network drawing information from a variety of public and private systems. It would require proactive monitoring, notification, and response based on standardized CONOPS and coordinated protocols across government agencies and the private sector.

Figure A.10 Chemical Sector

Chemical Sector
Plant Shutdown Impacts National Steel Production

- In 2005, Air Products and Chemicals' plants were damaged by Hurricane Katrina

- Disrupted market production of liquid hydrogen had a direct impact on the steel industry

- Complex production cycle depends on other infrastructures (petroleum, energy, transportation) in a complex, globally distributed supply chain

- Understanding how these industry sectors interface under normal and disrupted conditions is critical for supply chain management and policymaking

Source: Wikimedia Commons, Photo praxair plant.hydrogen.infrastructure, http://commons.wikimedia.org/wiki/File:Photo_praxair_plant.hydrogen.infrastructure.jpg.

The interrupted supply of liquid hydrogen in the aftermath of Hurricane Katrina provides an example of critical infrastructure interdependencies and the complex systems within a vital industry that experienced fragility and resiliency at different facilities within the same industry. On September 8, 2005, about one week after Hurricane Katrina made landfall in the Gulf of Mexico, a company named Air Products and Chemicals began experiencing problems with a pair of liquid hydrogen plants; these problems had a cascading adverse impact on the steel industry and regional economy as steelmakers faced a sudden shortage of a critical precursor material needed for steel production. Steel companies use the extremely cold liquid hydrogen to make galvanized, cold-rolled, and other specialized types of steel.

Air Products is one of two major North American suppliers of liquid hydrogen, and represents nearly half the market share. Liquid hydrogen is also used in aerospace, chemical processing, electronics, and other industries. Hurricane Katrina caused heavy damage to the company's liquid hydrogen plant in New Orleans, Louisiana. Another plant in Ontario, Canada, was offline for a scheduled two-month maintenance shutdown. And a third plant, in Pennsylvania, experienced the rippling effect of the hurricane when the plant laid off 70 workers after cutting production in order to conserve its limited supply of hydrogen.

That left just one operating liquid hydrogen plant in the Air Products arsenal (in California), with a capacity of only 2.3 million standard cubic feet a day. By comparison, the New Orleans plant produced 26.8 million cubic feet, while the Canadian facility generated 11.5 million cubic feet. Air Products reacted to the impact of Hurricane Katrina by trying to obtain liquid hydrogen for its customers from other sources and geographic areas. But the immediate impact on employees—and the local economies—rested with steelmakers who depended on Air Products. The steelmakers faced an uncertain future, because they did not know when the seriously damaged New Orleans facility would resume production.

Another steel company, Steel Dynamics of Fort Wayne, Indiana, reported it would not take orders for galvanized or cold-rolled steel until it could make other supply arrangements. Demonstrating a more resilient posture in the face of disaster, Nucor Corp., the nation's largest steel producer, avoided the same problems because it was self-sufficient, making its own liquid hydrogen. It was difficult to predict how a sustained shutdown of these plants would affect the steel industry because hydrogen supplies differ greatly from company to company.

Figure A.11 Norris Dam

Norris Dam
Pre–World War II Infrastructure in Tennessee Valley

- First major Tennessee Valley Authority (TVA) project, nearly 80 years old

- One of 29 hydroelectric plants that contribute to 10% of TVA power capacity; supports seven states

- Generates over 130,000 kilowatts, flexible operations, low-cost, emission-free

- Multisector resource supporting recreation, energy, transportation, water, and commercial facilities through a public-private partnership

Source: Wikimedia Commons, Norris-dam-west-tn1, http://commons.wikimedia.org/wiki/File:Norris-dam-west-tn1.jpg.

Of the 85,000 dams in this country—constructed an average of 50 years ago—there are some 4,000 that are considered structurally at risk. Furthermore, the Army Corps of Engineers (ACOE) maintains approximately 300 locks and dams in the U.S. inland waterways, and those facilities are an average of 70 years old. Given ACOE's reported maintenance and construction backlog of approximately $60 billion per year, these structures are a unique CIKR concern across the nation, because of the important role of dams in supporting the infrastructure sectors.

Norris Dam—at nearly 80 years old—is a hydroelectric and flood control structure located on the Clinch River in Campbell County, Tennessee. Its construction in the mid-1930s was the first major project for the Tennessee Valley Authority (TVA), which had been created in 1933 to bring economic development to the region and control the rampant flooding that had long plagued the Tennessee Valley.

A straight, concrete, gravity-type barrier, Norris Dam is 1,860 feet long and 265 feet high. Norris Lake, the largest reservoir on a tributary of the Tennessee River, has 33,840 acres of water surface and 809 miles of shoreline. The dam has a maximum generating capacity of 131,400 kilowatts and provides electricity to people in the Anderson County and Campbell County region across Tennessee. The dam is owned and operated by the TVA and represents a multipurpose resource, supporting the energy, water, transportation, recreational, and commercial facilities infrastructure sectors through flood prevention and reservoir management.

As early as 1911, the present site of Norris Dam—initially called the Cove Creek site—was identified as a prime location for a sizeable dam. Several government and private entities believed that a dam in the upper Tennessee Valley could provide badly needed flood control to East Tennessee and help keep the Tennessee River consistently navigable year-round. Beyond flood control and maritime navigation, this dam—like many strategically located across the country—is part of a regional CIKR network that supports cross-sector infrastructure capabilities.

Figure A.12 Western Rivers Regional Flooding

Western Rivers Regional Flooding
Record Levels of Rainfall/Snowmelt Cause Severe Floods

- In 2011, two major storm systems combined with spring snowmelt to create severe regional flooding

- Forced the U.S. Army Corps of Engineers to open all three regional spillways for the first time in history

- Cost of impact ranged from $30 to $40 billion

- An example of how an investment in mitigation (i.e., spillways) can avoid or reduce future disaster related costs

Source: Wikimedia Commons, Old Arcata Road Flood, https://commons.wikimedia.org/wiki/File:Old_Arcata_Road_Flood.jpg.

The Mississippi River floods that occurred in the spring of 2011 were among the largest and most damaging recorded along this waterway in the past century, comparable in extent to the major floods of 1927 and 1993. Many people do not realize 2011 was the first year in history that the U.S. Army COE opened all three regional spillways on the Missouri and Mississippi rivers due to major flooding—Morganza, Louisiana, north of New Orleans; Bonnet Carré near New Orleans; and Bird's Point–New Madrid, Missouri—and the first time the Morganza spillway was opened in 37 years.

Described as the perfect storm of circumstances for flooding, two major storm systems deposited record levels of rainfall on the Mississippi River watershed, and when that additional water combined with the springtime snowmelt, the river and many of its tributaries began to swell to record levels. The damage costs were an estimated $30–40 billion; still, according to the COE, "The Mississippi's flood control system functioned as designed and greatly reduced risk during the flooding." COE officials also indicated that the controlled flooding saved millions of dollars in damage to places like Baton Rouge and St. Louis.

The Mississippi/Missouri River spillways are a good example of valuable investments in preparedness, mitigation, and resilience, proving the accuracy of the emergency planners' rule-of-thumb—that every $1 invested in preparation yields a $4 savings in future response costs.

Figure A.13 Northeast Blackout of 2003

Northeast Blackout of 2003
Local Failures Trigger International Disruptions

- Cut power to 10 million people in Canada and 45 million people in eight U.S. states
- Cascading effects transformed a local problem into a regional and international power disruption
- Initial shutdown of one power plant due to mismanagement and high electrical demand resulted in over 100 other plants shutting down across the Northeast U.S. and Canada

Source: Wikimedia Commons, View south from 545 Sherbourne-at night, during that last big blackout-2003-08-15, http://commons.wikimedia.org/wiki/File:View_south_from_545_Sherbourne_-_at_night,_during_that_last_big_blackout_-_2003-08-15.jpg.

The Northeast Blackout of 2003 provides a dramatic example of how interconnected infrastructure sectors in the United States are vulnerable to local and isolated events, which in turn can expand the problem to a regional or national level due to cascading failures. The blackout of 2003 was a widespread power outage that occurred throughout parts of the northeastern and midwestern United States and Ontario, Canada, in August 2003. An estimated 10 million people in Ontario and some 45 million people in eight U.S. states were affected. At the time, it was the second most widespread blackout in history, after the 1999 Southern Brazil blackout.

Reports indicate that a series of interconnected events contributed to the cascading regional crisis brought on by the blackout. The localized source of the problem points to Cleveland, Ohio, where the electric utility FirstEnergy (FE) failed to assess the vulnerabilities of voltage instabilities and did not recognize the deteriorating condition of its system. Additionally, the electric company failed to manage tree growth in its transmission rights-of-ways and did not provide effective real-time diagnostic support. One of the triggering events was a generating plant in Eastlake, Ohio (a suburb of Cleveland), that went offline amid high electrical demand, putting a strain on high-voltage power lines that were subsequently downed when they came into contact with overgrown trees. The resulting cascading effect ultimately forced the shutdown of more than 100 power plants across the region.

From a cyber-security view, a software bug known as a *race condition* existed in General Electric Energy's Unix-based energy management system. Once triggered, the bug stalled FirstEnergy's control room alarm system for over an hour. System operators were unaware of the malfunction, and the failure deprived them of both audio and visual alerts for important changes in the operational state of the system. The lack of alarms led operators to dismiss certain calls and notifications and contributed to the chain of degrading power problems.

The reliability of the electrical grid was called into question because the weather was very hot in much of the affected region, and the high temperatures increased energy demand as people across the region turned on fans and air conditioning. This caused the power lines to sag as higher currents heated the lines. Most of the Amtrak Northeast Corridor service was interrupted (it uses electric locomotives) and electrified commuter railways also were shut down. The power outage's effects on international air transport and financial markets were widespread.

Telephone networks generally remained operational, but the increased demand for energy triggered by the blackout left many circuits overloaded. Water systems in several cities lost pressure, forcing "boil water" advisories to be issued. Cellular service was interrupted as mobile networks were overloaded with the increase in call volume. Major cellular providers continued to operate on standby generator power. Television and radio stations remained on the air, with the help of backup generators, although some stations were knocked off the air during the entire blackout.

"Even without the threat of cyberterrorism," assert global innovation experts (quoted in Zolli 2012), "the likelihood of repeating a disruption such as the 2003 blackout has increased," driven by a greater demand for power transfers over longer distances, underinvestment in power transmission systems, and consolidation of electric utilities. Furthermore, there are complexities associated with an expected wave of transformer failures (due to aging power infrastructures), complicated by the increased frequency of severe weather events and the possibility of U.S. automobile drivers plugging more electric vehicles into the power grid. "If we are ever to ensure that the grid meets the growing needs of the twenty-first century consistently, safely, and securely, it will need to be transformed—but how?" (Zolli 2012).

Figure A.14 Collective Action Theory

Collective Action Theory
Elinor Ostrom, 2009 Nobel Laureate

- Suggests a unique approach to managing common pool resources

- Treats homeland security, resilience, and infrastructure protection as a public good

- Positive and negative externalities are accounted for through a collective public-private enterprise

- Concept is rooted in "tragedy of the commons," where interconnected, common resources cannot be managed independently

- Collective action correlates with intergovernmental and public-private partnerships because parties are incentivized to act in the mutual interests of all parties vs. self-serving ethos

Source: Wikimedia Commons, Nobel Prize 2009-Press Conference KVA-30, http://commons.wikimedia.org/wiki/File:Nobel_Prize_2009-Press_Conference_KVA-30.jpg#filelinks.

To better understand collective action—the framework that underpins this study—and the basis for this social science theory, this case study highlights the work of Elinor Ostrom, the first (and only) woman to be awarded the Nobel Prize in Economics (2009). Her award-winning research suggests that people can cooperatively manage common resources such as fisheries, pastures, or forests without relying solely on government intervention or privatization. *Time* magazine named Ostrom one of its 100 Most Influential People in the World for 2012.

Since this study focuses heavily upon the criticality of interagency coordination and PPPs when strengthening homeland security and community resilience, Ostrom's work is of particular interest. The examination of multi-agency collaboration and expanded private-sector investment in collective security in the homeland, along with a need for greater redundancies across CIKR sectors, highlights the utility of collective action across all levels of the public and private sectors.

Social scientists had grappled with issues of sustainability since the 1960s, when "The Tragedy of the Commons"—a phrase popularized by American ecologist Garrett Hardin (1968) in his influential article for *Science*—emerged as the standard to explain the diminution of *public goods* such as air or water. Ostrom's research asked a question similar to the one that guides this study, considering national preparedness and community resilience when addressing specific requirements of critical infrastructure protection: What incentives do individuals, organizations, or communities have to conserve, protect, or manage resources *owned* by no one—such as safety, security, and environmental variables? As this study considers existing and novel ways the nation might significantly improve resilience and preparedness across CIKR sectors, Ostrom's groundbreaking work on collective action proved extremely helpful (Ostrom 1983, 1990).

Ostrom's answer to the question of handling public goods was that "communities with common interests in preservation—such as lobster fishermen in Maine, or farmers who share irrigation systems in Nepal—often come together to regulate resources more effectively than a remote government bureaucracy. She found that groups often protect or manage resources by establishing rules, then shaming or honoring [coercing or incentivizing] members depending on their behavior" (Miller 2012) and the situation. One of the hypotheses of this study is that security and resilience can be viewed as public goods that have clear benefits to the public and private sectors and are best managed by a dynamic relationship among governmental interagency stakeholders and private-sector investors and owners—leveraging the principles of collective behavior (Ostrom, Gardner, and Walker 1992, 1994).

Ostrom played a central role in persuading economists that "the tragedy of the commons" problem and other social dilemmas often could be solved by communities on their own. She acknowledged that there were complex and ill-defined public policy issues that entered into the mix and therefore "no panaceas," and she cautioned that planners should not expect simple formulas when dealing with some of these broad social problems. "Ostrom's specialty in institutional arrangements and resource management embraced topics as diverse as inner-city police emergency-response times and African forestry practices" (Miller 2012). One of her best-known works was *Governing the Commons* (1990), which this study draws upon in making the theoretical and operational case for collective action across the "security commons," which include homeland security imperatives such as preparedness, resilience, and infrastructure protection (see also Ostrom 1998; Ostrom et al. 1999).

"When Ostrom did field work, she did it literally, plodding around Swiss pastures and the Los Angeles water district for her work on the governance of property held in common" (*Economist* 2012b). "The rules she outlined governing when and how common property could be properly managed—for example, it had to have clearly defined boundaries, users of the property had to be able to monitor its use and 'punish' those who exploit it excessively—not only revolutionized the understanding of the so-called 'tragedy of the commons' (showing they didn't have to end in tragedy), but were part of a wider reconsideration of the importance of political institutions in economic life" (*Economist* 2012b). Ostrom's work reminds us that borders between disciplines, like those between the firm and the market (and perhaps the public and private sectors) can be profitably crossed. This is an important reminder for planners, policymakers, and practitioners as we seek to implement smart resilience and preparedness in the homeland security commons. A chemist and a biologist, for example, must work together to understand the application of certain chemicals, and a private-sector owner-operator must work with public-sector emergency and disaster management planners on areas of mutual concern. Innovation is introduced to the world by having new ideas introduced and tested, which is the strategic imperative in the area of community resilience and infrastructure protection (Ostrom 2000; Ostrom et al. 2002; Ostrom 2007).

Interestingly, on the day she died in June 2012, Ostrom published a short commentary about the Rio+20 United Nations Conference on Sustainable Development held in Brazil, asserting, "A single international agreement would be a grave mistake. . . . We cannot rely on singular global policies to solve the problem of managing our common resources" (quoted in Miller, 2012). In that same spirit, one might consider Ostrom's admonition when examining critical infrastructure resilience, because it is increasingly clear to state, local, regional, and federal planners that the nation cannot rely upon a singular approach in addressing the common challenges of preparedness, homeland security, and emergency response; rather, we must consider transformational collective approaches to strengthen national preparedness.

Notes

1. The population of New York City is approximately 8.2 million. By comparison, the next largest U.S. cities are Los Angeles (3.8 million) and Chicago (2.7 million), according to the 2011 U.S. census.

2. India is heavily dependent upon fossil fuel, which is driving the power sector's coal demand to grow at approximately 6 percent a year. China is the largest coal consumer globally. India could surpass America as the world's second-largest coal consumer by 2017 (*Economist* 2013b, 54).

Appendix B
Test Questions and Research Topics

Drawing from the findings and recommendations in chapters 7 and 8, as well as the case study summaries in Appendix A, expert interview themes in Appendix C, and range of public policy references, the following 30 questions are designed to stimulate further research, discussion, and analyses among students, practitioners, and policymakers seeking to strengthen homeland security, resilience, and disaster management.

These challenge problems could be assigned to students at the graduate or undergraduate level as a semester-long project or practicum requiring research, data collection, interviews, public policy review, and development of enabling practices—collected in a comprehensive format for class presentation. The questions that follow complement the more detailed operationalizing questions listed in the far right column of the Initial Themes and Expectations matrix of Appendix E:

1. At a macro level, what have we learned as a nation from major disasters such as the 9/11 terrorist attacks, Hurricanes Sandy/Irene, and the Japanese earthquake/tsunami?
2. As policymakers and planners, what would we do differently to improve preparedness and disaster management with the benefit of lessons learned from major crises over the past decade?
3. How can we galvanize the public through a national framework that helps operationalize resilience at the local and regional levels?
4. With complex dependencies and interdependencies across the infrastructure sectors, what are the areas of greatest concern and what are the potential remedies for them?
5. Leveraging collective action precepts, improved interagency coordination, and private-sector resources, how can we significantly recapitalize national infrastructure systems?
6. Given our nation's central role in the global economy, what tools or capabilities are needed to forge more resilient supply chains?
7. From a strategic perspective, what are the most significant challenges facing disaster management, emergency response, and homeland security planners since the 9/11 attacks and recent natural disasters?

8. What are some of the reasons the current risk assessment approach is considered insufficient to capture the nature and range of natural and human-made disasters that currently face our nation?

9. What is the difference between a capabilities-based approach to functional resilience and the traditional risk assessment model in which risk is considered a function of threat, vulnerability, and consequence? $R = f(T, V, C)$

10. What are some practical examples at the local, regional, or national levels that underscore the potential improvements in resilience and preparedness that can be derived from mitigation efforts?

11. Why do public policy planners consider *cultural* factors such a significant issue in transforming the way we think about resilience in twenty-first-century American society?

12. What is the role of a *national framework* in expanding public awareness of preparedness and critical infrastructure resilience challenges?

13. How does a *national framework* such as the resilience continuum model described in Chapter 2 (Figure 2.1) support implementation of national preparedness public policies?

14. What are the primary agencies and organizations within the government interagency that are responsible for critical infrastructure and national preparedness?

15. What national-level staff elements are responsible for facilitating the interagency process in support of national preparedness? Explain how national policy informs preparedness and disaster management at the local, state, and regional levels.

16. Why are maritime seaports considered a unique safety and security environment to study the complex nature of critical infrastructure resilience challenges?

17. What do the terms *whole-community* and *whole-of-nation* mean when examining the nationwide homeland security enterprise? Provide examples describing where they appear to work well and where they do not appear to work well.

18. Why do many policy planners and critical infrastructure experts consider public-private partnerships (PPPs) the most critical capability to significantly improve critical infrastructure resilience at all levels?

19. How can metrics and measurement tools help improve the understanding of national preparedness and areas of greatest concern to community resilience?

20. How do the 10 initial themes and expectations listed in Appendix E inform the resilience research that supports this study on critical infrastructure resilience?

21. What are the operating principles of collective action theory and why are homeland security, disaster management, and critical infrastructure resilience considered *public goods*?

22. In Chapter 5 there are 12 overlapping themes at the intersection of collective action theory and interagency coordination. Which ones do you consider most important to the improvement of preparedness and resilience policy and why?

23. If information sharing is considered to be the key to interagency coordination and organizational collaboration, why does it seem to be one of the most significant challenges in advancing public policy implementation?

24. Some say that critical infrastructure and key resource (CIKR) interdependencies are a mixed blessing in the area of critical infrastructure resilience. While increased speed and efficiency result from interconnected systems, how do they make us more vulnerable? Provide several examples from the case studies.

25. Why is personal preparation at the household level the key to community resilience, and how can we—at the local, state, and federal levels—encourage and incentivize a culture of preparedness and resilience?

26. After Superstorm Sandy in October 2012, what were the most significant community challenges facing public and private leaders as well as DHS/FEMA officials, and how could a resilient approach help address those challenges?

27. Develop a list of five to 10 organizational policies to support the execution of information assurance and cyber security. Defend each policy item by linking it to an existing national strategy or public policy and summarize how it would be implemented.

28. Select a business or organization and:
    a. determine its dependencies and interdependencies within the local or national economy (whom it depends on, who depends on them)
    b. identify its vulnerabilities to various all-hazards events or disasters and associated risks to business continuity
    c. develop a business strategy to sustain the business functions (given the identified vulnerabilities and business risks) and to strengthen resiliency.

29. Develop a disaster management plan for a local-, regional-, or state-level organization that includes a:
    a. mission statement outlining the strategic objectives to support preparedness and resilience
    b. literature review that identifies relevant policy guidance to inform the plan
    c. list of supporting agencies and organizations in adjacent markets or regions
    d. list of primary themes that must be operationalized in a cross-domain, all-hazards environment.

30. What short phrase or national slogan—similar to World War II examples—would you suggest to elevate the visibility of, and galvanize commitment to, national resilience and whole-of-community preparedness? Explain the rationale for your selection.

Appendix C
Subject Matter Expert Interviews

Figure C.1 Subject Matter Expert Interviews

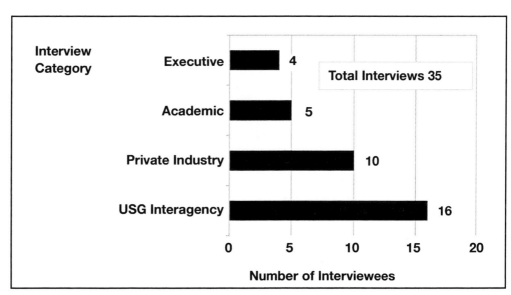

In the process of interviewing security experts across the community of government policymakers, academic scholars, field practitioners, and private industry, it became increasingly clear that the initial research theme of critical infrastructure protection (CIP) would expand to a broader focus on risk mitigation, preparedness, and functional resilience.

The following section divides the results of 35 expert interviews into 17 broad categories, reflecting the major themes that emerged in response to research questions. The interviews were conducted over a five-month period within the United States (primarily in Washington, DC, New York City, and Los Angeles/Long Beach) and with national security and emergency management experts in London, England, especially the Cabinet Office, Civil Contingencies Secretariat.

This appendix is devoted exclusively to recording the response of interviewees—in some cases, it documents their exact words (cited in quotations)—with a nexus to resiliency issues; the views or opinions of the author are not reflected in this chapter. The names of the specific interviewees are protected by a reference system listed in Appendix G. The responses of the individuals interviewed are derived from private notes of the interviews capturing their remarks and answers to research questions.

STRATEGIC CONTEXT

The 1996 Presidential Commission on Critical Infrastructure Protection (PCCIP) provided President Bill Clinton with a comprehensive examination of infrastructure protection in two directions: (1) physical and (2) cyber systems, with a principal focus on cyber security. The White House promulgated a Presidential Decision Directive (PDD-63) in 1997 asserting the criticality of cyber security. The emphasis was not placed on physical infrastructure protection until the terrorist attacks of September 11, 2001, when the vulnerabilities inherent in American vital infrastructure were revealed. That change was reflected in the Global War on Terror (GWOT), when public awareness and perception of safety and security were altered even though a similar risk existed before and after the events of 9/11. The traumatizing events of 9/11 galvanized society to create security structures that did not previously exist in U.S. history, placing greater emphasis on critical infrastructure protection (CIP) and national preparedness. There were major increases in financial investments to improve security by both the private and public sectors. From 2006 to 2008, there was a new level of attention placed on physical *and* cyber security, highlighted by public policy, governmental programs, and congressional funding recognizing the importance of forming partnerships across the interagency (Interview 9).

When the U.S. Department of Homeland Security (U.S. DHS) was formed, critical infrastructure protection was viewed from a physical security perspective. Largely considered "guns, gates, and guards," it later matured to include human and cyber-security themes. DHS and FEMA place strategic emphasis on supporting state governors with the most important physical infrastructure requirements, electricity (Emergency Support Function [ESF]-12) and telecommunications (ESF-2) (Interview 9).

Our greatest challenge to resilience is facing the impact of increased complexity and unpredictability caused by major interconnectivity and interdependencies across all sectors and supply chains. The challenge is that a disaster in another part of the world can have a serious downstream impact on regional economies, which is very difficult to predict and model (Interview 11).

Consider the Japan earthquake-tsunami-nuclear disaster that had a cascading impact on computer and vehicle production in the United States due to disruptions in parts delivery and supply-chain security. Other examples are Iceland's volcano (Eyjafjallajökull) in 2010, when erupting magma hit a glacier and ash exploded into the sky, causing aviation officials to ground European flights for days because of the dangers of flying through volcanic ash. Further, Boeing's fleet of aircraft must track and monitor tens of thousands of parts and supplies that impact the world aviation market and associated global supply chains. Another example of surprises that surface from increased risk and complexity is the Deepwater Horizon Oil Spill in the Gulf of Mexico, where it was discovered that we as a nation did not have the capability to cap an offshore deepwater oil well (Interview 11).

The year 2011 was important for disaster response and resilience policy as we drew lessons from previous events in shaping current models. We were also reminded that disasters must be handled on a case-by-case basis because they are all different. Hurricanes and tornadoes are like "boutique events" because they are "specialized and exclusive" in a response sense. The 2010 Haiti earthquake was a turning point because it impacted our subsequent response to the Deepwater Horizon oil spill and application of both the National Oil and Hazardous Substances Pollution Contingency Plan and National Contingency Plan (NCP). It also impacted efforts supporting Israel in responding to the unusual earthquake there in August 2011 and helping Japan after the 2011 earthquake-tsunami-Fukushima nuclear disaster. Earlier, the Haiti earthquake required national planners to work extensively with USAID, Departments of State and Defense (particularly SOUTHCOM) (Interview 12).

A University-Affiliated Research Center (UARC) like the Johns Hopkins University Applied Physics Laboratory (JHU/APL), along with academic scholars and experts across the private sector, can play a unique role in helping the U.S. government close the gaps between national-level policies and both local and regional all-hazards planning and execution. Many universities, owners, and operators also want to be part of addressing resiliency and collaboration challenges at the regional level. While JHU/APL can coordinate action with federal agencies and departments, private-sector associations and organizations (such as the All-Hazards Consortium) can concurrently bring together regional and local efforts to establish a new approach. The key is to achieve a blend of efforts that reinforces organizational values and corporate respect (Interview 13).

In response to lessons learned from Hurricane Katrina, the Director of National Intelligence (DNI) General Flynn said, "The greatest future threat is not working together" (Interview 16).

Understanding our current world of infrastructures requires a level of complexity in an environment where technology is expanding rapidly—and we often see a learning and leadership deficit in this area. Consider the post–World War II generation that "saved the world from disaster" by growing the economy and building the infrastructures that we have enjoyed over the past 60 years. With resilience, we are seeing how the human-built and natural systems interface. There are *wicked problems* (where we know the problem but cannot solve it) and there are *black swan* events one cannot predict with existing data (events that are a surprise and have a major impact), a theory developed by the philosopher Nassim Nicholas Taleb (Interview 17).

The speed with which data sources and information are growing exceeds the ability of government to process them. In an era when we need more public-private partnerships (PPPs), there is a growing gap between government and private businesses.

The private companies want their privacy protected during any activity, yet if a crisis occurs, they want government to respond to support their private interests. We are at a strategic inflection point where we need innovation across community boundaries (Interview 17).

Within the Department of Homeland Security, Infrastructure Protection (IP) has matured as an organization over the past five years. From a strategic perspective, DHS has solid CIP databases and a relationship with the field through our protective security advisors and homeland security advisors, but we need:

1. a mechanism—and a pilot to lay the groundwork—to open the "data aperture" and distribute the information to the states; pushing the data back to those who can utilize it, helping state fusion centers better understand CIP capabilities and evaluate threats from a local perspective;

2. a data integration system that will integrate information from various sources and fuse it in an automated manner across multiple rule sets and input streams. Our current system, Automated Critical Asset Management System (ACAMS), is functional but falls short because it is not compatible with cohort systems and roadmaps around the country;

3. an expansion of our strategic partnerships with international interlocutors to address supply-chain issues, undersea cables, and broader CIKR issues in a regional manner;

4. a closer alignment with the missions of cyber and physical security (CIP) by integrating best practices and planning efforts (Interview 18).

Education partners are critical when developing infrastructure policy, and the academic community has much to offer in understanding the projects, trends, and challenges of the future. The year 2040 seems distant, but the challenges of moving transportation and planning for the future are current events. The question is how to identify and prioritize infrastructure deficiencies in the twenty-first century. Where is the transportation system gridlock on our major corridors, and what policy is needed to move projects of national significance forward? Our future economy depends on resilient infrastructures and a transportations system free of congestion (Interview 19).

CULTURAL FACTORS

A basic question when considering changes needed to improve CIP and resilience is, Are we even capable of reforming or transforming our government institutions to better prevent or respond to crises? In 2013, some within the interagency see U.S. government bureaucracies having reached a form of the Laffer curve[1] saturation, making them unwilling—or highly resistant—to develop significant policy changes. This leads to an inability to see the chance of attack and failure to think creatively about the threat environment. Therefore, absent a traumatic event, there is likely to be little change because of the culture of denial, risk, and cost avoidance (Interview 6).

There is also a cultural barrier to a whole-of-community approach due to a common practice at the local level of asking for financial assistance for even minor emergency events. For example, during local flooding in Maryland, the local government contacted the state to request bottled water they could have easily procured on their own. Rather than exploring community vendors first, the local authorities can sometimes immediately seek assistance from higher authorities in order to avoid costs. This attitude fosters unnecessary dependency rather than local readiness and capability (Interview 7).

Asserting the role of thought-leader requires a "defining venue" and discourse around a strategic issue: that is, when and why is the private sector included in government planning, and how can that be improved? A culture of "conference-convening power" can create breakthroughs at crucial junctures in shaping infrastructure protection policies (Interview 14).

The Romans had ombudsmen counselors—politicians who could overrule determinations in order to "do the right thing," regardless of applicable regulations. Perhaps this provision should be incorporated into current public policy development in supporting critical infrastructure resilience. Another potential tool for application in this field is "disruptive technology" (Interview 14).

NATIONAL FRAMEWORK

How do we implement an effective national framework that cultivates a "culture of preparedness" and integrates resilience in all areas? Currently, there is no "organizing principle" that reduces risk and provides rewards to "keep people engaged." While it is a good program, we need more than a "See Something—Say Something" slogan (Interview 9).

Private industry has discovered the importance of business recovery plans and individual preparedness plans. For example, after the Gulf Coast region started recovering from Hurricane Katrina, the shipyard in Pascagoula, Mississippi, was back in operation, but many employees did not return to work because daycare facilities were not open. The local and regional economy was ready to resume operation, but it was impeded by the lack of resilience in neighborhood daycare services. Resilience is not a separate program or budget line item; rather, it is a behavior and a quality that needs to be embedded within all systems, programs, activities, and behavior. This example highlights the need to stitch together a framework, governance, or family of recovery plans to raise the level of resiliency in communities:

1. government at the strategy/policy level
2. private industry at the company level
3. families at the human/personal level (Interview 9).

Examples of dependencies and interdependencies (regional economy, shipyard workforce, employees, children, availability of daycare services) point to a "gap in partnerships" within our society. Significant effort is being poured into national preparedness and resilience at the national policy level, but we must close the divide between federal programs and local, community, family, and individual efforts. We need a national-level framework that offers a "consistent, integrated, and systemic process to coordinate preparedness." To close this "gap" between national and local systems, we need a self-sustaining framework (i.e., organizing principle) recognizing that response and recovery activity takes place largely at the local level (Interview 9).

We need to map infrastructure dependencies and interdependencies nationwide to understand the unique ligaments involved in resilience by geographic regions, including policies, statutes, operations, systems, networks, organizations, funding, incentives, and people—identifying the many interconnected codependent utilities and services by region. This idea is similar to what has been done at some State Fusion Centers (SFCs) and State Emergency Operations Centers (EOCs) by mapping the network of public/private first responders: police/law enforcement, emergency management representatives, and port security/Area Maritime Security Committees, which provides a comprehensive roadmap of interconnected interagency players for that region. Right now, it is a "volunteer" self-forming community-of-interest, but we need a framework that would be a catalyst to formalizing and structuring these relationships. The Sector Coordinating Committees (SCC) galvanized the private sector at the national level (2003–2004) but never replicated it at the local level. The unit of measure is local/regional geographic communities of interest that need to be identified, mapped, and leveraged to develop a nationwide framework to keep communities engaged, but it cannot be mandated or prescribed top-down from the national level (Interview 9).

The path to a resilient society and culture of preparedness does not lie in "disaster" references. Politicians do not run for elected office on a platform of "disaster" preparedness. Building a compelling national framework and galvanizing a community resilience movement is better achieved by leveraging *existing* needs and requirements of the general public—not adding new programs or budgetary requirements. It requires a simple appeal to implement resilience through current concerns and interests: e.g. crime reduction, improved health, better education, economic housing, and food quality. Build a culture of resilience that complements and reinforces big issues that the public currently cares about by integrating preparedness and community resilience into everything we do. Good engineering sciences, environmental designs, and education programs have resiliency embedded within their design and implementation (Interview 11).

It would be helpful if a "framework for action" could be developed for national resilience. For example, during World War II, there was a campaign to galvanize an entire nation with four words: "Defeat Germany—Hold Japan." What is the equivalent charge to forge a culture of preparedness—the framework to create a resilient posture within our society? (Interview 12).

Managing events at the White House through the National Security Staff involves coordinating the interagency, especially black swan events (unforeseen, surprise events). The scale and scope of each disaster is unique, but there should be a basic national capability to surge and flex, drawing upon the necessary participants in a seamless, coordinated manner (White House, interagency, international partners, United Nations, USNORTHCOM, NGOs, and so on). We know the events are coming and we should anticipate disasters. As Solomon said, "There is nothing new under the sun." The key to success is unity-of-effort. In a community sense, we must "unify the tribe." Although there are different cultures, funding, governance, authorities, and responsibilities, we are essentially a tribal society that must pull together under a national framework to "create and sustain resilience" (Interview 12).

Identifying and prioritizing essential functions are prerequisites for federal continuity and disaster management planning because they drive an agency's preparedness efforts. This is necessary because disruptive events that trigger implementation of a continuity plan usually result in an agency's resources and staffing being restricted when compared to normal operations. Therefore, the government as a whole and each individual agency must predetermine what normal functions in their organization are considered essential during and after a disaster (Interview 12).

Academic and research organizations can play a unique role in developing a national framework and raising strategic issues. Their prior performance as thought leaders allows them to leverage existing relationships with government sponsors, and study rigorous analytics that bridge policy and technical areas. Nationally, we need a Goldwater-Nichols-like provision for local, state, and regional first responders and government officials by cross-training and educating practitioners beyond their service organization. As seen in joint professional military education (PME) requirements, the expansion of cross-agency experience can best be accomplished by linking the training to promotion and career opportunities. We should encourage a culture of resilience and preparedness by forming a Homeland Security volunteer arm similar to Air Force's Civil Air Patrol (CAP) and Coast Guard's Auxiliary (CGAUX), changing the model from compelling compliance to incentivizing service. Drawing from economic principles, we need to employ "incentive-compatible mechanisms," especially for the private sector, to reshape our national culture of preparedness (financial, training, trust) (Interview 14).

Looking at National Preparedness (PPD-8), the first two plans ("prevent, protect") are more applicable as cultural factors in the social sciences that seek deterrence through policies and the political process. The last two plans ("respond, recover") draw from the engineering sciences calling for physical action and emergency services. "Mitigation" bridges both categories, offering systemic means to reduce the impact of disaster through preventive measures across all sectors (Interview 15).

RESILIENCE

It is a challenge to define *community resilience*. It doesn't follow jurisdictional boundaries, but instead requires new thinking about preparedness, determining risk-based security needs and business continuity to identify critical capacity linkages (Interview 15).

Resilience is difficult to quantify in the planning process and hard to capture in statutes and policymaking. The key is to apply performance standards and incentivize states to use resilience as a criterion for their infrastructure investments, and to show a value proposition and return on investment (ROI) for public and private stakeholders (Interviews 8, 19).

Resilience is considered the ability to reduce downtime after a disaster by re-establishing services as quickly as possible. Planning will always require a risk-based approach—accounting for vulnerability, threat, intent, probability, and consequences—to determine the criticality of the infrastructures impacted. Private industry is more focused on natural disasters and business continuity because counterterrorism is a low probability event (Interview 4).

Preparedness and resilience go together. The key is a systemic capability to absorb disruptions and minimize the structural and functional impact of disasters. Hurricane Katrina reminded us that resiliency allows a community to restore services sooner than it otherwise could. Adopting a whole-community approach, FEMA Director Craig Fugate has said that resilience is "getting people to take care of themselves; not just providing shelter, but enabling the general public to get back to work . . . and establishing a stable tax base five years after the disaster." Resilience means minimizing the disruption of an attack or disaster: being able to take a hit and keep working (Interview 9).

Building on the *National Security Strategy*'s definition of resilience (The White House 2010), DHS's focus is on the ability to *withstand* an attack. There is a primary emphasis on mitigation, response, and recovery (with FEMA leading), and mitigation is largely directed toward building structures and homes. Prevention and protection is focused on industry sectors (with DHS/IP leading). To operationalize this the DHS department-wide Resilience Integration Team (RIT) was formed to incorporate the input of all DHS components and resolve differences between components. Experts within DHS questioned if the RIT had the necessary authorities and resources to impact strategic resilience objectives across the public and private sectors (Interview 10).

Resilience should be designed into all aspects of CIP sectors. For example, structures should be designed to support multiple objectives within cost constraints, incorporating all factors (environmentally green, physical security, and natural disaster) within architectural planning. Similarly, resiliency should be integrated into academic curriculums, disaster management, and EMS training so that national education standards support a culture of preparedness, resilience, and infrastructure protection (Interview 11).

How do we create a resilient nation? We must view it as a system of systems, starting with personal resilience, recognizing every person and family has a unique set of planning variables and challenges. One can conceptually view resilience as a series of concentric circles—a layered system—with national resilience being an aggregate of all levels from the personal domain outward to the national level. For example, during Hurricane Katrina, the post-event assessment uncovered lack of resilience within all elements of the emergency response and disaster management systems; human, infrastructure, and organizational resilience across the government and local communities was very fragile (Interview 12).

We need to move away from a "protection" mind-set that focuses on securing national assets and instead seek "continuity of function in the face of risk" or "continuity of resilience." The reason for this approach is that infrastructure, systems, and networks collectively provide "functions—a means to an end." The key is to understand the function of the asset. Following this approach, the two ends of the preparedness continuum are "physical hardening" at one end and "functional resilience" at the other. For example, the Alaskan oil pipeline delivers critical hydrocarbons from the North Slope through a single pipeline. This is a resource that primarily requires a level of physical hardening with a security system to monitor its protection. In order to be more resilient, it would be wise to pre-position pipeline repair equipment and train a pipeline security response team to accomplish pipeline repairs within a 24-to-48-hour period (Interview 15).

The Electric Sector Pilot will provide an assessment of cyber readiness as a major portion of functional resilience, evaluating the role government should play in the process. What are the policy and vulnerability gaps? Where is there a need for collective action or establishing formal memorandums of understanding (MOUs)? Participants were identified by working through the U.S. Department of Energy's (DOE) Pilot lead, the U.S. Department of Homeland Security (DHS), and the existing DHS relationship with the Critical Infrastructure Protection Advisory Council (CIPAC). There will be an assessment of the electric grid and the maturity level of grid capabilities, which will require that the public sector learn the right questions to ask of private-sector utilities. An effort like this allows collective learning to take place within the critical infrastructure sectors identifying dependencies, interdependencies, surveillance and applicable laws, and the like (Interview 2).

DHS/Office of Infrastructure Protection (OIP) has launched the Regional Resilience Assessment Program (RRAP) with a series of nationwide pilots, including those in Georgia and New Jersey. The focus is on local and regional programs "capable of making a difference on the ground" because federal authorities are limited if communities are not prepared—as was learned during Hurricane Katrina (Interview 10).

The RRAP attempts to standardize how resiliency is evaluated across various sectors and facilities. RRAP is an interagency assessment of specific critical infrastructure and key resources (CIKR), combined with a regional analysis of the surrounding infrastructure, including key interdependencies. It evaluates critical infrastructure "clusters," regions, and systems to reduce the nation's vulnerability to all-hazard threats by coordinating efforts to enhance CIKR resiliency and security across geographic regions. Participation in RRAP is voluntary, and the information collected is protected under the Protected Critical Infrastructure Information Program (PCIIP) (Interview 3).

The private sector operates based on profit margins. Unless there are quantifiable cost savings, it will be difficult to incentivize corporate investments in resilience, preparedness, and mitigation, so DHS must find ways to make the business case to the private sector, showing an economic benefit. Insurance rates could be reduced if underwriters observe a quantifiable reduction in lives/property lost due to preparedness (emergency management plans, evacuation exercises, and so on); but the research, modeling, and empirical data must be developed across infrastructure sectors and business areas to support the investments by commercial enterprise and equity investors (Interview 4).

Measures of resilience should not be administered as merely an organizational plan that is inactive until a disaster occurs. Rather, it should be a habitual practice that is constantly integrated into the public and private sectors with standardized training in assessment measures and critical infrastructure resilience (Interview 7).

"Community resilience" involves a dynamic combination of public and private infrastructures. There needs to be an economic incentive that shows the business sector that advance preparation and investment in resilience will restore the flow of commerce more quickly, and most importantly, allow for a prompt return to revenue-producing activity. Consider the Volkswagen plant in Alabama that recovered from Hurricane Katrina and was back in operation only 5 days after the storm because of pre-disaster resiliency planning efforts. We also need to consider the role of labor unions (positive or negative) when evaluating the ability to recover and restore operations (Interview 9).

The Homeland Security Advisory Council (HSAC)—through the 2010 Quadrennial Homeland Security Review (QHSR)—initiated the Community Resilience Task Force that published a report in June 2011. The report addresses a spectrum of issues and recommendations based on lessons learned since 9/11 and Hurricane Katrina (Interview 10).

DHS is seeking "high-value programs to incentivize and encourage the private sector" to invest in community resilience. For example, there is the Rick Rescorla National Award for Resilience. On September 11, 2001, Rescorla was vice president of Security for Morgan Stanley at their headquarters in the World Trade Center. Before losing his life that day, he personally led the evacuation of Morgan Stanley's 2,700 employees, and all but six of Morgan Stanley's workers in the South Tower survived. Following the earlier terrorist attacks on the World Trade Center (in 1993), Rescorla drilled his Morgan Stanley employees in disaster preparedness and response, and his actions ensured employees knew how to evacuate. The *Rick Rescorla National Award for Resilience* was awarded for the first time in September 2012 (Interview 10).

DHS launched the Resilience STAR Pilot (patterned after the DOE's Energy STAR program)—a voluntary certification program that aims to make homes and buildings more secure and resilient to all hazards. The Resilient Homes Pilot brings DHS together with local officials, private-sector insurers, and builders in risk-prone communities to rebuild private residences recently destroyed by hazards. During the Secretary's testimony to the Senate (April 2012), she indicated that DHS is exploring expanding DHS's "Resilience STAR" program into the transportation sector to highlight and advance security and resiliency standards for key supply-chain nodes and infrastructure. The goal is to achieve "mission sustainability" through simple, economizing procedures, leveraging existing programs and priorities (Interview 10).

DHS is partnering with the Insurance Institute for Business and Home Safety (IBHS) and the insurance industry to strengthen "building standards" through IBHS programs such as FORTIFIED. Applying building science solutions to reduce risks, FORTIFIED plans help improve the quality of residential and light commercial buildings, offering solutions for new and existing structures across the country that are exposed to some type of natural hazard. Ultimately, the goal is to see home insurance premiums reduced for those homes certified through the Resilience STAR program;

interagency work is under way on this effort, particularly in the Department of Housing and Urban Development (HUD), the Small Business Administration (SBA), and General Services Administration (GSA) (Interview 10).

How can we embed resilience within the culture of our society and government interagency? First of all, resilience is a "good business practice" and should be part of all disciplines as they work toward:

1. creating and sustaining an elastic capability within individual and organizational areas of interest;
2. absorbing the impact of minor disruptions or major disasters;
3. reinforcing the ability to adapt and change, which is not a new requirement, but something we have faced since the founding of this country. For example, good public policies reflect resilient thinking. In both the public and private sectors, resilience is essential, not optional (Interview 12).

Resilience can be considered a precursor to preparedness—a planning variable embedded within response and also a strategic outcome of CIKR efforts. Health care and personal wellness as a system of systems provide a helpful metaphor for understanding community resilience. For example, the medical industry is a group of professionals supporting health care resilience, all essential parts of a broader resiliency objective (dental hygienists, psychologists, cardiologists, pediatricians, emergency room staff, nurses, and so on). When an individual gets sick, the patient has personal requirements, and a team of health care professionals is there to assist when needed. Health patterns are unique to the person, family, and society, and the collective outcome is a level of resilient health. Further, the body has many parts, and each individual system within the broader system of the body requires a unique approach to healthy behavior and outcomes that contributes to the overall welfare: heart, eyes, and diet—all contribute to physical health, performance, and resilience. And a healthy immune system—like community resilience—allows the body to rebound and recover more quickly from internal and external attacks (disease or disaster). Finally, we know how to operationalize health care at a personal level, and we must likewise operationalize and implement resilience at a personal, community, and national level (Interview 12).

Personal-level resilience is at the center of building community resilience. Human nature dictates that work and community priorities will fall below family concerns. "People will not stay at work if their families are at risk"; therefore, the primary focus must be placed on advance preparations at the personal, human, and family level with pre-trained and pre-positioned efforts. Building resilience doesn't mean protecting ourselves from every contingency but from risk-based impacts—and having a system to determine how much should be spent on infrastructure protection. Part of the risk-based program is the Common Vulnerability Scoring System (CVSS) that applies limited resources to the most critical resources and reflects DHS requests for greater emphasis on more vulnerable locations based upon a quantitative scoring and mapping system (Interview 14).

"Every complex system will fail, but the speed of recovery is the best measure of a healthy system. . . . Resilience is reflected in how well infrastructure can absorb external impacts." The key to resilience and continuity centers on "local interdependencies" because there is a local and regional "self-forming community-of-interest" that organizes around a hazard or incident. "Resilience challenges us to look more at consequences than causalities." When recovering from or withstanding an impact, the cause is less important (at that point), and mitigation is more important to overcome the consequences. For example, we may not know the precise cause or origin of an epidemic or pandemic, but we know that the immediate consequence will be the loss of workforce personnel and essential employees, which brings an organization to a standstill—as the Japanese experienced during the earthquake-tsunami of 2011 with respect to local and regional governments. Some of the major entities that were responsible for coordinating the regional response and recovery to the incidents were missing, displaced, evacuated, or the buildings where they normally worked were gone (Interview 18).

Investing in resilience programs—at the personal, community, or state level—can be difficult to motivate or incentivize because it is viewed the same way as buying insurance; consumers (who are already budget-constrained) are being asked to add another item to their budget. So, the key is to find something they (individuals, companies, organizations, etc.) already value, which offers a return on investment (ROI) and has a clearly understood value proposition. Otherwise, resilience investments will usually be considered a costly distraction that does not provide a tangible return (Interview 18).

Some hazardous events demand experience and capabilities beyond what we currently have as a nation—usually low-probability, high-consequence disasters. The electric power companies are perhaps the most effective at "putting things back together" because they have significant experience in repairing power systems to rapidly restore services. For maritime emergency response, the Deepwater Horizon Oil Spill in the Gulf of Mexico (2010) represented a new level of maritime-environmental disaster management that required capabilities and capacities beyond our existing national experience. If a New Madrid earthquake occurs in the Midwest United States, how would we manage major power disruptions and subsequent rationing of electricity? That scenario would exceed our existing plans and thrust us into a low-frequency, high-impact condition. Therefore, rather than try to defend and protect against all the consequences of extreme black swan scenarios, we need to establish a capabilities-based resilience posture that rapidly restores the most important infrastructures across all the sectors, based on large-scale optimization and predetermined mapping of essential services (Interview 18).

POLICY FACTORS

Promulgation of National Preparedness (PPD-8) represents a major policy effort and contains five frameworks (prevent, protect, mitigate, respond, recover), with the *National Response Framework (NRF)* (2008) serving as a "unifying mechanism," since the document has been rewritten and provides a common lexicon along with the other policy documents. The White House has worked on the biosurveillance strategy, coordinating the efforts of the Departments of Health and Human Services (HHS), Homeland Security (DHS), and Defense (DOD) with an emphasis on a whole-of-community approach. The goal is to get the federal policy level in order first, which can then inspire and motivate coordination with lower levels—expanding the ability to "surge capabilities across local, state, and regional levels" (Interview 20).

Within DHS, there are seven operational components: U.S. Citizen and Immigration Services (USCIS), Customs and Border Protection (CBP), the Federal Emergency Management Agency (FEMA), Immigration and Customs Enforcement (ICE), U.S. Secret Service (USSS), U.S. Coast Guard (USCG), and Transportation Security Administration (TSA). The National Protections and Programs Directorate (NPPD) might become the eighth component on the list, especially since NPPD is increasingly more operational in its roles and missions (Interview 18).

For CIP, the *National Infrastructure Protection Plan (NIPP)* is the basic planning document (2009). To help understand where improvements are needed in national-level resilience, consider the National Infrastructure Advisory Council (NIAC) reports on information sharing and public-private partnerships (Interview 3).

The DHS policy needed to operationalize Sector Coordinating Committees (SCCs) at the local level is lacking. And the *NIPP* is more of a "strategy" than an "action plan" to execute protection and resilience (Interview 9).

Since 9/11, some $18.5 billion (approximately $8 billion on interoperability, $10.5 billion on other support) has been spent on FEMA grant programs. The past decade has seen a proliferation of strategies and plans across the federal, state, and local preparedness communities, without a comprehensive organizing framework to inform their development and execution. For example, there needs to be a simple national-level strategy for action that implements PPD-8 (National Preparedness) (Interview 10).

The annual National Preparedness Report (March 2012)—required by Presidential Policy Directive-8 (PPD-8)—reflects the current state of national-level preparedness based on input from all 56 states and territories. In May 2011, the White House published the Implementation Strategy for PPD-8, which seeks to operationalize whole-of-nation, all-hazards preparedness policy, and represents a paradigm shift in our national approach to emergency management by taking a community-oriented approach to resilience. The national preparedness system will describe how the cycle of planning, organizing, equipping, training, and exercising support the achievement of the National Preparedness Goal. The strategy draws from the National Incident Management System (NIMS), National Planning System, National Training and Education System, National Exercise Program, and Remedial Action Management Program to track progress on lessons learned and corrective actions taken to build and sustain preparedness (Interview 11).

We must identify the gaps in policy implementation. Policy documents, including HSPDs, are being revised to move beyond a post-9/11 counterterrorism focus to include an all-hazards/resilience approach, attempting to integrate the safety and security communities within the interagency. The departments are looking at the Emergency Support Functions (ESFs) and expanding application to "all hazards," with a "whole-of-community" approach that recognizes the central role of the private sector (Interview 1).

One of the biggest problems for DHS is identifying and resolving "issues that are in the seams that nobody has the responsibility to solve, but are in fact threats." These are often issues that are "between dependencies." Sometimes it takes a catastrophic event to reveal the biggest problem: In 1989, Exxon was a very successful company, but was unaware of a corporate deficiency in crisis and disaster management until the oil tanker Exxon Valdez ran aground in Alaskan waters and caused a major environmental disaster (Interview 18).

Preparedness policies must be integrated across departments and agencies to provide guidance on critical infrastructure, homeland security funding, public health, safety, and environmental protection—recognizing that interagency responsibilities are not isolated issues but reside at the intersection of multiple agencies: health (HHS), safety (FEMA), and the environment (EPA). It is also useful to examine the eight national-level essential functions that have been identified from the broader list of 72 (Interview 12).

Due to advanced technology and supply-chain complexities, global threats can rapidly materialize in the homeland and become a serious domestic threat. At the strategic level, the Office of the Director of National Intelligence (ODNI) provides resources to the intelligence community (IC) and facilitates efforts such as the National Intelligence Manager (NIM) Pilot to formulate a Western Hemisphere/Homeland Unified Intelligence Strategy (UIS). And the UIS incorporates homeland (public and private) variables, which feeds the Suspicious Activity System and the FBI's E-Guardian database—providing law enforcement leads for first responders (Interview 16).

Federal partnerships include all IC components as well Departments of State, Treasury, Energy, and non-Title 50 agencies (Title 50 refers to war and national defense). HSPD-8 directs the development of an organic capability to share intelligence and forge relationships with interagency partners. For resiliency/CIKR objectives, the goal is to ensure the interagency is connected at all levels, including health safety (HHS), water supplies (EPA), and nuclear facilities (NRC) (Interview 16).

The Electric Sector Pilot program (U.S. Department of Energy and U.S. Department of Homeland Security 2012) is designed to determine the security and cyber posture of a mature system, offering a potential model for other utilities to determine how to mitigate cyber-security risks. The electric sector was selected because the power grid is a well-bounded service, heavily regulated (relative to some other sectors), and has an established community-of-interest. The pilot addresses key elements of the DOE's roadmap, allowing the DOE to coordinate directly with industry partners on Energy Delivery System Cyber Security, including participation by the North American Electric Reliability Corporation (NERC)—an organization of U.S. electric grid operators—and informed by the Energy Policy Act of 2005 (Interview 2).

The Office of the Assistant Secretary of Defense/Homeland Defense/American Security Affairs (ASD/HD/ASA) is the executive agent for the Defense Critical Infrastructure Program (DCIP), through the Defense Critical Infrastructure Office (DCIO), collaborating with other military services and coordinating with STRATCOM on prioritization of critical databases across DOD. NORTHCOM, as geographic Combatant Commander (COCOM) for the homeland, supports Defense Critical Infrastructure (DCI) policy with a focus on any cyber, SCADA (Supervisory Control & Data Acquisition), and power grid issues that will affect the Defense Department in the homeland. The DOD-DCIP helps identify, prioritize, assess, and remediate issues of concern, employing the Critical Asset Identification Process (CAIP). The focus is on threats to the homeland civil infrastructure where there is a direct or indirect impact on assets needed by the war fighter (Interview 5).

There needs to be more application of social sciences and examination of human behavior factors. Things like collective action theory, cultural factors, tragedy of the commons, and integration of economic, environmental, safety, and security planning need to be better understood in conjunction with national preparedness—applying a national framework for critical infrastructure priorities and functional resilience, not just disaster preparation. There are lessons that can be learned and useful security principles to be applied from our international partners, working through DHS/NPPD/ Infrastructure Protection and appropriate embassy staff elements to examine Critical Foreign Dependency Initiatives (CFDIs) (Interview 10).

LEGISLATION

In some cases, legislation, laws, and statutes need to be updated. The *National Response Framework (NRF)* is structured around ESFs, informed by the Disaster Relief and Emergency Assistance Act (August 2007). The Stafford Act and Economy Act are also important to the role of DHS/FEMA, as well as the Post-Katrina Emergency Management Reform Act (PKEMRA). For example, the historic environmental legislation known as the Oil Pollution Act of 1990 (OPA-90), enacted after the Exxon Valdez case in Alaska (1989), was inadequate for addressing the Deepwater Horizon Oil Spill case in the Gulf of Mexico (2011). Exxon Valdez was a near-shore, coastal mishap involving refined oil with one responsible party, and Deepwater Horizon was an off-shore event involving unrefined oil with multiple responsible parties. The laws and statutes from OPA-90 (as well as the Emergency Management and Assistance Act, CFR 44, October 2008) were insufficient to address the incident response in 2010 (Interview 1).

Across the infrastructure sectors, there are areas of preparedness that can be advanced by interagency strategies and policies, presidential executive orders, and government regulations, but some initiatives will require congressional legislation. For example, the Energy Independence and Security Act of 2007 (EISA) is an Act of Congress concerning the energy policy of the United States. The purpose of the act is "to move the United States toward greater energy independence and security; to increase the production of clean renewable fuels; to protect consumers; to increase the efficiency of products, buildings, and vehicles; to promote research on and deploy greenhouse gas capture and storage options; and to improve the energy performance of the Federal Government, and for other purposes." The bill originally sought to cut subsidies to the petroleum industry in order to promote petroleum independence and different forms of alternative energy. These changes were ultimately dropped after opposition in the Senate, and the final bill addressed automobile fuel economy, development of biofuels, and energy efficiency in public buildings rather than a broader focus on strategic resilience across the energy sector (Interview 4).

We need more effective policy and legislation to enable national preparedness for all-hazards national scenarios across all CIKR sectors. We don't "subtract" previous legislation when it is time to move forward, but simply keep adding on more statutes. A comprehensive review of all existing legislation and statutes that impact emergency/disaster response is crucial to ensure complementary and synchronized guidance, informed by valuable lessons learned over the past 10 years. In the field of hazardous material (ESF-14) and oil pollution, the last major oil pollution legislation—before Deepwater Horizon in the Gulf of Mexico—was the Oil Pollution Act of 1990 (OPA-90). OPA-90 was insufficient to address the wide-ranging issues experienced 20 years later. And the latest version of the National Contingency Plan (NCP) was promulgated in 1994 to reflect the oil spill requirements of OPA-90, so major environmental policies are clearly outdated. Furthermore, updated legislation for human-made environmental disasters should address scenarios where "private polluters are required to pay." There also needs to be a comprehensive examination of disaster preparedness and resilience-related items in the Code of Federal Regulations (CFRs), incorporating twenty-first-century threats and preparedness realities. The "response" guidance over the past 20 years has migrated from the *Federal Response Plan (FRP),* to a *National Response Plan (NRP),* to the current *National Response Framework (NRF)* that reflects the maturity of national guidance, but also may lack the enduring principles necessary for comprehensive whole-of-nation, public-private imperatives (Interview 12).

Shortly after 9/11, the National Infrastructure Advisory Council (NIAC) was established by executive orders to address cyber-security issues; it was later expanded to include all other industrial sectors. The first project was to review existing laws and information, which led to Congress passing a law exempting CIP information provided to the federal government from Freedom of Information Act requests. This helped ease concerns in the business sector about providing information about weaknesses in operations (Interview 14).

Legislation must include waivers for human intervention, considering how laws could interfere with or support personnel participating in disaster management or recovery operations. Also, first responder credentialing is a factor: Fire departments are more integrated in their qualifications than police, allowing them to respond to a broader range of emergencies, but 11,000 local police departments across the country represent potential resources—currently limited by their range of authorities—that could be trained to support a more extensive range of disaster management and response roles (Interview 14).

Authorities and jurisdictions add to the complexity of coordination challenges. A maritime study with a fire and hazardous material (HAZMAT) environmental spill involved 97 different jurisdictions, offering a case study that highlights the barriers to interagency collaboration and collective action (Interview 14).

NIAC looked at things like insurance when considering legislation that would establish laws applicable in an emergency. The goal is to have people think about all personal factors in preparation for a natural or human-made disaster—including insurance as part of personal preparedness (Interview 14).

The Title 5 regulatory process is deficient, and the Regulatory Flexibility Act of 1980 should be updated. The latter requires federal agencies to analyze the impact of regulatory actions on small entities (small businesses, small nonprofit organizations, and small jurisdictions of government) and, where the regulatory impact is likely to be "significant," seek less burdensome alternatives for them (Interview 17).

The Stafford Act needs to be updated based upon the requirements of government in a twenty-first-century all-hazards environment. As DHS/FEMA learned during hurricane events in the U.S. Virgin Islands, the Stafford Act only allows restoration of infrastructure that was previously in place; it does not allow for changes or improvements in post-disaster reconstruction. Perhaps there should be a mechanism added to the act that would allow for more flexibility in that area, because the reason the structure or system was vulnerable in the first place may have been due to where it was located or how it was designed/constructed—calling for changes in location or design (Interview 18).

When developing legislation, too often the biggest "political guerrilla" dominates the political process through a system that is still focused on "fixing things." The process must be revised. Different parts of the country are ready for infrastructure investments at different times. The goal is to move goods, people, and services as necessary and keep businesses and the economy going, and achieving this goal requires a critical examination of mass transit with an integrated approach geared to meeting overall needs of the country. New transportation legislation must incentivize investors to build local and state infrastructure across all sectors: air, land, sea, rail, and highway (Interview 19).

Some have suggested establishing a National Infrastructure Bank, but it has not yet proved to be a viable approach. Thirty-three states have already tried it, but it doesn't yield the expected funds. As an alternative, Congress is considering increased federal participation in the Transportation Infrastructure Finance and Innovation Act (TIFIA) loan process. The current administration tried to stimulate the economy through "shovel-ready" infrastructure projects, but it's not possible due to the amount of red tape and lengthy permitting process; after two and a half years, only 35 percent of the stimulus money has left Washington, DC. The solution is to move infrastructure funds from the central government to the local and state governments, which would reduce the red tape and strengthen regional economies and job markets. As an example, the mayor of Los Angeles used TIFIA funds to accelerate a project and accomplished in a few years what might have taken 10 years to achieve (Interview 19).

Whole-of-Community

Whole-of-community starts with expanded communications, information, and the building of trust. A logical place to start is in areas vulnerable to floods and hurricanes to apply lessons learned. As FEMA expands its efforts to implement the whole-of-community approach, how will the local, county, and state governments be included in what is currently largely a regional, federal, and national system of governance? How will a preparedness culture be incorporated into regulatory and legal communities across the nation (Interview 1)?

A whole-of-community approach should be characterized by a mind-set of handling a situation through the least-centralized and most-local competent authority. A request for assistance from the state or adjoining jurisdictions should occur only when the local authorities are not capable of addressing the threat on their own. Likewise, federal involvement should only occur when the state cannot properly mitigate the threat. Clear and effective baseline planning is needed on the state and local levels to establish a strong preparedness posture. States could provide a common inventory database for local authorities to coordinate implementation of mutual support agreements. By creating an effective one-stop-shop for local municipalities in assessing the capabilities of neighboring governments, they can quickly and effectively assess whether or not they require state or federal assistance for a given incident (Interview 7).

The "limitations of government" are often revealed during disasters—large and small—and highlight a need to understand and map the existing capabilities in the private sector. For example, during the Deepwater Horizon Oil Spill, the government did not possess the technical expertise or the experience to secure the oil spill, and coordination efforts were delayed due to lack of knowledge concerning where the response capabilities existed across the country and how/where they could be activated. This principle needs to be recognized across many preparedness areas to either (1) improve government capabilities, or (2) turn to the private sector for resolution. Since 1991—during military operations in the Middle East—we have witnessed impressive displays of military, technological, command-and-control, communications, and warfighting skills that exist in the U.S. government, yet in 2005, when Hurricane Katrina destroyed New Orleans and presented the challenges of evacuation management at the Super Dome, the government was unable to execute the necessary actions. This highlights a graphic and painful example of limitations within government (Interview 11).

The whole-of-community concept needs to move from a U.S. government-centric preparedness focus to a societywide emphasis that is integrated within all levels of society. "Community" means public, private, and societywide, because preparedness requirements overlap and impact public and private sectors. There needs to be a greater understanding of how to cope with crises across the public and private sectors. Sometimes, the public sector does not understand or recognize its own limits—complicated further by the private sector failing to understand the government's capabilities—which causes a failure to prepare or properly share response and recovery operations. "Fluidity across all sectors" needs to be achieved; this, in turn, will serve as a catalyst to collective action and cooperation across local, state, and federal sectors (Interview 11).

In addition, there is a need for regional information derived from mapping of infrastructure interdependences across civil society. The Ports of Los Angeles/ Long Beach—similar to the Port Authority of New York and New Jersey—provide a bellwether for the future of the country because they are geographic, economic, and transportation hubs with large public-private communities-of-interest fueling the economic engine of the country with cargo/freight, oil distribution, complex infrastructures, and cyber security across all domains (Interview 15).

PUBLIC-PRIVATE PARTNERSHIPS

We need to better understand the links between players, barriers to participation, and proprietary hurdles that hinder or help partnerships. This is an area that requires an integrated approach across all sectors, including application of common linguistics, terms of reference, and social psychology (Interview 1).

There are many different ways to engage in public-private relationships (PPPs). The Electric Sector Pilot program offers a practical effort to expand understanding of cyber-related issues in a field that has clearly identified leadership, oversight, and regulation—offering a potential PPP model for other critical infrastructure sectors to learn from. The study will shed light on how much private-sector CEOs and CIOs are willing to invest in cyber security. It will require government and industry to compare terms-of-reference, since they often use a different "language" (Interview 2).

PPPs are joint ventures between private-sector firms and public-sector agencies. An excellent example of a PPP—and a potential model for other sectors—is the DOE's Advanced Research Projects Agency–Energy (ARPA-E) partnership with Duke Energy (one of the largest electric power companies in the United States), and with the Electric Power Research Institute (EPRI), a nonprofit research organization that focuses on the electric power utility industry in the United States and abroad to identify opportunities for testing and deploying ARPA-E–funded projects that will bolster the electric grid (Interview 4).

The DHS "Resiliency Star" Pilot is taking an innovative approach to incentivize participation during the economic recession. By working with insurance companies, DHS is promoting the shared benefit of building more resilient homes and businesses with hopes that lower insurance premiums and other benefits will spur participation by the private sector. DHS is modeling their program after the DOE Energy Star program to identify potential consumer savings as a reward for investing in resilience safeguards. If a single inspector can be trained to conduct both the Energy Star and Resiliency Star assessments, rather than requiring separate inspections for both programs, this would enable further economies. As an example of uncoordinated programs among agencies, both the Department of Transportation (DOT) and the Transportation Security Administration (TSA) conduct separate inspections for airport security, rather than joining efforts into a single inspection protocol that would reduce costs without sacrificing security (Interview 7).

The Protected Critical Infrastructure Information (PCII) program was intended to be a voluntary program in order to gather information on infrastructure protection and vulnerability assessments while fostering trust between the public and private sector. To ensure the private-sector information is protected, legislation requires that the system for processing collected information be modeled after the traditional classification regime with need-to-know criteria. This has had the unintended result of data used for emergency response becoming too restricted and limiting the formation of PPPs (Interview 8).

Since 9/11 and Katrina, there have been encouraging examples of PPPs formed around the country. Perhaps we need to form a national auxiliary program for homeland security that places a unique PPP focus on resiliency, preparedness, and cyber security, similar to the FBI's InfraGard, the U.S. Coast Guard (USCG) Auxiliary, and USAF's Civil Air Patrol—citizen volunteers who devote significant interest and effort to an area of interest to them that also supports homeland security and safety. The FBI has established auxiliary chapters around the country through the InfraGard program. InfraGard is an information-sharing and analysis effort combining the knowledge base of a wide range of members. It is a partnership between the FBI and the private sector, and an association of businesses, academic institutions, state and local law enforcement agencies, and other participants dedicated to sharing information and intelligence to prevent hostile acts against the United States. InfraGard chapters are geographically linked with FBI Field Office territories, similar to the USCG's Auxiliary—a network of some 50,000 volunteers who help the USCG perform its missions across the country in a PPP relationship. The goal of InfraGard is to promote ongoing dialogue and timely communication between members and the FBI. Members gain access to information that enables them to protect their assets and, in turn, give information to government that facilitates its responsibilities to prevent and address terrorism and other crimes (Interviews 3, 9, 16).

The DHS's launch of a nationwide PPP auxiliary program that supports resilience and preparedness would require a new level of engagement and the ability to leverage incentives for information sharing, training, and funding. It could be formed around local chapters that offer a qualification and promotion program and periodic group meetings—a volunteer, qualified, and recognized community of professionals (Interview 9).

Another good PPP example is the Southeast Region Research Initiative (SERRI), a groundbreaking program managed by Oak Ridge National Laboratory (ORNL) for the U.S. Department of Homeland Security to assist local, state, and tribal leaders in developing the tools and methods required to anticipate and forestall terrorist events and to enhance disaster response. Combining science and technology with validated operational approaches, SERRI addresses regionally unique requirements and suggests regional solutions with potential national implications. The partnership of ORNL, the Y-12 National Security Complex, and the Savannah River National Laboratory provides links to a range of regional and national research universities, showcasing cutting-edge science and technology development (Interview 9).

The *Maersk-Alabama* piracy case, which involved the hijacking of a container ship by Somali pirates in 2009, included private-sector participation in the Maritime Operational Threat Response (MOTR) process, but the commercial maritime representative was excluded from the interagency coordination conference calls when kinetic operations started—an action that reflects potential gaps in a real-world example supporting maritime transportation infrastructure. We underperform when excluding those in the private sector who know the most in the field. This represents a noteworthy case study that can be generalized across broader security principles and operational scenarios (Interview 14).

NIAC examined ways to involve the private sector in infrastructure protection projects of concern to the government. One primary lesson is that "one size does not fit all." For example, the railroad industry is highly organized with professional standards, and the other extreme is the apartment building industry, which is uncoordinated due to fragmented ownership by small apartment owners or Real Estate Investment Trusts (REITs) (Interview 14).

We also need to expand PPPs to include the academic community, exploring new ways to "infiltrate the world of scholars." It's not just public-private, it's also academic (PPAP) (Interview 15).

The ODNI has initiated a nationwide private-sector partnership effort, focused on five sectors: nuclear, cyber, financial, transportation, and communications. "Private" includes commercial companies, CIKR organizations, nongovernmental organizations (NGOs), think tanks, and academia. The Intelligence Reform & Prevention of Terrorism Act of 2004 allows the private sector to "receive information." Also, IC Directive 205 (2008)—created by ODNI's Analytic Outreach Coordinator—establishes a monthly meeting to produce analyses that incorporate all-source information. These ODNI-sponsored outreach programs take a holistic approach, including input from private contractors. They seek to educate the private sector about unclassified (UNCLAS) intelligence information and manage expectations. The approach is to go where the private sector has already organized itself (Interview 16).

The question is, How can we incentivize the general public to participate? The FBI can educate people about how other nations are stealing intellectual property and proprietary information, and DHS can develop relationships with company CSOs/CIOs, but we need to spark a grassroots movement that galvanizes society. Clearly, the ingredients are there:

1. DHS's "See Something—Say Something" campaign,
2. all disasters/crises are "local" events, and
3. CIKR priorities are in the local/regional environment. Usually, private-sector associations will organize themselves around a collective concern, but CIKR, CIP, resilience information sharing has not gained traction: only three or four of the 76 state and regional fusion centers have established private-sector coordinators (Interview 16).

In a postindustrial-, postinformation-age environment, everything is coproduced with the private sector (Kettl 2008). PPPs formed by networking and collaboration are not new; we need more "cognitive diversity," where we agree on the problem, share values, share a common vision, engage in critical thinking, build trust in diverse communities, and create solutions. We are at a point where our infrastructure is crumbling, budgets are down, and so we must explore new sources of funding through private investors and equity markets (Interview 17).

In 2010, DHS launched the Private Sector Preparedness Accreditation and Certification Program (PS-Prep), based upon legislation titled Implementing the Recommendations of the 9/11 Commission Act of 2007. This legislation created a federal program to encourage companies to develop business continuity and emergency management plans for catastrophic events. The act encourages organizations to establish robust business continuity and emergency management plans. PS-Prep is a partnership between DHS and the private sector that enables private entities to receive emergency preparedness certification from a DHS accreditation system created in coordination with the private sector. The standards—developed by the National Fire Protection Association, the British Standards Institution, and ASIS International—are designed to improve business continuity and organizational resilience. AT&T was the first commercial company to be awarded the PS-Prep certification (Interview 18).

DHS/FEMA have placed an increased focus on sustainable communities—minimizing operational disruptions to the local community. FEMA leaders ask the question, What are you restoring? And the answer often given is that "the goal of restoration is a community with a stable tax base five years after the incident" (Interview 18).

In this budget climate, we must identify new revenue streams and offer programs that attract private capital and invite "users to participate." While PPPs come with some legal and administrative limitation, we must ensure they work because they represent major sources of venture capital. We need to look at things like commuter and inner-city high-speed rail, maritime highways, short-sea shipping (between domestic regional ports), and improved rail connections to ports (Norfolk and LA/LB have railway access directly to the docks). Another challenge is the 7- to 15-year permitting process, which is too long for the private industry—they may not invest in programs that take that long. The I-35 highway bridge over the Mississippi River in Minnesota was rebuilt in only 437 days, a relatively short period of time, because it received cross-governmental focus and leveraged PPPs (Interview 19).

CAPABILITIES APPROACH

We need a preparedness system that is flexible, adaptable, and postured to uniquely respond to any disaster or crisis event in an all-hazards environment. In 2003, the critical infrastructure focus was on "protection" (CIP). When Hurricane Irene hit the East Coast in 2011, it highlighted the need for increased emphasis on "mitigate, respond, and recover" capabilities. During Irene, the electric sector was reminded of the importance of local factors because private residents wanted their trees for neighborhood aesthetics, and the power companies wanted to cut and trim trees before the storm to mitigate the damage to power lines due to high winds (Interview 1).

Beyond the post-9/11, post-Katrina mind-set to "protect and secure the infrastructure," there needs to be a broader societal look across all functional elements of the system with a focus on interdependencies and the cascading effect of crisis management, ensuring a "spectrum of capabilities" (Interview 1).

Budget realities affect mission areas and capabilities. The FY14 DHS budget request indicates a 20 percent reduction in CIP funding and a 15 percent increase in cyber-related appropriations. After nine years of operations, DHS needs to ask itself, How do current structures and processes help or impede what capabilities we need for the nation? (Interview 3).

When considering preparation approaches, it makes more sense to develop generic functional resilience rather than focus on trying to predict a single security threat. First responders provide the initial reaction to a disaster, but as a nation, we need to develop "fungible capabilities" that are interchangeable, or can be easily exchanged or shifted to match the nature of the threat or disaster. Perhaps the best examples are found within metropolitan forces (NYPD, LAPD), where they have developed a whole-of-community approach. Resilience capabilities are difficult to establish because they "don't believe an attack will really happen in their world" (Interview 6).

The Automated Critical Asset Management System (ACAMS), while federally funded and developed, was crippled by project management issues. The process of assessment and data collection is labor intensive, resulting in an underpopulated database. After DHS hired protective security advisors, ACAMS was abandoned and advisors focused their attention instead on an assessment tool in DHS/NPPD, splitting funding between both programs without consensus on a choice of systems. States often use their own assessment tools that lack interoperability, creating barriers to both information sharing and cooperation across jurisdictions. Additionally, there has been a lack of local leadership in enforcing standard risk assessment methodologies (Interview 8).

Gaps within government elements often stem from conflicting capability priorities. At the federal level, the probability of attacks (anthrax, WMDs, etc.) are low, and the potential consequences are high; but at the local level, the probability of disasters (flooding, tornados, etc.) are high, and the consequences are also high. So FEMA is shifting planning efforts from a scenario-based focus to a capabilities approach, incentivized through the DHS grant program, emphasizing communications and information sharing. There are 15 National Planning Scenarios listed in the *National Response Framework (NRF)*. These scenarios are divided into eight key categories: explosive attack, nuclear attack, radiological attack, biological attack, chemical attack, cyber attack, natural disaster, and pandemic influenza (Interviews 9, 10).

Through the National Exercise Program (NEP), supported by the interagency, 37 core capabilities have been identified to ensure adequate national-level preparedness and disaster management capabilities (Interview 10).

We desperately need a "comprehensive decision support tool" that works across organizations and data boundaries. We can eventually find the infrastructure-related information we seek, but we lack the ability to collect, sort, and analyze it in a systemic and automated manner. Our situational awareness is impeded by a lack of detection and monitoring capabilities and persistent surveillance that feeds information to senior decision makers. The United States is data-heavy, but it supports infrastructure-light (Interview 11).

We need to "map crisis communities" and build resilience factors into widely used technologies such as social networking sites (SNS), geographic information systems (GIS), and global positioning systems (GPS) in a next generation fashion. Examples of cell phone use in times of crisis support this observation: Industry has developed a smartphone and other technologies (Facebook, Twitter, etc.) that would allow us to leverage and integrate the power of SNS, GIS, and GPS. During Hurricane Katrina, cell phones were ineffective, but texting was used extensively, pointing to the utility of handheld analog technology. Similarly during the 2010 earthquake in Haiti, texting across the country was the only reliable network and offered a virtual emergency communications system (Interview 11).

We must first understand, define, and quantify our requirements. We (DHS/FEMA) are not very good at defining capability-based operational requirements. Future planning and preparation must be made based upon empirical data—data "layers" vs. data "feeds." It is not just about producing GIS maps—it's about data "streams" vs. data "products." We need collaborative tools with the ability to handle unstructured, loosely coupled data that provide the capability to analyze, search, and employ. But first, we must clearly identify our requirements at the front end (Interview 11).

INFORMATION SHARING

Since 2004, DHS has maintained infrastructure protection field operations through the protective security advisor (PSA) program to enhance infrastructure protection, assist with incident management, and facilitate information sharing. Regional directors are supervisory PSAs, responsible for the activities of eight or more PSAs and geospatial analysts who ensure OIP critical infrastructure protection programs and services are delivered to state, local, territorial, and tribal stakeholders and private-sector owners and operators. As of December 2011, 93 regional directors and PSAs were deployed in 74 districts within 50 states and Puerto Rico (Interview 3).

Northern Command (NORTHCOM) in Colorado works with DHS Infrastructure Protection (DHS-IP) to identify information-sharing barriers that exist within the homeland and leverage the capabilities of tools such as GIS. DHS-IP coordinates Sector Coordination Councils (SCCs) across the country and meets with the Government Coordinating Councils (GCCs) to establish a network of open dialogue on national- and local-level infrastructure protection issues. DHS-IP oversees private-sector interface and maintains the National Infrastructure Coordinating Center (NICC), operated by the Transportation Security Administration, located at the Freedom Center in Dulles, Virginia. Additionally, DHS-IP publishes a DHS Daily Open Source Infrastructure Report through the National Transportation Advisory System (NTAS), highlighting noteworthy activities across the 16 infrastructure sectors (Interview 5).

A recent cyber article series in the *Washington Post* (O'Harrow 2012b) should serve as a wake-up call because it shows what twenty-something computer amateurs can do to adversely impact our systems. Reports like this highlight that across CIP and cyber areas, we need significant improvements in information sharing, but there are so many institutional barriers, we are often unable to share (Interview 6).

Our British counterparts have some effective preparedness and information-sharing programs that we could learn from. For example, they have published "Business Continuity for Dummies," which lays the groundwork for a nationwide initiative by starting with the foundation of small businesses at the heart of the private sector—the financial lenders and suppliers that support the small business community. Using critical relationships central to the small business sector, the UK government worked with banks to assert the criticality of resilience, publishing a "Business Continuity Guide." In addition, they have experienced success with implementation of public "outreach strategies," which would be a useful reference for our private-sector engagement efforts and improved disaster management (Interview 11).

The most important commodity across all public and private organizations is building relationships of trust. Senior U.S. government officials need to forge trusting relationships with industry CEOs through personal engagements *before* the crisis. It is important to know "when to contact the CEO of certain sectors/properties directly in order to consult on infrastructure security issues" (Interview 14).

The U.S. Secret Service (USSS) has elevated information-sharing opportunities with financial sector CEOs through a vibrant PPP, taking a top-down approach that bypasses corporate security officers (CSOs) to ensure open executive-to-executive communications. USSS increased the level of dialogue by conveying government needs during a National Security Special Event (NSSE). It is crucial to bring sector leaders into discussions at the beginning of the process; for example, DHS working groups addressing financial issues should engage the Finance Sector Services Coordinating Council (FSSCC) leadership early in their deliberations (Morgan Stanley, Goldman Sacks, etc.) (Interview 14).

Overclassification of homeland security information remains a challenge in a field that requires a need-to-share approach to increase the flow of information across agencies and homeland security officials. Some highly regulated sectors (telecommunications, airlines, nuclear power plants) already have highly cooperative exchanges of information with the federal government, while others are less engaged and need to establish new information-sharing capabilities (Interview 14).

We must nurture efficient mechanisms that foster information sharing across all levels of the interagency. We need to be intentional, forming working groups that are composed of the right people and identify policy as well as operational requirements. We must continue to systematically define collective priorities surrounding disaster management and national preparedness. For example, while the National Incident Management System (NIMS) is a helpful mechanism, it is not responsive enough for some situations (Interview 20).

Mitigation

Infrastructure protection and preparedness requires risk mitigation—taking steps to make a condition or consequence less severe. National and regional planners need to learn from manufacturing, especially transit authorities, transportation systems, and electric power utilities—organizations that operate in a culture that measure performance on recovery time and continuity of services. For example, we should be building safety and material science codes emphasizing structural integrity and human safety. The standard should be continuity of operations (COOP) and ensuring delivery of critical services, as practiced every day by utilities in the private sector (Interview 4).

The mid-Atlantic storm known as a *derecho* that impacted the Maryland–Washington, D.C. area on Friday night, June 29, 2012, and the disastrous Waldo Canyon urban wildfires in Colorado Springs that occurred that same summer underscore the rapidity and power that natural or human-made disasters can present to local and regional communities, sometimes with little or no warning. Those events, as well as Hurricane Irene (late August 2011) on the East Coast, followed by Tropical Storm Lee in the Gulf Coast region, highlight the challenges of establishing a culture of preparedness in our society and emphasizing mitigation before the storms arrive. Hurricane Irene impacted one-eighth of the U.S. population as it crossed 12 states along the East Coast. In the case of Hurricane Irene, Tropical Storm Lee, and the June 29th derecho, areas went without power for weeks, and one of the major causes was the failure to mitigate damage by trimming trees. Above-ground power lines run through communities that often fail to remove or trim trees, which is an issue that local counties, municipalities, and boroughs must address through disaster mitigation before the storm arrives (Interview 12).

Hurricane Irene also pointed to the importance of local, state, and regional Mutual Assistance Agreements (MAAs) and Emergency Management Assistance Compacts (EMACs). The EMAC is a national mutual aid partnership program that pre-coordinates and organizes state-to-state assistance during governor or federally declared emergencies. EMACs enable governors to support fellow governors during times of need. When DOE officials visited Connecticut in the wake of the Hurricane Irene, they observed how some states fail to take adequate mitigation efforts before disasters, which compounds the challenge of an already fragile and rigid infrastructure system. Not only did Connecticut have widespread tree damage to electrical power lines, but it lacked MAAs or EMACs to pre-identify sources of assistance and activate a network of support from adjacent states (Interview 12).

Although it can be expensive, difficult to define the return on investment (ROI), and challenging to motivate the public and private sectors to devote resources to it, *mitigation* matters. In reality, mitigation efforts actually improve resiliency across all sectors. When applying mitigation to flood insurance, we need to ensure the system is solvent and also consider where reconstruction and rebuilding are appropriate. In some cases, structures are being rebuilt in places clearly subject to future flooding threats (Interview 20).

INTELLIGENCE

There is an increased focus upon the IC building partnerships with homeland security and law enforcement communities. This initiative has attempted to work through the 76 local/state fusion centers that have been established since 2005, with IC participation in developing the Domestic Architecture for National Intelligence, working through DHS and the FBI (Interview 16).

The question for the IC is where federal entities fit in the domestic picture. Clearly, the Joint Terrorism Task Forces (JTTFs) across the country are a public-private touchpoint. There are 17 government agencies in the National Intelligence Program, and non-IC domestic organizations are connected to U.S.-based IC elements through NSA, National JTTF Center, and IC partners, and attempt to define critical infrastructure requirements through existing relationships and working groups. There is a common CIP vocabulary, and POCs have been designated across domestic IC organizations to support networking and information sharing. NSSEs such as the Super Bowl provide real-world missions to exercise relationships, test risk models, and evaluate the level of operations/intelligence integration (Interview 16).

Areas of interest to DHS/FBI involving a potential nexus to Foreign Terrorist Organizations (FTOs) are reviewed with the National Counterterrorism Center (NCTC) through the Interagency Threat Assessment Coordination Group (TACG), which is connected to the HS/LE Partnership Advisory Board, and interfaces with state and local law enforcement representatives. Specific threat concerns include "lone wolf" actors—homegrown violent extremists of any background or nationality; therefore, it is critical to work closely with agencies inside our national borders. No single agency can accomplish its mission alone, especially given the increased domestic threat. There are senior intelligence coordinators assigned within all departments in the interagency, but too often interagency relationships are based upon personalities. The objective is to establish a standardized system of working relationships that reinforce a repeatable and structured process—to ensure the intelligence-sharing coordination and protocols are not overly personality dependent (Interview 16).

RISK ASSESSMENTS

The greatest threat challenges are in cyber security and physical security, because DHS programs and organizations are often stovepiped and lack the necessary integration to enable a coordinated approach. Supervisory Control and Data Acquisition (SCADA) systems represent a significant vulnerability because they are largely controlled by disparate private enterprises with economic limitations. Furthermore, industrial control systems have unique security requirements that extend beyond validating compliance and event correlation. Effective SCADA security has very specific requirements, including the ability to quickly receive, store, and correlate very large data sets at both an application and source level. If the systems are connected to the Internet, hackers can find ways to exploit them and gain access to steal or manipulate data (Interview 3).

What is the standard calculus for risk and criticality? What are the independent variables that contribute to the outcome of criticality ranking, given functional interdependencies such as seasons, demand schedules, supply, safety, security requirements, economic impact, environmental standards, quality of life, and culture? PPD-8 discusses infrastructure protection in the context of national preparedness. We focus on critical infrastructure protection (CIP) because (1) there is a threat and infrastructure sectors represent "likely targets" for our enemies, and (2) critical infrastructures represent "essential capabilities that need protection." Resilience is the cumulative outcome of the five pillars of preparedness:

1. prevent (DHS);
2. protect (DOJ/FBI);
3. mitigate (FEMA);
4. respond (FEMA); and
5. recover (FEMA).

Risk mitigation is not always calculated, but risk is linked to "delivery of goods and services," which is why the economics of resilience has changed in the last 10 years from a vertical, centralized, dependency-based approach to a horizontal, decentralized, interdependent global supply chain operating on just-in-time delivery of cargo, goods, and products (Interview 9).

Single points of failure across all critical infrastructure sectors help identify areas of criticality on the disaster management list. Electricity and communications are the most important. All other sectors depend upon them. We need to look at undersea cables and civil GPS, which are "hidden utilities" and ubiquitous yet uniquely vulnerable capabilities with limited surge capacity or redundancy. When discussing cyber issues, one senior military executive recently said, "There are approximately 750,000 military users, and 750,000,000 civilians on the web," which helps explain the magnitude and nature of the cyber-security challenge. The challenges are primarily in the private sector, because the majority of critical infrastructure is owned and operated by the private sector (Interview 9).

Hurricane Irene (2011) revealed that we have not applied many of the lessons learned from Hurricane Katrina—or too often they were lessons *observed* rather than lessons *learned*. Exercises and training are good, but it is human nature to lose the valuable lessons of preparedness, infrastructure protection, and resilience unless we have an actual disaster occur frequently enough to retain our situational awareness and sense of urgency. The complexity of risk calculations include seasonal factors: (1) a major sports venue is a low risk unless it is football season and they are hosting the Super Bowl, and (2) regional electric power plants are higher criticality in August during high heat/AC season than fall/spring. Some critical areas may not emerge or be fully understood by senior decision makers in the public or private sector until a major disaster occurs. For example, consider the steel industry's need for liquid hydrogen and the cascading impact of Hurricane Katrina on Air Products & Chemicals Inc.—a primary source of hydrogen for the steel industry—and the subsequent impact of local economies due to workforce layoffs (see Figure A.6) (Interview 9).

Significant data sources are available for natural disasters, but fewer are available for counterterrorism. There is a Strategic National Risk Assessment (SNRA) program available to the states, including the Comprehensive Preparedness Guide (CPG) 201 and the CPG 201 toolkit (April 2012), as well as the Threat and Hazard Identification and Risk Assessment (THIRA) Guide. In order to push the focus down to the community level, local jurisdictions assign their own risks and coordinate with state-level officials. Then, each of the 10 FEMA regions consolidate input across their states and submit a holistic national picture. In addition to hazard and risk assessments, the THIRA process incorporates an assessment of "core capabilities," which has replaced "target capabilities." FEMA has developed disaster management training for states to learn the THIRA process and procedures (Interview 10).

The concept of "risk pooling" has surfaced with policymakers and within the insurance industry. Risk pooling is an important concept in supply-chain management, suggesting that demand variability is reduced if one aggregates demand across locations; because demand is aggregated across different locations, it becomes more likely that high demand from one customer will be offset by low demand from another. Infrastructure protection and computational models are currently too static and need to be more dynamic, with the ability to incorporate a broader range of emerging variables. For example, climate change has altered environmental and transportation patterns, opening new areas of risk and hazard that need to be considered (Interview 11).

DHS has instituted a CIP risk assessment program across the private-sector working through a voluntary program. It involves owners and operators and the value they can bring to the relationship. The current methodology is to collect an aggregate of valuable data showing trends and gaps, which in turn allows us to determine where to focus national attention. There is an Infrastructure Survey Tool (IST) to help "index and analyze risk." For example, for counterterrorism we bring in the subject matter experts (SMEs) from all the CIP sectors, and weighted values are assigned to risks based upon CIP security and resilience criteria, attempting to bring objective judgments to the process and value to the private companies. The ultimate goal is to develop a practical dashboard tool that provides a comparison index of security and resilience across facilities at the local level and sectors at the macro level to strengthen disaster management skills across the homeland security enterprise (Interview 18).

The post-Katrina energy sector has 29 facilities in four Gulf Coast states, with an increased focus on functional resilience by providing redundancies. A valuable tool is available to aggregate data and allow for comparisons across the entire energy sector. DHS determines the "level of priority one's and two's" based on potential consequences. To gain a regional perspective on CIP risk assessments, DHS examines states with mature disaster management and preparedness organizations like Florida, New Jersey, Mississippi, California, and Texas (Interview 18).

As noted earlier, current risk assessment tools do not capture criticality variables such as seasonal factors. DHS is aware of other risk assessment methods employed for public safety programs in locations such as the state of Maine, Saudi Arabia, and Canada. Furthermore, DHS has conducted cross-border infrastructure analyses with Canada's public safety and disaster management counterparts, which contribute to a CAN-US action plan (Interview 18).

We—as a nation—must find "creative ways to distribute risk across the homeland security enterprise." For example, we need to retool the Homeland Security Grant program from one that is focused on buying equipment for local emergency and disaster management organizations to more of a regional "capabilities approach," aggregating essential functions at regional locations where resources can be shared by jurisdictions and municipalities. By working with state and local authorities and private insurance companies, there may be ways to "buy down financial burdens of risk coverage" with a dynamic mixture of public-private support (i.e., 25 percent insurance and 75 percent Stafford Act coverage) (Interview 20).

OPERATIONAL APPLICATION

We need a next-generation Incident Command System (ICS) that is scalable and flexible because the current National Incident Management System (NIMS), as a disaster management model, "does not scale" adequately. The system is currently "too brittle" and fails to meet the needs of a complex disaster; for example, it is too large as an operational model for a local tornado, and too small for major incidents such as Hurricane Katrina or the Deepwater Horizon Oil Spill. The Japan earthquake of 2011 provides a valuable reference point to understand what is needed for a new ICS/NIMS—not because the disaster was handled well, but because of what was learned from mistakes and failures. The NIMS works well (administratively, person-nel accounting, information workflow, and so on) up to a certain threshold, but when the incident reaches a certain level of complexity, the system appears to "collapse." Why does this occur? Perhaps because the ICS was designed as a top-down unity-of-command tool rather than a coordinated unity-of-effort construct that seeks to integrate efforts horizontally across a complex set of actors (Interview 11).

An Integration Planning Model for ports (and other sector hubs) will require a comprehensive understanding of sector operational requirements and the fusion of a variety of databases, informed by the mapping of infrastructure gaps, threat risks, and cross-sector interdependences. To highlight regional efforts with potential intermodal connectivity, DOT has allocated $11 million for local state efforts, including emergency evacuation planning over the next 20 years, and $500 million (over 5 years) to plan rural highway transportation. This reflects additional opportunities to link cross-domain planning efforts and demonstrate multi-agency, disaster management collaboration—showing the interconnected nature of twenty-first-century transportation networks (Interview 13).

An example of a complex business continuity project on the mid-Atlantic corridor is the DHS-funded pilot partnering with the State of New Jersey and the private sector, focused on the New Jersey Turnpike/Exit 14, where there is a major geographic node and potential regional choke point at the intersection of oil, shipping, fiber, rail, highway, banking, data processing, cell phone, and power systems. This $10 million project involves the application of dynamic modeling and collaborative tools—and no federal agencies. Another example of highly complex and interconnected intermodal networks is the Port Authority of New York and New Jersey (PANYNJ), where disaster management and emergency response challenges are compounded by the fact that there are over 250 companies with interests and trade partnerships across all business sectors (Interview 13).

Major ports of entry with complex interdependent infrastructures "harden the facilities where they can, isolate and separate systems to strengthen security, and physically protect SCADA systems." There are FEMA-funded pilot efforts under way to operationalize regional resilience and enhance disaster management in:

1. Annapolis/Arundel, MD
2. Greenwich, CT
3. St. Louis, MO
4. Anaheim, CA
5. Gulfport, MS
6. Charleston, SC
7. Memphis/Mt. Pleasant, TN; with initial studies beginning at Memphis, Charleston, and Gulfport (Interview 15).

During Hurricane Katrina, the situation called for more cooperative unity-of-effort than controlled unity-of-command. Faced with a disaster declaration and potential loss of civil society, there was an immediate demand to work across stovepiped organizations, which required cultivating a common set of values and shared vision within the joint, interagency, and private communities. When operating in a disaster or crisis environment where there is no legal mandate or authority over cohort organizations (i.e., interagency process), unity-of-effort is the primary organizational and leadership challenge (Interview 17).

Some elements within FEMA have asserted the importance of building a nationwide "emergency resource database" so the federal government and disaster management planners have a continuous tracking system for all physical inventories of emergency materials and resources. That represents a "physical protection" mind-set that would be impossible to maintain because static inventories of equipment are always changing. If we focus on "community resilience," it is more important that we "map the existing processes" because disasters are usually complex, chaotic, and uncertain events that require planners to agree on "methods, processes, and where to find the necessary information" [regarding resources] rather than know continuously where are all physical supplies are located. For example, rather than develop a new resource database that needs continuous updates, PPPs are established with companies (Home Depot, Walmart, Walgreens, etc.) that already maintain highly sophisticated global supply-chain inventory systems. This is another example of how resilience-focused capabilities based assessments (CBAs) are more useful than traditional infrastructure protection methodologies (Interview 18).

The Blackout of August 2003, which hit the Northeast and Midwest sections of the United States and parts of Canada, serves as a good example. DHS was working across the CIP sectors in the disaster response mode and found that cellular phone companies were running their transmitters on emergency generators that required diesel fuel; when they ran out of diesel, they sought help from DHS in locating the fuel providers across the region. Since this disaster—as is usually the case—was an unusual event that required coordination activity outside normal channels, the communications sector did not have an existing market relationship with diesel fuel providers. However, DHS, despite not knowing all the fuel-service providers in the region (no resource database), did have relationships with regional contacts that maintained habitual relationships with fuel companies. Knowing the process and methods in the region for fuel distribution and activating pre-established relationships, the cellular companies were rapidly connected with the diesel fuel providers. This example highlights that in disaster management, it is less about having a database of diesel fuel sources and more about knowing the functional process for storing and moving fuel across the region—and maintaining a relation-ship with those entities that routinely interact with resource providers and suppliers (Interview 18).

CYBER SECURITY

Many questions remain unanswered when facing cyber-security challenges in the twenty-first century. How do we implement the Homeland Security Act of 2002 with the growing emphasis on cyber security? Is critical infrastructure always physical or human, or can it also be virtual? Where does cyber security fit into HSPD-7, since it crosses all 16 critical infrastructure sectors? What is the interface between the exist-ing interagency government structures for infrastructure protection (IP) and emerging organizations responsible for cyber security? These issues are reflected across the interagency and industry where one can see fragmented policies and strategy imple-mentation caused by organizational conflict. One community emphasizes physical security (led by the CSO), while the other is focused on cyber security and information assurance (led by the CIO). This is particularly important to resolve because cyber events can become physical events, impacting the banking industry, water systems, or electric grids (Interview 1).

The cyber Interagency Policy Committee (IPC) draws upon the chief informa-tion officers (CIOs) of cross-governmental, multi-agency federal networks with an all-hazards emphasis on the Department of Homeland Security (DHS) and the Department of Defense (DOD). The IPC is still working through how best to reflect cyber security within national preparedness policy. Howard Schmidt was the cyber-security coordinator of the Obama Administration, operating in the Executive Office of the President of the United States, until retiring in May 2012. One of his primary policy objectives was the development of a "National Strategy for Trusted Identities in Cyberspace," designed to enable private industry to create electronic identities that can be relied upon in cyber space, similar to the way that businesses rely upon the combination of drivers' licenses and credit cards to authenticate identities in physical space (Interview 2).

The cyber-security system is very complex. DOD/CYBERCOM is a microcosm of the nation—reflecting the ubiquitous and complex nature of establishing and executing cyber-security strategy and policy across all domains and sectors. And while all sectors are unique and distinct in their cyber security, vulnerabilities, risks, strengths, and public-private interface, the goal within cyber policy is to examine each area (sector by sector), building on lessons learned (Interview 2).

DHS recognizes from a safety and security perspective that cyber security cannot be separated from physical security requirements. Cyber is embedded across all the CIP sectors. Within NPPD, their divisions—Infrastructure Protection (IP), Cyber Security & Communications (CS&C), US-VISIT, and Federal Protective Service (FPS)—combine efforts on joint risk assessments and integrate resources as appropriate. And the private sector is wrestling with the same cyber challenges that face the public sector (Interview 18).

In the cyber arena, we continue to review the lessons learned from National Level Exercises (NLEs) to identify the most crucial legislative, regulatory, and policy gaps and determine what parts of cyber-security systems can be addressed through CIP policies (Interview 20).

MARITIME SECURITY

Ports offer a unique security environment, intermodal trade space, and disaster management challenge. An integrated planning model allows us to better understand and experiment with the role of PPPs and whole-of-nation precepts as they relate to ports. Although every port is geographically, organizationally, and physically different, each possesses common planning and policy qualities that can be generalized across regions—and since 2011, significant public and private capital has been invested in port security risk assessments, interagency operation centers, and technology innovations—albeit in an ad hoc and uncoordinated fashion (Interview 13).

Ports represent a cross-modal intersection of overlapping resources and vulnerabilities due to small vessel threats (e.g., USS *Cole*-like attack); potential dirty bomb or WMD in containers; underwater attacks or harbor mining; vital commodities moved via highways, railway bridges, and tunnels; high volumes of human traffic through cruise ship terminals; and conveyances of hydrocarbons and volatile products such as fertilizers and liquid natural gas. Therefore, they deserve special consideration in building whole-of-nation resilience. Instead of a strategy that revolves solely around the pursuit of DHS port security grant funds (which has been the focus since 2001), there needs to be an all-hazards, cross-domain, fully integrated port security strategy that expands upon the current interagency planning efforts by DHS/USCG and Area Maritime Security Committees to establish a culture of resilience based on mapping of essential functions and capabilities (Interviews 13, 14, 15).

America's 361 major ports are geographic "borders" and ports-of-entry as well as economic, operational, and environmental hubs of transportation, pipelines, railways, tunnels, telecommunications, food distribution, agriculture requirements, water treatment, power, wastewater, medical supplies, chemicals, hazardous materials, freight-shipping, treasury policies, law-enforcement, immigration, and customs. They employ large numbers of people and serve as the foundation of a globalized economy and supply-chain network that supports the fragile arteries of local, regional, and national economies[2] (Interview 13).

Ports operate in a complex mixture of dependences/interdependences that touch a host of counties, municipalities, and counties, with policy, political, and fiscal ligaments across local, urban, state, regional, and federal authorities and jurisdictions. And research indicates that major ports in the country (e.g., NY/NJ, LA/LB, Tidewater Virginia, New Orleans, Baltimore) often have a fragmented network of multi-agency, multijurisdiction, multiscale projects that are uncoordinated (at best) and conflicting (at worst). The entities within the ports (and between different cities) are competing for the same disaster management resources and grant dollars, with no executive agent to coordinate enterprise-level initiatives based upon operational requirements, risk assessments, or functional mapping (Interview 13).

Sometimes mature federal agencies with robust planning capabilities and potential funding resources (the Department of Energy, for instance) can bring experience, relationships, and interagency skills that don't exist in another lead federal department (DHS). This should be considered when addressing port-related issues. For example, DOE can leverage experience across specific areas such as D&M with camera systems, safe transport of nuclear material, gas pipeline safety, coordination of utilities in the power sector, regional issues crossing state lines, overlapping jurisdictions, federal projects with private investment, interoperability of communications and video systems, and existing collaborative with state and federal actors (Interview 13).

"The ports touch everything," and there are opportunities for significant whole-of-nation coordination at all levels with the potential for dramatic improvements that could serve as models for other geographic regions and infrastructure sectors. By simply integrating planning and execution of disaster management federal projects that intersect with adjacent local, regional, and state initiatives, there would be immediate improvements in efficiency and effectiveness with projects, including video surveillance, railway safety, highway security, agriculture hubs, local business impacts, chemical containment, refineries, maritime transportation, and freight shipping[3] (Interview 13).

As an example that underscores the specific resilience advancements in maritime security—forging new levels of consensus across disaster management planning, funding, and execution functions—consider 15 video-camera projects alone in a local port that extend across three state authorities, 12 federal agencies, seven owner-operators, and multiple labor unions—all impacted by cyber-security requirements and the application of social media. An effective port security initiative must integrate overlapping efforts across the Departments of Homeland Security, Transportation, Commerce, Energy, and State and leverage the opportunities for joint planning, synchronization of procedures and systems, and collective action with commercial maritime industry, military homeland defense planners (NORAD/NORTHCOM), private investors, and labor unions (Interview 13).

Realistically, one must begin a port security planning effort with some practical assumptions from a PPP perspective:

1. Recognize that there will be resistance from many stakeholders for fiscal self-protecting reasons.
2. Start by working on one specific project that serves as an exemplar to be generalized to other sectors/projects in the port of entry.
3. Make the secondary priority to coordinate and integrate incrementally by adding other projects.
4. Emphasize unity-of-effort by downplaying "lead agencies."
5. Take a bottom-up approach and allow tangible progress to attract further participation.
6. Owners-operators and labor unions must be involved at the front end.
7. Recognize that it requires relationships, holding meetings—and it takes time to build organizational and personal trust.
8. Take a collaborative "whole-of-nation" approach that respects the "sovereignty" of all stakeholders (Interview 13).

MEASUREMENTS

There is increased emphasis on operations research, metrics, and the ability to measure capabilities, preparation, response, and assessments across all parts of the disaster management system: prevent, protect, mitigate, respond, and recover (Interview 1).

And we are emphasizing metrics, capability-based assessments, and measurable performance within DHS/FEMA, applying "systematic scoring methods" of risks and capabilities to attempt to quantify response readiness. There needs to be agreement and scientific consensus on standards across the critical infrastructure protection (CIP) sectors, including engineering and construction codes. DHS grants need a disciplined system to reinforce those standards with performance measures and quantitative risk thresholds (Interview 10).

More quantitative information should be used in preparedness planning to reduce the amount of guesswork. "Everyone is surprised by natural disasters, but should they be?" FEMA research indicates that there are disaster cycles within geographic regions that can support improved decision making regarding preparedness and disaster management. For nearly 50 years (1964–2010), disaster statistics were mapped across the country by type of event and national-state level declaration. Some of the findings were that there are certain locations across the country where no disasters occur, but for other areas of the country there are clear regional trends that can inform preparation and mitigation and disaster planning, allowing individuals and agencies to "buy down risk based on empirical data." PPD-8 (National Preparedness) suggests the need for a capabilities-based approach across the preparedness pillars (prevent, protect, mitigate, respond, recover). Perhaps we need a national "risk map" and practical plan based on scientific data—building upon existing organizational boundaries (10 FEMA regions), and DHS grant programs (Interview 12).

DHS/IP needs to better understand private-sector operational requirements at the local and state levels and forge a better regional focus/capability across the FEMA regions. We are consistently being asked to provide more training and education across the local, state, and regional levels. Much can be learned from studying the ports because they are a microcosm of the country: They integrate and share data across all infrastructure sectors and multiple agencies; require modeling, training and exercises; and represent a crossroads of all-domain, whole-of-government intermodal transportation requirements (Interview 18).

The national preparedness and disaster management system is not designed to reward performance. In fact, sometimes the federal government's policies penalize success. For example, if a state institutes systemic measures for monitoring water treatment or standardized regional emergency communications—which enhance resilience and disaster management—it risks losing the opportunity to compete for federal homeland security grants or recurring funding. The Federal Aviation Administration offers a positive example, where the agency was rewarded for internal innovations that ultimately resulted in the Next-Generation Air Traffic Control (ATC) capability, and strengthened security and resilience within the national aviation transportation system (Interview 19).

NOTES

1. The "Laffer curve" is an economic term suggesting that increasing tax rates beyond a certain point will be counterproductive for raising further tax revenue.

2. Nearly 80 percent of freight and cargo entering the Port of Norfolk is shipped to locations in the Midwest United States.

3. All-Hazards Consortium, a private nonprofit organization focused on implementation of homeland security policies at the local and state level, reports there are over 20 port-related projects in the Port of Baltimore. These projects are funded through state-level UASI grants that overlap with: private-sector owner-operators, state-local governments, and federal projects.

Appendix D

Supporting Data for Major Findings

NATIONAL FRAMEWORK

Building on Chapter 2 (Figure 2.1), the subject matter expert (SME) interviews in Appendix C, as well as major findings (Chapter 7), one can see that a comprehensive national framework for critical infrastructure resilience is a major undertaking. While there are resilience and preparedness policy improvements being made at the national level, they often remain detached from local, community, or regional efforts. Thus, resilience is not a separate program or budget line item but rather an active virtue that must be embedded within personal, community, organizational, and governmental systems, programs, and attitudes at all levels. An effective national resiliency framework must also leverage the capabilities and capacity of public-private partnerships (PPPs)—operationalizing the whole-of-nation concept.

A national framework that enables critical infrastructure resiliency requires a culture of preparedness across all levels of the public and private sectors. Private industry has discovered the importance of developing business recovery plans and individual preparedness plans but often lacks a mechanism to move beyond these organic programs to integrate efforts with the public sector. A lack of resilience at the individual or community level can undermine local business continuity, decreasing the availability of goods and services when disaster strikes. For example, as the Gulf Coast region recovered from Hurricane Katrina, the commercial shipyard in Pascagoula, Mississippi was ready to resume operations, but the employees could not return to work because daycare facilities were not open, and many parents had to remain at home with their children. The shipyard was unable to resume operations—causing a disruption to the local and regional economy—because of a community resilience (daycare children) issue. This illustrates a *gap in partnerships* within our society that a national framework could help address.

DHS Auxiliary "NDUR"

It is clear that PPPs are the key to the implementation of national preparedness policies and disaster management improvements. One of the practical ways to operationalize PPPs in the post-9/11 security environment is to leverage the collective effort of community volunteers and professional organizations. In this spirit, the U.S. Department of Homeland Security (DHS) could develop an auxiliary program modeled after a whole-of-community principle to enhance national resilience on an individual and community basis. As a proposed name for the program, the National Drive for Unified Resilience (NDUR; pronounced "endure") would be a PPP between DHS and existing auxiliaries, local institutions, and volunteer organizations to leverage state and community resilience through projects and awareness.

America is a serving nation, and there is a volunteer spirit that inspires a tradition of community service and is fueled by a desire to be part of something significant. Programs promoting homeland security and resilience can tap into the potential of these qualities in our culture. A great example of this dynamic is found in the history of the Boy Scouts of America (BSA), a youth leadership and volunteer organization that has pioneered the involvement of private citizens in assisting families at the grassroots level. During World War I, the BSA raised over $350 million for the U.S. war effort through government bond drives. They also led volunteer efforts leveraging government functions throughout both world wars, including "planting war gardens to raise food, conducting a census of black walnut trees to identify timber needed for airplane propellers and gun stocks, collecting peach pits and nut shells for use in filters of gas masks, [and working] as dispatch bearers or government literature distributors and [providers of] general assistance to other wartime organizations" (McDermott 2002).

Skilled American citizens, patriotic volunteers, and community organizations are a potential resource that could be energized to support homeland security and resiliency efforts. For this reason, the DHS should develop a PPP in the form of an auxiliary service to forge more sustainable communities through local resiliency initiatives in geographic communities of interest. This would galvanize a cadre of citizens who desire to serve their country and build better communities as stewards of their neighborhoods. Existing service or volunteer organizations such as the FBI-sponsored InfraGard, U.S. Coast Guard Auxiliary, Air Forces Civil Air Patrol (CAP), American Red Cross, FEMA Corps, and Salvation Army provide models for this proposal.

Perhaps no agencies are more familiar with this concept than the local networks of first responders who comprise regional Emergency Operations Centers (EOCs), including police, firefighters, and emergency medical services (EMS). These communities-of-interest have already developed disaster/emergency plans, mutual aid agreements, and operational support systems in the region and identified the local stakeholders. Consider the legacy of firefighting organizations: They have long traditions of standardized training, Incident Management Systems (IMS) development, and support for grassroots civic organizations. Building on that legacy, the DHS could form an effective resiliency auxiliary, as well. The International Association of Fire Chiefs (IAFC) has tapped into this form of community engagement and PPPs for years, seeking to improve firefighting awareness and cultivate a culture of prevention and preparedness. The reasons to join a resilience and national preparedness community organization are virtually the same as those offered for joining the IAFC:

- to receive clear, concise, and trusted information that helps you do your job more efficiently;
- to gain support and solutions from peers who face similar challenges;
- to get 24/7 access to the latest data, research, and best practices in the fire and emergency service;
- to get access to thought leadership articles on current and emerging trends;
- to gain professional development opportunities through leadership and training programs;
- to build a network of contacts to whom you can turn when you need assistance and advice; and
- to have an advocate in Washington, D.C., working for funding and resources that support your department, your personnel, and your community.

A DHS auxiliary could draw upon these same resources by offering incentives from the broader missions of homeland security components such as U.S. Citizen and Immigration Services (USCIS), Customs and Border Protection (CBP), the Federal Emergency Management Agency (FEMA), Immigration and Customs Enforcement (ICE), U.S. Secret Service (USSS), U.S. Coast Guard (USCG), Transportation Security Administration (TSA), and the National Protections and Programs Directorate (NPPD). The Infrastructure Protection (IP) and Cyber Security and Communications (CS&C) divisions within NPPD would be a possible staff within DHS to design and implement the program, placing initial emphasis on community preparedness, resilience, and cyber-security themes.

By drawing in community groups and volunteer organizations, the private sector would share in major homeland security imperatives, participating directly as partners in promoting community resilience and personal preparedness. Additionally, the private sector might further leverage the capabilities of the department and strengthen whole-of-nation capability in the following ways:

- draw from a pool of existing personnel and resources—"patriots-citizens" willing to assist in securing the homeland;
- provide the opportunity to establish a cultural identity for DHS as a relatively young government organization;
- strengthen open communications, information sharing, and public relations on national, state, regional, and local levels; and
- operationalize infrastructure resilience, preparedness, and security on community, household, and individual levels.

Similarly, a coastguardsman in Michigan participating in a disaster preparedness workshop suggested drawing from the older generation and legacy programs by passing on the knowledge to modern students in the area of preparedness. Federal dollars, he suggested, could go toward education, drills, and learning materials featuring "Pete, the Preparedness Puppy" as a school mascot modeled after the post–World War II U.S. Forest Service's "Smokey the Bear" campaign that raised forest fire safety awareness, thus elevating self-reliance and preparedness education among K-12 students (DomPrep 2012, 47).

SOCIAL MEDIA

Drawing from the Japan earthquake Fukushima case study, SME interviews, Appendix C regarding information sharing, as well as major finding 7.60 (on social networking), we need to better understand how to leverage the capabilities of technology and the benefits of innovation in social networking. With expanded broadband connectivity, fiber optic networks, and increased availability of digital technology, social networking sites (SNS) have become a powerful medium of mass communication over a very short period of time. The study of disaster cases reveals both the current importance of SNS and new capabilities in dissemination of critical information, situational awareness, and other critical functions in disaster management supporting resilience. SNS and social media can also distribute information rapidly among demographics normally not aware of or attentive to official channels of emergency information.

As detailed in the case study of the Japan earthquake, there are "spikes" in Internet, Facebook, and Twitter account activity during and immediately after natural disasters, with social media trends outpacing traditional media outlets and other official means of notification. Individuals are also increasingly dependent on SNS for seeking help and sharing information. An American Red Cross study found that many people use social media to inform others of a disaster or to request help, with 74 percent expecting more rapid action from emergency response if the appeal for assistance was made through social media (American Red Cross 2010). SNS is also an expanding source of news coverage and awareness of ongoing disaster activity. A study by the Pew Research Center revealed that a growing number of viewers are turning to the video site YouTube for coverage and raw video of disasters (Coyle 2012).

Appendix E
Initial Themes and Expectations

1. INTERAGENCY COORDINATION

CIP and resilience themes	Strategic imperatives and definitions	Collective action theory	Operationalizing questions
Within the U.S. government (USG) interagency, all departments, agencies, and organizations must expand the level of coordination and cooperation to close gaps that could be exploited by nefarious elements (National Research Council [NRC] 2008).	Significantly expand whole-of-government connectivity among USG agencies, offices, departments, and military elements at federal, state, and local levels (Wilson 1989; Raach and Kaas 1995; Donley 2005). Collective action offers a range of factors that affect decisions, especially the importance of efficacy and concern about the collective good (Olson 1965).	**Public Goods** Goods that are hard (or impossible) to produce for private profit, because the market fails to account for large positive externalities. Maritime security is a nonrivalrous, nonexcludable public service—consumption of goods by one member does not reduce availability for others, and no one can be excluded from using the good (Samuelson 1954).	• Did departments and agencies of the USG engage in coordinated planning and execution? • Did interagency actions reflect a common view and commitment to the public good (resilience)? • Is there an established organization focused on the integration of interagency capabilities and leveraging collective efforts to achieve functional resilience?

2. INTERNATIONAL COLLABORATION

CIP and resilience themes	Strategic imperatives and definitions	Collective action theory	Operationalizing questions
The post-9/11 asymmetric threat environment requires a higher level of collaboration across international boundaries. A globalized supply chain depends on collective safety, security, economic, and environmental priorities (The White House 2010).	Build a global CIP information exchange system to expand international engagement and foreign disclosure authorities (Haas 1980; Carafano and Weitz 2007; NRC 2008). Global collective action involves principles of international cooperation—factors that promote it or inhibit it at the global level (Sandler 2004).	Tragedy of commons Public goods exist and will be destroyed if exploitation is not controlled through external intervention. Action must be taken to align personal gain with group good. Those who pursue self-interest impose collective costs; when the common resource is lost, all members face ruin because they tried to maximize self-interest (Hardin 1968; Sandler 2004).	• Is there a global urgency that views vulnerability of critical infrastructure as a tragedy of commons? • What role did international infrastructure organizations play in execution of the cases? • Was there a methodology in place to incorporate international cooperation? • Is there a culture of global resilience that recognizes the need to align national gain with collective security requirements?

3. PRIVATE SECTOR PARTICIPATION

CIP and resilience themes	Strategic imperatives and definitions	Collective action theory	Operationalizing questions
The role of the private sector and industry in planning and execution of CIP and resilience is fragmented. Owners and operators in the private sector can be adversely impacted by any disaster or attack causing infrastructure failure in the private domain (U.S. GAO 2006).	Provide a framework and process for commercial- and private-sector participation with government (1) to achieve policy objectives, and (2) to appropriate the role of the private sector (Frittelli 2008). Public-private partnerships directly impact collective action and foster movement of groups across private and public boundaries (Bratman 1993).	Free riders There is a natural tendency for groups to withhold their contribution to support collective efforts while enjoying the benefits of the broader group. Members defect when they consider that their support to the collective enterprise will not impact its success or failure. Government may use laws and statutes to induce participation, through coercion or incentives, and prevent parties from reneging (Olson 1965).	• Was the private sector involved in execution of functional resilience? • Is the private sector incentivized to participate? • What hurdles impede private-sector partnerships in CIP and resilience? • Is the private sector enjoying the benefits of public security while failing to contribute to policy execution? • What role should the private sector play in supporting CIP and resilience objectives?

4. INFORMATION SHARING

CIP and resilience themes	Strategic imperatives and definitions	Collective action theory	Operationalizing questions
Isolated silos of information are maintained within closed systems. Organizational policies, statutory regulations, and culture are factors that impede the sharing of information across USG. Policy changes are needed to establish mandatory sharing of information across agency boundaries (Ostrom 1998; NRC 2008).	Open the lines of communication and close barriers based on data controls, system certification and authentication, privacy and security classification concerns (Relyea 2004; U.S. GAO 2006; NRC 2008). Collective action in the global economy requires movement of information across organizational seams by government, industry, and private and public organizations (Melucci 1996).	**Social dilemmas** While supportive of group action, some stakeholders pursue activities that reward them individually, despite being contrary to their commitment to collective efforts. Each party must yield something of value so the "exchange" will make them better off. Repeated trials aid mutually valued coordinated action, so resolution is based on trust and experience (Weimer and Vining 2005).	• How transparent was the sharing of CIP information among joint, interagency, multinational interests? • Did information sharing help or hinder execution of CIP and resilience in these cases? • How might elements of the interagency be incentivized to participate and share information more openly? • What external forces could be applied to increase confidence that counterparts will honor their obligations?

5. STRATEGY IMPLEMENTATION

CIP and resilience themes	Strategic imperatives and definitions	Collective action theory	Operationalizing questions
National CIP strategies have been implemented and enforced in a fragmented and uneven manner. The uncoordinated execution of CIP programs and lack of a systems approach are the most significant symptoms of this strategic shortfall (U.S. Department of Homeland Security 2008).	Clarify lines of responsibility within the CIP community-of-interest (COI) and operationalize measures of resilience to facilitate implementation. Collective action among elements of government and instruments of national security must leverage costs to implement policies (Gilbert 2006). Transaction costs can be divided into three categories: search, negotiation, and monitoring/enforcement.	**Transaction costs** Participants desire to achieve benefits of collective action while minimizing costs—time, efforts, and resources—to contribute to collective decisions. Without mechanisms to effectively negotiate collective efforts, costs can overwhelm players, forcing them to withdraw. With well-designed institutions, agreements and costs are better managed (Hardin 1982).	• How did collective efforts of participating elements of interagency and the private sector reflect policy execution? • Could field execution improve through better policy implementation? • Do the current programs serve as effective policy to incentivize stakeholders to participate? • Have transaction costs played a role in the fragmented and incomplete execution of CIP and resilience? • How do costs break down by subcategories?

6. SYSTEMS INTEGRATION

CIP and resilience themes	Strategic imperatives and definitions	Collective action theory	Operationalizing questions
Interoperable fusion analysis and anomaly detection tools must be integrated into enterprise architectures that support common operating and user-defined operational pictures. This holistic system of systems should support all technologies and rule sets (NRC 2008).	Develop an integrated and automated service-oriented architecture (SOA) to fuse databases and technology systems that leverage best practices across intelligence and information providers (Panayides 2004). Each collective action player can initiate corrective measures to improve group action due to interconnectivity and costs (Searle 1990).	**Conformity costs** There is a need to impose costs on individual groups to achieve collective goals despite their objection. These costs occur when the collective decision differs from that of an individual's ideal preference. Integrating and negotiating common courses of action will require trade-offs. Governments are continually weighing what costs its citizens are prepared to bear (Ostrom 1990).	• Were responders able to leverage the benefits of an integrated information and intelligence system? • Were there successes or failures linked to systems and databases? • Should the USG impose standards for systems integration and allow conformity costs and outside forces to compel compliance? • Do existing costs contribute to agency actions that create free riders and nonparticipation?

7. INTELLIGENCE COOPERATION

CIP and resilience themes	Strategic imperatives and definitions	Collective action theory	Operationalizing questions
Despite the formation of new national-level organizations to coordinate and standardize intelligence products, the collection, analysis, and dissemination of intelligence data and information remain an acute vulnerability within all domains, including the maritime sector (The White House 2006).	Optimize intelligence collaboration and dissemination to improve notification and warning indicators as well as detection and monitoring (Betts 1978; Hughes-Wilson 1999; Donley 2005) Individuals will not always act voluntarily to achieve the common interest without coercion or incentives to compel action (Ostrom 1990).	**Coordination** Group members must decide individually what they want, how prepared they are to contribute to the collective enterprise, and how to coordinate their efforts for the greater good. Coordination problems are especially pervasive for large and multiple competing groups (Carney 1987).	• Treating CIP, resilience and intelligence as public goods, are there coordinated plans that enabled senior leaders to make timely decisions? • How can intelligence sharing be improved to avoid a crisis of infrastructure? • Is there a holistic approach within the USG that views intelligence as a collective good that must be produced and distributed jointly? • What signals, warnings, and notifications are made available through intelligence systems?

8. Governance and Leadership

CIP and resilience themes	Strategic imperatives and definitions	Collective action theory	Operationalizing questions
Unlike other national strategies, CIP and resilience lacks a single global synchronizer, integrator, or executive agent to oversee and enforce joint, interagency, multinational requirements of complex and interconnected national-level CIP and resilience policies (NRC 2008).	Establish a single global synchronizer or executive agent within the U.S. government who is responsible for maintaining and executing the strategy (Freidrich and Mason 1940; Miyakawa 2000; NRC 2008). Collaborative governance involves the conflict between individual interests and achievement of shared interests for a group of individuals (Donahue and Zeckhauser 2006).	**Focal points** Coordination will occur if participants identify a leader to organize efforts and target energy to common purposes. Coordination is a prerequisite to successful collective action, and problems often surface from uncertainty or insufficient information. Once members agree on the rules and lines of responsibility, problems are often solved (Medina 2007).	• Was there a focal point that provided an integrated and fully coordinated command and control process? • What steps could be taken to improve the operational and strategic organizations? • Who is the interagency focal point to synchronize and integrate all preparedness and resilience action within the USG? • Is there a designated agency or executive agent that is attempting to provide the consolidated leadership and oversight of CIP enforcement and analysis?

9. Cross-Domain Solutions

CIP and resilience themes	Strategic imperatives and definitions	Collective action theory	Operationalizing questions
The inability to move data and information across security classification levels impedes CIP and resilience. Rigid protocols based on need-to-know v. need-to-share, and lack of a nonclassified enclave aggravate existing security gaps (DOT 2006; U.S. Navy Department 2007).	Expand capability of moving information among security classification levels to minimize overclassification and maximize flow of information (Davis 1952; Kaiser 1989; Hubbard 2005). Collective action highlights the value of groups sharing intentions through common activity that requires common knowledge. Mutual obligations and collective behavior also need to be addressed (Gilbert 1989).	**Externalities** Government is expected to (1) prevent "public bads" that jeopardize safety or security, and (2) remedy threats to public welfare (i.e., security, pollution control, zoning, and uncoordinated maritime security). Because consumption of public goods is disconnected from their production, consumers will be tempted to overuse or waste them (Sandler 2004).	• Did cross-domain externalities such as access to information and intelligence impede execution of the cases? • Was adequate classified and nonclassified info available to support the mission? • Was information overclassified such that operations were hindered? • Are there negative externalities within the security systems that contribute to the uncoordinated nature of maritime security efforts?

10. CONCEPTS OF OPERATIONS

CIP and resilience themes	Strategic imperatives and definitions	Collective action theory	Operationalizing questions
Given the existing governance protocols, operational activity, and technology systems, there must be bridging mechanisms to operationalize CIP and resilience. Concepts of Operations (CONOPS) are the action plans and rule sets that enable execution of operational requirements (U.S. GAO 2006).	Synchronize operational planning, standard operating procedures, and rule sets across joint interagency coalition organizations (Goertz 2006; NRC 2008). Collective action includes groups of principals organizing to voluntarily retain the residuals of their own efforts and collectively solve common problems (Ostrom 1990).	Principal-agent Costs must be managed by those in authority delegating action to agents who carry out certain decisions for collective action. Principals possess authority to make certain decisions and try to align agent preferences with their own to minimize agency loss. Delegation entails a trade-off between the benefits of having agents taking action and the effort required to monitor their behavior (Olson 1965).	• Have principal-agents established an organized CONOPS to inform coordinated field actions? • Was there consensus on how to proceed in conducting the cases, informed by standard operating procedures? • Have national infrastructure leaders delegated the requirement to develop and employ standardized CIP CONOPS?

Appendix F

External Documents

The primary sources of research material for this study were subject matter expert (SME) interviews, case studies, and policy documents from government agencies, as well as external references addressing critical infrastructure resilience and national preparedness capability gaps. External reports include documents published by the White House, U.S. Government Accountability Office (GAO), Congressional Research Service (CRS), and the National Infrastructure Advisory Council (NIAC). The following 18 documents—whether cited specifically within the text or not—provide valuable information that influenced the content of this report; each one represents important efforts that inform and catalyze our way forward as a nation in need of a more resilient society.

THE WHITE HOUSE (FEBRUARY 12, 2013)

Executive Order No. 13636: Improving Critical Infrastructure Cybersecurity. Addresses the national security and homeland security concerns associated with repeated cyber intrusions into critical infrastructure by increasing the volume, timeliness, and quality of cyber-threat information shared with private-sector entities. The Department of Homeland Security (DHS) secretary, the U.S. attorney general, and the director of National Intelligence are given responsibility to implement this policy under the U.S. National Security Council (NSC).

NATIONAL ACADEMIES (AUGUST 1, 2012)

Disaster Resilience: A National Imperative. Prepared by the Committee on Increasing National Resilience to Hazards and Disasters, Committee on Science, Engineering, and Public Policy. Increasing the nation's resilience to natural and human-caused disasters will require complementary federal policies and locally driven actions that center on a national vision. Improving resilience should be seen as a long-term process, but it can be coordinated around measurable short-term goals that will allow communities to better prepare and plan for, withstand, recover from, and adapt to adverse events.

STRONG ACT (DECEMBER 19, 2012)

Strengthening the Resiliency of Our Nation on the Ground (STRONG) Act (S-3691), sponsored by Senators John Kerry (D-MA), Frank Lautenberg (D-NJ), and Kirsten Gillibrand (D-NY). Referred to the Committee on Commerce, Science, and Transportation on December 19, 2012. This legislation requires the White House Director of the Office of Science and Technology Policy establish an interagency working group with cabinet-level representation from all relevant federal agencies in order to:

1. provide a strategic vision of extreme weather resilience;
2. conduct a gap and overlap analysis of federal agencies' current and planned activities related to achieving short- and long-term resilience to extreme weather and its impacts on the United States, such as flooding and drought; and
3. develop a National Extreme Weather Resilience Plan. It also requires the plan to include the establishment of an online, publicly available information clearinghouse to be used by federal agencies and other stakeholders to inform resilience-enhancing efforts and to build upon and complement existing federal efforts. (Kerry, Lautenberg, and Gillibrand 2012)

CONGRESSIONAL RESEARCH SERVICE (CRS) (AUGUST 23, 2012)

Critical Infrastructure Resilience: The Evolution of Policy and Programs and Issues for Congress. This report aids Congress in its oversight of critical infrastructure programs and resilience policy efforts at the DHS (R42683).

U.S. GOVERNMENT ACCOUNTABILITY OFFICE (GAO) (MARCH 2007)

Critical Infrastructure: Challenges Remain in Protecting Key Sectors. Addresses DHS attempts to implement strategy through the establishment of public- and private-sector councils, including the extent of their establishment, key facilitating factors and challenges affecting their formation and the formation of sector plans, and the status of DHS efforts to fulfill key cyber-security responsibilities (GAO-07–626T).

GAO (MARCH 2010)

Critical Infrastructure Protection: Update to National Infrastructure Protection Plan Includes Increased Emphasis on Risk Management and Resilience. Summarizes evolution of the policy and programs at the DHS that could promote resiliency of the nation's critical infrastructure systems (GAO-10–296).

GAO (July 2011)

Cybersecurity: Continued Attention Needed to Protect Our Nation's Critical Infrastructure. Describes cyber threats facing cyber-reliant critical infrastructures, recent actions taken by the federal government in partnership with the private sector to identify and protect them, and the ongoing challenges to defending these infrastructures (GAO-11-865T).

GAO (May 2012)

Critical Infrastructure Protection: DHS Could Better Manage Security Surveys and Vulnerability Assessments. Recommends DHS develop plans for its efforts to improve the collection and organization of data and the timeliness of survey and assessment results, and gather and act upon additional information from asset owners and operators about why improvements were or were not made (GAO-12-378).

National Infrastructure Advisory Council (NIAC) (January 13, 2004)

Cross Sector Interdependencies and Risk Assessment Guidance. Concludes that cross-sector crisis management coordination is fundamental to the rapid restoration of critical infrastructure and integral to sustain the public's confidence in those infrastructures.

NIAC (April 13, 2004)

Best Practices for Government to Enhance the Security of National Critical Infrastructures. Identifies the conditions under which selected government intervention could be beneficial and uses a framework that allows exploration of the efficacy of market forces in any sector. It then applies the findings to different sectors, yielding preliminary ideas of where market intervention may be more or less applicable.

NIAC (October 12, 2004)

Common Vulnerability Scoring System. Supports the use of CVSS as a common metric by all federal departments and agencies in assessing the level of vulnerability within sectors of critical infrastructure; contends that DHS should promote the use of the scoring system by other governments and private owners and operators in conjunction with coordination with NIAC in identifying a host organization.

NIAC (October 11, 2005)

Risk Management Approaches to Protection. Identifies specific positive federal government actions under way that indicate significant resources and attention are being applied to the nation's risk management challenge, and recommends continued investment in risk management to improve national capabilities.

NIAC (JULY 11, 2006)

Public-Private Sector Intelligence Coordination. Makes recommendations to improve trust between the intelligence community and critical infrastructure owners and operators, the quality and timeliness of intelligence analysis, dissemination to the right decision makers in a timely manner, protection of sensitive government and private-sector information, and administrative processes required for effective public-private coordination.

NIAC (JANUARY 16, 2007)

Convergence of Physical and Cyber Technologies and Related Security Management Challenges Working Group. Outlines the rapidly growing threat to critical infrastructure control systems posed by cyber vulnerabilities in the midst of convergence between physical and information technology systems.

NIAC (JANUARY 16, 2007)

The Prioritization of Critical Infrastructure for a Pandemic Outbreak in the United States Working Group. Identifies critical services and resources through a survey of the public sector in order to pursue identification, criteria, definitions, and principles of effective implementation in the case of a pandemic.

NIAC (SEPTEMBER 8, 2009)

Critical Infrastructure Resilience: Final Report and Recommendations. Calls for a renewed focus on resilience efforts by examining what steps government and industry should take to best integrate resilience and protection into a comprehensive risk-management strategy; features six strategic-level recommendations to advance government policy and improve government coordination to advance national-level critical infrastructure resilience.

NIAC (OCTOBER 19, 2010)

A Framework for Establishing Critical Infrastructure Resilience Goals Final Report and Recommendations. Provides a common definition of resilience and employs a case study approach of selected sectors to clarify sector-specific strategies and practices, starting with the electricity and nuclear sectors, proposing a framework for setting resilience goals within all critical infrastructure sectors.

NIAC (March 23, 2012)

Regional Resilience Scoping Study. Lays groundwork for further study, applying the resilience framework developed by the NIAC to a region within the United States to determine how public and private CIKR partners can work together to establish goals for improving resilience. Special emphasis is given to goals that would be relevant at the national level.

Appendix G
Subject Matter Expert Interviewees

1. White House, National Security Staff (NSS), Office of Resilience Policy (April 2, 2012; Washington, DC)
2. White House, National Security Staff (NSS), Cyber Security Directorate (April 2, 2012; Washington, DC)
3. DHS/NPPD, Office of Infrastructure Protection (April 5, 2012; Arlington, VA)
4. DHS/S&T Disaster Management (April 12, 2012; Washington, DC)
5. NORAD/USNORTHCOM staff elements (April 20, 2012; Colorado Springs, CO)
6. DIA Intelligence Official; Senior Executive, Intelligence Community (June 4, 2012; Washington, DC)
7. JHU/APL Asymmetric Operations Department, Homeland Protection (June 27, 2012; Laurel, MD)
8. JHU/APL Asymmetric Operations Department, Homeland Protection (June 28, 2012; Laurel, MD)
9. DHS/NPPD, Infrastructure Protection Senior Executive (April 26, 2012; Washington, DC)
10. DHS, Office of Resilience Policy Senior Staff Planner (June 5, 2012; Washington, DC)
11. FEMA Office of Policy Program Analysis, Strategic Foresight Initiative (July 15, 2012; Washington, DC)
12. Red Cross Senior Executive, Former White House, National Security Staff Senior Director (July 13, 2012; Washington, DC)
13. All Hazards Consortium, Private Sector Executive (May 16, 2012; Laurel, MD)
14. National Infrastructure Advisory Council (NIAC), Senior Executive (June 7, 2012; Baltimore, MD)
15. Homeland Security Research Center, Northeastern University, Senior Executive (May 9, 2012; Boston, MA)

16. Office of the Director of National Intelligence (ODNI) staff elements (May 17, 2012; McLean, VA)
17. Private Sector Senior Executive, Former DHS Official (July 23, 2012; Washington, DC)
18. DHS, NPPD, Infrastructure Protection Senior Policy Official (June 19, 2012; Washington, DC)
19. Congress, House Committee on Transportation and Infrastructure (July 23, 2012; Washington, DC)
20. White House, National Security Staff (NSS), Senior Resilience Policy Planner (June 28, 2012; Washington, DC)

Note: Some of the 20 interviews included multiple participants at a single location, offering the opportunity to gather information from more SMEs (35 total).

Appendix H
Acronyms and Abbreviations Key

ACAMS	Automated Critical Asset Management System
ACOE	U.S. Army Corps of Engineers
ADA	All-Domain Awareness
AMSC	Area Maritime Security Committee
BSA	Boy Scouts of America
CAIP	Critical Asset Identification Process
CAL	Critical Asset List
CBP	Customs and Border Patrol
CDC	Centers for Disease Control and Prevention
CFDI	Critical Foreign Dependency Initiatives
CFR	Code of Federal Regulation
CIKR	Critical Infrastructure and Key Resources
CIMS	Critical Incident Management System
CIO	Chief Information Officer
CIP	Critical Infrastructure Protection
CIPAC	Critical Infrastructure Protection Advisory Council
CIR	Critical Infrastructure Resilience
CNP	Center for National Policy
COCOM	Combatant Commander
COG	Continuity of Government
COI	Community of Interest
CONOPS	Concept of Operations
COOP	Continuity of Operations
CPG	Comprehensive Preparedness Guide
CSI	Container Security Initiative
CSO	Chief Security Officer
CYBERCOM	U.S. Cyber Command
DCA	Defense Critical Asset
DCI	Defense Critical Infrastructure
DCIO	Defense Critical Infrastructure Office

DCIP	Defense Critical Infrastructure Program
DCMA	Defense Contract Management Agency
DHS	U.S. Department of Homeland Security
DIA	Defense Intelligence Agency
DIB	Defense Industrial Base
DOD	U.S. Department of Defense
DOT	U.S. Department of Transportation
ECIP	Enhanced Critical Infrastructure Protection
EISA	Energy Independence and Security Act
EMAC	Emergency Management Assistance Compact
EOC	Emergency Operations Center
EPRI	Electric Power Research Institute
ESF	Emergency Support Function
FCC	Federal Communications Commission
FEMA	Federal Emergency Management Agency
FMAG	Fire Management Assistance Grant
FOIA	Freedom of Information Act
FRP	Federal Response Plan
GAO	Government Accountability Office
GCC	Government Coordinating Council
GIS	Geographic Information Systems
GPS	Global Positioning System
GWOT	Global War on Terror
H1N1	Influenza A Virus Subtype H1N1
HHS	Department of Health and Human Services
HILP	High-Impact, Low-Probability
HPLI	High-Probability, Low-Impact
HSAC	Homeland Security Advisory Council
HSAS	Homeland Security Advisory System
HSPD	Homeland Security Presidential Directive
IBHS	Institute for Business and Home Safety
IC	Intelligence Community
ICS	Incident Command System
IED	Improvised Explosive Device
IPC	Interagency Policy Committee
IT	Information Technology
IW	Irregular Warfare
JHU/APL	Johns Hopkins University Applied Physics Laboratory
MAA	Mutual Assistance Agreement
MOU	Memorandum of Understanding
MSA	Mutual Support Agreements
MTA	Metropolitan Transportation Authority
NCP	National Contingency Plan
NEI	Nuclear Energy Institute
NEP	National Exercise Program

NERC	North American Electric Reliability Corporation
NGB	National Guard Bureau
NIAC	National Infrastructure Advisory Council
NICC	National Infrastructure Coordinating Center
NIMS	National Incident Management Systems
NIPP	National Infrastructure Protection Program
NISAC	National Infrastructure Simulation and Analysis Center
NLE	National Level Exercise
NOAA	National Oceanic and Atmospheric Administration
NORAD	North American Aerospace Defense Command
NORTHCOM	U.S. Northern Command
NPPD	National Protection and Programs Directorate
NPR	National Preparedness Report
NRF	National Response Framework
NSC	National Security Council
NSCT	National Strategy for Counterterrorism
NSMS	National Strategy for Maritime Security
NSS	National Security Strategy
NTAS	National Transportation Advisory System
NYC	New York City
NYPD	New York Police Department
OIG	Office of the Inspector General
OIP	Office of Infrastructure Protection
OMB	Office of Management & Budget (White House)
OPA-90	Oil Pollution Act of 1990
PANYNJ	The Port Authority of New York and New Jersey
PCCIP	Presidential Commission on Critical Infrastructure Protection
PCII	Protected Critical Infrastructure Information
PDD	Presidential Decision Directive
PHEP	Public Health and Emergency Preparedness
PKEMRA	Post-Katrina Emergency Management Reform Act
POLALB	Ports of Los Angeles/Long Beach
PPD	Presidential Policy Directive
PPP	Public-Private Partnership
PSA	Protective Security Advisor
PSCD	Protective Security Coordination Division
QHSR	Quadrennial Homeland Security Review
RCPGP	Regional Catastrophic Preparedness Grant Program
RECP	Regional Emergency Coordination Plan
RIT	Resilience Integration Team
ROI	Return on Investment
RRAP	Regional Resiliency Assessment Program
SBA	Small Business Administration
SCADA	Supervisory Control and Data Acquisition

SCC	Sector Coordinating Committee
SERRI	Southeast Region Research Initiative
SFC	State Fusion Center
SME	Subject Matter Expert
SNL	Sandia National Laboratories
SNRA	Strategic National Risk Assessment
SNS	Social Networking Sites
SOCMA	Society of Chemical Manufacturers and Affiliates
SOP	Standard Operating Procedure
SOUTHCOM	U.S. Southern Command
SSA	Sector-Specific Agency
STRATCOM	U.S. Strategic Command
TCA	Task Critical Asset
TEPCO	Tennessee Electric Power Company
THIRA	Threat and Hazard Identification and Risk Assessment
TSA	Transportation Security Administration
TTPs	Tactics, Techniques, and Procedures
TVA	Tennessee Valley Authority
UASI	Urban Area Security Initiative
USA	U.S. Army
USAF	U.S. Air Force
USCG	U.S. Coast Guard
USG	U.S. Government
USMC	U.S. Marine Corps
USMM	U.S. Merchant Marine
USN	U.S. Navy
USSS	U.S. Secret Service
UW	Unrestricted Warfare
WMDs	Weapons of Mass Destruction

References

Agranoff, R. 2006. "Inside Collaborative Networks: Ten Lessons for Public Managers." Special issue, *Public Administration Review* 12 (December): 56–65.

Allen, T. 2012. *The Future of Homeland Security: The Evolution of the Homeland Security Department's Roles and Missions*. Testimony before the U.S. Senate Committee on Homeland Security and Government Affairs, Washington, DC, July 22.

Allison, G. 1971. *Essence of Decision: Explaining the Cuban Missile Crisis*. New York: HarperCollins.

American Red Cross. 2010. "Web Users Increasingly Rely on Social Media to Seek Help in a Disaster." ARC Disaster Online Newsroom, August 9. http://newsroom.redcross.org/2010/08/09/press-release-web-users-increasingly-rely-on-social-media-to-seek-help-in-a-disaster/.

American Society of Civil Engineers (ASCE). 2009. *Guiding Principles for the Nation's Critical Infrastructure*. Reston, VA: ASCE Publications.

———. 2013. *2013 Report Card for America's Infrastructure*. Reston, VA: ASCE Publications.

Anderson, C. 2012. "Japan Earthquake Social Media Coverage: Disaster by the Numbers." *Huffington Post*, March 9. http://www.huffingtonpost.com/2012/03/09/japan-earthquake-social-media_n_1332853.html.

Andreas, P. 2003. "Redrawing the Line: Borders and Security in the Twenty-First Century." *International Security Journal* 28, no. 2: 78–111.

Applegate, E. 2013. "In Davos, the World Economic Forum's Big, Unintelligible Ideas." *Bloomberg BusinessWeek*, January 25. http://www.businessweek.com/articles/2013-01-25/in-davos-the-world-economic-forums-big-unintelligible-ideas#r=hp-ls.

Associated Press (AP). 2011a. "Impacts from Irene, State-to-State." *CBS News*, August 29. http://www.cbsnews.com/2100-201_162-20098379.html?tag=cbsSMPB.

———. 2011b. "State-by-State Look at Irene's Impact." *Wall Street Journal*, August 30. http://online.wsj.com/article/AP6cc31521a2234afa8d2566476b103e9a.html.

———. 2012. "India Businesses Weather Blackouts, but at a Cost." *The Big Story*, August 1. http://bigstory.ap.org/article/power-restored-across-india-after-historic-failure.

Australian National Security Strategy (ANSS). 2013. "Strong and Secure—A Strategy for Australia's National Security." Australian Government, Department of the Prime Minister and Cabinet, January 23. http://www.nationalsecurity.gov.au/.

Axelrod, R. 1984. *The Evolution of Cooperation*. New York: Basic Books.

Bandyopadhyay, P. 2012. "A Few Lessons and the Way Ahead, from the Big Blackout." Mumbai: Diligent Media Corporation. August 6. http://www.dnaindia.com/analysis/column_a-few-lessons-and-the-way-ahead-from-the-big-blackout_1724376.

BBC News. 2012. "Japan Quake: Loss and Recovery in Numbers." British Broadcasting Company, March 11. http://www.bbc.co.uk/news/world-asia-17219008.

Betts, R.K. 1978. "Analysis, War, and Decision: Why Intelligence Failures Are Inevitable." *World Politics* 31, no. 1: 61–89.

Blackburn, B. 2011. "Japan Earthquake and Tsunami: Social Media Spreads News, Raises Relief Funds." *ABC News*. March 11. http://abcnews.go.com/Technology/japan-earthquake-tsunami-drive-social-media-dialogue/story?id=13117677.

Borenstein, S. 2013. "Climate Talk Shifts from Curbing CO_2 to Adapting." *Associated Press*. June 15. http://hosted.ap.org/dynamic/stories/U/US_SCI_CLIMATE_ADAPTATION?SITE=AP&SECTION=HOME&TEMPLATE=DEFAULT.

Brashear, J., and W. Jones. 2010. "Risk Analysis and Management for Critical Asset Protection (RAM-CAP Plus)." In *Wiley Handbook of Science and Technology of Homeland Security*, ed. J.G. Voeller. Hoboken, NJ: John Wiley & Sons.

Bratman, M. 1993. "Shared Intention." *Ethics* 104, no. 1: 97–113.

Bruneau, M., S. Chang, R. Eguchi, G. Lee, T. O'Rourke, A. Reinhorn, M. Shinozuka, K. Tierney, W. Wallace, and D. von Winterfelt. 2003. "A Framework to Quantitatively Assess and Enhance the Seismic Resilience of Communications." *Earthquake Spectra* 19, no. 4: 733–752.

Buchanan, J. (1972). "Towards Analysis of Closed Behavioral Systems." In *Theory of Public Choice: Political Applications of Economics*. Ann Arbor: University of Michigan Press.

Byram, D., ed. 2009. *Introduction to Homeland Security*. New York: Pearson Custom Publishing.

Carafano, J., and R. Weitz. 2007. "Enhancing International Collaboration for Homeland Security and Counterterrorism." *Heritage Foundation Backgrounder,* no. 2078 (October 18): 1–3.

Carmel, S. 2011. Senior Vice President, Maritime Services, Maersk Line Limited, Norfolk, Virginia. Interview with the author, June 16.

Carney, M. 1987. "The Strategy and Structure of Collective Action." *Organization Studies* 8, no. 4: 341–362.

Carroll, J., and K. Montgomery. 2008. "Global Positining System (GPS) Timing Criticality Assessment—Preliminary Performance Results." Paper presented at 40th Annual Precise Time and Time Interval (PTTI) meeting, Reston, VA, December.

Carroll, R. 2012. "Climate Change Threatens California Power Supply." July. http://www.reuters.com/article/2012/08/01/us-usa-california-climate-idINBRE87001Q20120801.

Chen, D., and M. Navarro. 2012. "For Years, Warnings That It Could Happen Here." *New York Times,* October 30. http://www.nytimes.com/2012/10/31/nyregion/for-years-warnings-that-storm-damage-could-ravage-new-york.html?_r=0.

Christensen, T., and P. Laegreid. 2007. "The Whole-of-Government Approach to Public Sector Reform." *Public Administration Review* 67, no. 6: 1059–1066.

Clark, B. 2011. "Hurricane Irene Infrastructure Woes Worry U.S. Chemical Producers." Houston, TX: ICIS, August 27. http://www.icis.com/Articles/2011/08/27/9488496/hurricane-irene-infrastructure-woes-worry-us-chemicals-producers.html.

Congressional Research Service (CRS). 2007. *Maritime Security: Potential Terrorist Attacks and Protection Priorities*. CRS Report prepared for Members and Committees of Congress, Washington, DC. May 14.

———. 2012. *Critical Infrastructure Resilience: The Evolution of Policy and Programs and Issues for Congress*. CRS Report prepared for Members and Committees of Congress, Washington, DC. August 23.

Contestabile, J.M. 2011. *Concepts on Information Sharing and Interoperability*. Laurel, MD: The Johns Hopkins University Applied Physics Laboratory.

Cooper-Ramo, J. 2009. *The Age of the Unthinkable: Why the New World Disorder Constantly Surprises Us*. New York: Back Bay Books.

Coyle, J. 2012. "Study: Viewers Turning to YouTube as News Source." July 16. http://apnews.myway.com/article/20120716/DA01PLR81.html.

Creswell, J. 2007. *Qualitative Inquiry and Research Design—Choosing Among Five Approaches*. 2d ed. Thousand Oaks, CA: Sage.

Crichton, M., C. Ramsay, and T. Kelly. 2009. "Enhancing Organizational Resilience Through Emergency Planning: Learnings from Cross-Sectoral Lessons." *Journal of Contingencies & Crisis Management* 17, no. 1: 24–37.

Daalder, I., and I.M. Destler. 2001. *Organizing for Homeland Security.* Statement prepared for the Committee on Governmental Affairs, U.S. Senate, Washington, DC. October.

Davis, E. 1952. "Security and the News." *Public Administration Review* 12, no. 2: 85–88.

Dawes, R. 1980. "Social Dilemmas." *Annual Review of Psychology*, 31, 169–193.

Dawson, C. 2011. "Quake Still Rattles Suppliers." *Wall Street Journal*, September 29. http://online.wsj.com/article/SB10001424053111904563904576586040856135596.html.

deLeon, P. 1988. *Advice and Consent: The Development of the Policy Sciences.* New York: Russell Sage Foundation.

DomesticPreparedness.com (DomPrep). 2012. *DomPrep Action Plan: Building Resilient Regions for a Secure and Resilient Nation.* Prepared by John Morton and Catherine Feinman. Severna Park, MD: IMR Group, Inc.

Donahue, J., and R. Zeckhauser. 2006. "Public-Private Collaboration." In *The Oxford Handbook of Public Policy.* Oxford, UK: Oxford University Press, pp. 508–509.

Donley, M. 2005. "Rethinking the Interagency System." Occasional Paper 05-01. McLean, VA: Hicks & Associates, Inc.

Economist. 2012a. "The Benefits of Hindsight: The Need for More Monitoring of Domestic Terrorism." August 18, p. 27.

———. 2012b. "Elinor Ostrom: Defender of the Commons, Died on June 12th, Aged 78." June 30, p. 65.

———. 2012c. "Zombie-Proof Architecture: When the Dead Start to Walk You'd Better Start Building." August 25, p. 14.

———. 2013a. "Everything Is Connected." January 5, pp. 17–19.

———. 2013b. "The Mixed Fortunes of a Fuel." January 5, p. 54.

El Nasser, H. 2012. "American Cities to Millennials: Don't Leave." *USA Today*, December 4.

Electromagnetic Pulse (EMP) Commission. 2008. *Report of the Commission to Assess the Threat to the United States from Electromagnetic Pulse (EMP) Attack.* Critical National Infrastructures Report, April.

Federal Emergency Management Agency (FEMA). 2011. *A Whole Community Approach to Emergency Management: Principles, Themes, and Pathways for Action.* Washington, DC. FDOC 104-008-1/December.

———. 2012a. *Crisis Response and Disaster Resilience 2030: Forging Strategic Action in an Age of Uncertainty.* Washington, DC. January.

———. 2012b. "Hurricane Irene, Tropical Storm Lee Survivors Continue to Receive Disaster Assistance," March 5. http://www.fema.gov/news-release/2012/03/05/hurricane-irene-tropical-storm-lee-survivors-continue-receive-disaster.

Fielding, N., and Fielding, J. 1986. *Linking Data.* Beverly Hills, CA: Sage.

Flynn, S. 2004. *America the Vulnerable: How Our Government Is Failing to Protect Us from Terrorism.* New York: HarperCollins.

———. 2006. *The Continued Vulnerability of the Global Maritime Transportation System.* Testimony before a hearing of the Subcommittee on Coast Guard and Maritime Transportation, Committee on Transportation and Infrastructure, U.S. House of Representatives on Foreign Operations of U.S. Port Facilities, Washington, DC. March 9.

———. 2007. *The Edge of Disaster—Rebuilding a Resilient Nation.* New York: Random House.

Flynn, S., and S. Burke. 2012. *Critical Transportation Infrastructure and Societal Resilience.* Report, March. Washington, DC: Center for National Policy.

Frazier, I. 2013. "The Toll: Sandy and the Future." *New Yorker,* February 11. http://www.newyorker.com/reporting/2013/02/11/130211fa_fact_frazier.

Friedman, M. 1984. "The Methodology of Positive Economics." In *The Philosophy of Economics,* ed. D. Hausman. Cambridge, UK: Cambridge University Press, pp. 145–178.

Friedrich, C., and E. Mason, eds. 1940. *Public Policy.* Cambridge, MA: Harvard University Press, pp. 3–24.

Frischmann, B. 2013. *Infrastructure: The Social Value of Shared Resources.* New York: Oxford University Press.

Frittelli, J. 2008. "Port and Maritime Security: Background and Issues for Congress; Maritime Security: Overview of Issues." In *Port and Maritime Security,* ed. Jonathon Vesky. New York: Nova Science, pp. 11–47.

Funabashi, Y., and H. Takenaka, eds. 2011. *Lessons from the Disaster: Risk Management and the Compound Crisis Presented by the Great East Japan Earthquake.* Tokyo: The Japan Times.

George, A., and A. Bennett. 2005. *Case Studies and Theory Development in the Social Sciences.* Cambridge, MA: MIT Press.

Gerencser, M. 2011. "Re-Imagining Infrastructure." *American Interest Journal* 6 no. 4. www.the-american-interest.com/article.cfm?piece=926.

Gerencser, M., R. Van Lee, F. Napolitano, and C. Kelly. 2008. *Megacommunities: How Leaders of Government, Business, and Non-Profits Can Tackle Today's Global Challenges Together.* New York: Palgrave Macmillan.

Gerring, J. 2007. *Case Study Research: Principles and Practices.* New York: Cambridge University Press.

Gilbert, M. 1989. *On Social Facts.* Princeton, NJ: Princeton University Press.

———. 2006. *A Theory of Political Obligation: Membership, Commitment, and the Bonds of Society.* Cary, NC: Oxford University Press.

Goertz, G. 2006. *Social Science Concepts: A User's Guide.* Princeton, NJ: Princeton University Press.

Gonzalez, A. 2011. "The Japan Earthquake and Supply Chain Risk Management." Logistics Viewpoints (blog), March 16. http://logisticsviewpoints.com/2011/03/16/the-japan-earthquake-and-supply-chain-risk-management.

Grynbaum, M., and C. Haughney. 2011. "New York Subway Running in Time for Morning Commute." *New York Times,* August 29. http://www.nytimes.com/2011/08/29/nyregion/new-york-expects-lengthy-recovery-of-transit-system.html?_r=1&ref=michaelmgrynbaum.

Gunderson, L., C. Holling, and S. Light. 1995. *Barriers and Bridges to the Renewal of Ecosystems and Institutions.* New York: Columbia University Press.

Gunderson, L., C. Holling, and D. Ludwig. 2002. *Panarchy: Understanding Transformations in Human and Natural Systems.* Washington, DC: Island Press.

Haas, E. 1980. "Why Collaborate? Issue-Linkage and International Regimes." *World Politics* 32, no. 3: 357–405.

Hardin, G. 1968. "The Tragedy of the Commons." *Science* 162 (December 13): 1243–1248.

Hardin, R. 1982. *Collective Action.* Baltimore, MD: Johns Hopkins University Press.

Harris, R. 2011. "What Went Wrong in Fukushima: The Human Factor." *Morning Edition.* National Public Radio Special Series, July 5. http://www.npr.org/2011/07/05/137611026/what-went-wrong-in-fukushima-the-human-factor.

Homeland Security Council. 2007. *National Strategy for Homeland Security (NSHS).* Homeland Security Digital Library, October. http://www.hsdl.org/?view&did=479633.

Homeland Security News Wire. 2012. "New York Overhauls Emergency Response Capabilities Post-Irene." February 27. http://www.homelandsecuritynewswire.com/dr20120226-new-york-overhauls-emergency-response-capabilities-postirene.

Hubbard, P. 2005. "Freedom of Information and Security Intelligence: An Economic Analysis in an Australian Context." *Open Government: Journal on Freedom of Information* 1, no. 3: 1–11.

Hughes-Wilson, J. 1999. *Military Intelligence Blunders.* New York: Carroll & Graf Publishers.

Hunt, S. 2005. "Whole-of-Government: Does Working Together Work?" *Policy and Governance.* Discussion Paper 05-01. Asia Pacific School of Economics and Government, Australian National University.

Infosec Island. 2011. "Hurricane Irene Critical Infrastructure Conference Call." http://www.infosecisland.com/blogview/16113-DHS-Hurricane-Irene-Critical-Infrastructure-Conference-Call.html.

Ingraham, P. 2005. "You Talking to Me? Accountability and the Modern Public Service." *Policy Science & Politics* 2, no. 1: 17–21.

Insurance Institute for Business and Home Safety (IIBHS). 2012. *Know Your Plan: Prepare for a Disaster.* http://disastersafety.org/earthquake/disaster-planning-there%e2%80%99s-an-app-for-that/.

Kachi, H., and Y. Takahashi. 2011. "Plant Closures Imperil Global Supplies." *Wall Street Journal*, March 14. http://online.wsj.com/article/SB10001424052748704027504576198961775199034.html.

Kahn, C. 2011. "Hurricane Irene Power Outages: Electricity Blackouts Affect 4 Million Homes and Businesses." *Huffington Post*, August 28. http://www.huffingtonpost.com/2011/08/28/hurricane-irene-power-outages_n_939441.html.

Kaiser, F. 1989. "The Amount of Classified Information: Causes, Consequences, and Correctives of a Growing Concern." *Government Information Quarterly* 6, no. 3: 247–266.

Katayama, F. 2011. "Hurricane Irene Travel Recovery Could Take Days, Says Expert." Reuters, August 29. http://www.reuters.com/video/2011/08/29/hurricane-irene-travel-recovery-will-tak?videoId=218794855.

Kerry, J., F. Lautenberg, and K. Gillibrand. 2012. Strengthening the Resiliency of Our Nation on the Ground (STRONG) Act (S-3691). Washington, DC: U.S. Government Printing Office, December 19. http://beta.congress.gov/bill/112th-congress/senate-bill/3691.

Kettl, D. 2002. *The Transformation of Governance: Public Administration for Twenty-First Century America.* Baltimore, MD: Johns Hopkins University Press.

———. 2004. *System Under Stress: Homeland Security and American Politics.* Washington, DC: CQ Press.

———. 2006. "Managing Boundaries in American Administration: The Collaboration Imperative." Special issue, *Public Administration Review*, 66, 10–19.

———. 2008. *The Next Government of the United States: Why Our Institutions Fail Us and How to Fix Them.* New York: W.W. Norton.

Klein, K. 2011. "Obama: Irene Impact to Be 'Felt for Some Time.'" Voice of America, August 27. http://www.voanews.com/content/obama-irene-impact-to-be-felt-for-sometime-128567668/144474.html.

Kumar, A. 2011. "Hurricane Irene's Impact on Virginia Agriculture Assessed." *Washington Post*, September 2. http://www.washingtonpost.com/blogs/virginia-politics/post/hurricane-irenes-impact-on-virginia-agriculture-assessed/2011/09/02/gIQASd17wJ_blog.html.

Lee, D., and D. Pierson. 2011. "Disaster in Japan Exposes Supply Chain Flaw." *Los Angeles Times*, April 6. http://articles.latimes.com/2011/apr/06/business/la-fi-quake-supply-chain-20110406.

Leverett, E.P. 2011. *Quantitatively Assessing and Visualizing Industrial System Attack Surfaces.* Master's thesis, University of Cambridge, Cambridge, UK.

Lewis, N. 2011. "Hurricane Irene Sparks Talk of HIT Disaster Strategy." *Information Week*, September 6. http://www.informationweek.com/news/healthcare/security-privacy/231600792.

Livingston, I. 2012. "Could Forecasters Have Better Predicted the June 29 Derecho?" *Washington Post*, July 3. http://www.washingtonpost.com/blogs/capital-weather-gang/post/could-forecasters-have-done-better-with-the-june-29-derecho/2012/07/03/gJQAbgkwKW_blog.html.

Lobb, A. 2011. "Japan Earthquake on Twitter: Social Media Trends During Disaster." Justmeans, March 11. http://www.justmeans.com/Japan-Earthquake-on-Twitter-Social-Media-Trends-During-Disaster/46835.html.

Lovett, R.A. 2011. "Japan Earthquake Not the 'Big One'?" *National Geographic News*, March 14. http://news.nationalgeographic.com/news/2011/03/110315-japan-earthquake-tsunami-big-one-science/.

Lukasik, S., S. Goodman, and D. Longhurst. 2003. *The Adelphi Papers—Special Issue: Protecting Critical Infrastructures Against Cyber-Attack,* 43, issue 359.

Luman, R., ed. 2007. *Proceedings on Combating the Unrestricted Warfare Threat: Integrating Strategy, Analysis, and Technology.* Unrestricted Warfare Symposium, March 20–21. The Johns Hopkins University Applied Physics Laboratory, Laurel, MD.

Luthra, S. 2011. "India's Energy Policy and Electricity Production: An Interview with Charles Ebinger." *Policy Q & A.* National Bureau of Asian Research, Washington, DC. October 26. http://nbr.org/research/activity.aspx?id=181.

Maloof, F.M. 2012. "Understand EMP Threats? U.S. Enemies Do: Anti-ballistic Missile Defense System Ill-Prepared for Assault." WND.com. December 30. http://www.wnd.com/2012/12/understand-emp-threat-u-s-enemies-do/.

Marshall, C., and G. Rossman. 2006. *Designing Qualitative Research.* 4th ed. Thousand Oaks, CA: Sage.

McCoy, K., and G. Strauss. 2012. "Destruction Potential of Sandy's Storm Surge Nearly Tops Scale." *USA Today,* October 29, 3A.

McDermott, T.P. 2002. "USA's Boy Scouts and World War I Liberty Loan Bonds." *SOSSI Journal* 51 (May/June): 68–73. http://www.sossi.org/journal/scouts-ww1-liberty-bonds.pdf.

McGuire, M. 2006. "Collaborative Public Management: Assessing What We Know and How We Know It." Special issue, *Public Administration Review,* 66, 33–42.

McKibben, P., and J. Morse. 2012. "Derecho Shut Down Warren 911 for 90 Minutes." Cincinnati.com, August 6. http://news.cincinnati.com/article/20120806/NEWS/308060082/Derecho-shut-down-Warren-911-90-minutes.

McKinney, M. 2012. "A Formidable Foe." ModernHealthCare.com. October 27. http://www.modern-healthcare.com/article/20121027/MAGAZINE/310279922.

McNicholas, M. 2008. *Maritime Security: An Introduction.* Burlington, MA: Butterworth-Heinemann.

Medina, L. 2007. A *Unified Theory of Collective Action and Social Change.* Ann Arbor: University of Michigan Press.

Melucci, A. 1996. *Challenging Codes: Collective Action in the Information Age.* New York: Cambridge University Press.

Micheletti, M. 2003. *Political Virtue and Shopping: Individuals, Consumerism, and Collective Action.* New York: Palgrave MacMillan.

Microsoft. 2013. "What Is a Botnet?" In *Safety and Security Center.* July 3. http://www.microsoft.com/security/resources/botnet-whatis.aspx.

Miller, C. 2005. "Electromagnetic Pulse Threats in 2010." Center for Strategy and Technology, Air War College, Air University. Montgomery, AL: Maxwell Air Force Base, November.

Miller, S. 2012. "Only Woman to Win Nobel Prize in Economics." *Wall Street Journal,* June 12. http://online.wsj.com/article/SB10001424052702303444204577462810744310888.html.

Miyakawa, T. 2000. *The Science of Public Policy: Essential Readings in Policy Sciences II.* New York: Routledge.

Mukherji, B., S. Chaturvedi, and S. Choudhury. 2012. "In India, Weak Monsoon Adds to Power Crisis." *Wall Street Journal,* August 2. http://online.wsj.com/article/SB100008723963904435455045775564900963094424.html.

Mussington, D. 2002. *Concepts for Enhancing Critical Infrastructure Protection: Relating Y2K to CIP Research and Development.* Research conducted by RAND's Science and Technology Policy Institute for the Office of Science and Technology Policy.

National Academies. 2012. *Disaster Resilience: A National Imperative.* Committee on Increasing National Resilience to Hazards and Disasters/Committee on Science, Engineering, and Public Policy. Washington, DC: National Academies Press.

National Commission on Terrorist Attacks upon the United States. 2004. *The 9/11 Commission Report.* http://www.911commission.gov/report/911Report.pdf.

National Infrastructure Advisory Council (NIAC). 2004a. *Best Practices for Government to Enhance the Security of National Critical Infrastructures.* Final Report and Recommendations by the Council. http://www.dhs.gov/xlibrary/assets/niac/NIAC_BestPracticesSecurityInfrastructures_0404.pdf.

———. 2004b. *Common Vulnerability Scoring System.* Final Report and Recommendations by the Council. http://www.first.org/cvss/cvss-dhs-12-02-04.pdf.

———. 2004c. *Cross Sector Interdependencies and Risk Assessment Guidance.* Final Report and Recommendations by the Council. http://www.dhs.gov/xlibrary/assets/irawgreport.pdf.

———. 2005. *Risk Management Approaches to Protection.* Final Report and Recommendations by the Council. http://www.dhs.gov/xlibrary/assets/niac/NIAC_RMWG_-_2-13-06v9_FINAL.pdf.

————. 2006. *Public-Private Sector Intelligence Coordination.* Final Report and Recommendations by the Council. http://www.dhs.gov/xlibrary/assets/niac/niac_icwgreport_july06.pdf.

————. 2007a. *Convergence of Physical and Cyber Technologies and Related Security Management Challenges Working Group.* Final Report and Recommendations by the Council. http://www.dhs.gov/xlibrary/assets/niac/niac_physicalcyberreport-011607.pdf.

————. 2007b. *The Prioritization of Critical Infrastructure for a Pandemic Outbreak in the United States Working Group.* Final Report and Recommendations by the Council. http://www.dhs.gov/xlibrary/assets/niac/niac-pandemic-wg_v8-011707.pdf.

————. 2009. *Critical Infrastructure Resilience.* Final Report and Recommendations by the Council. http://www.dhs.gov/xlibrary/asset/niac/niac_critical_infrastructure_resilience.pdf.

————. 2010. *A Framework for Establishing Critical Infrastructure Resilience Goals.* Final Report and Recommendations by the Council. http://www.dhs.gov/xlibrary/assets/niac/niac-a-framework-for-establishing-critical-infrastructure-resilience-goals-2010-10-19.pdf.

————. 2012a. *Intelligence Information Sharing.* Final Report and Recommendations by the Council. http://www.dhs.gov/xlibrary/assets/niac/niac-intelligence-information-sharing-final-report-01102012.pdf.

————. 2012b. *Regional Resilience Scoping Study.* http://www.dhs.gov/xlibrary/assets/niac/niac-regional-resilience-white-paper-032412.pdf.

National Oceanic and Atmospheric Administration (NOAA). 2012. "About Derechos." Part of the NOAA-NWS-NCEP Storm Prediction Center website, July 26. http://www.spc.noaa.gov/misc/AbtDerechos/derechofacts.

National Research Council (NRC). 2008. *Maritime Security Partnerships.* Naval Studies Board. Washington, DC: National Academies Press.

————. 2011. *Building Community Disaster Resilience Through Private-Public Collaboration.* Washington, DC: National Academies Press.

National Security Telecommunications Advisory Committee. 2008. *NSTAC Report to the President on Commercial Communications Reliance on the Global Positioning System (GPS).* February 28.

New York City. 2013a. "Mayor Bloomberg Outlines Ambitious Proposal to Protect City Against the Effects of Climate Change to Build a Stronger, More Resilient New York." *The Blue Room*, June 11. http://www.nyc.gov/portal/site/nycgov/menuitem.c0935b9a57bb4ef3daf2f1c701c789a0/index.jsp?pageID=mayor_press_release&catID=1194&doc_name=http%3A%2F%2Fwww.nyc.gov%2Fhtml%2Fom%2Fhtml%2F2013a%2Fpr201-13.html&cc=unused1978&rc=1194&ndi=1.

————. 2013b. "A Stronger, More Resilient New York." *PlaNYC.* June.

New York City Department of Environmental Protection Communications and Intergovernmental Affairs. 2011. "Department Completes Repairs to Gilboa Dam Spillway Damaged During Hurricane Irene." http://www.nyc.gov/html/dep/html/press_releases/11-107pr.shtml.

Newman, S. 2013. "Earthweek: A Diary of the Planet." *Ventura County Star* (CA), January 27.

Norris, F., S. Stevens, B. Pfefferbaum, K. Wyche, and R. Pfefferbaum. 2008. "Community Resilience as a Metaphor, Theory, Set of Capacities, and Strategy for Disaster Readiness." *American Journal of Community Psychology* 41, nos. 1–2: 127–150.

North, D. 1990. *Institutions, Institutional Change, and Economic Performance.* Cambridge, UK: Cambridge University Press.

Nuclear Energy Institute (NEI). 2011. "Impact of Hurricane Irene on U.S. Nuclear Energy Facilities." News release, August 28. http://www.nei.org/newsandevents/newsreleases/impact-of-hurricane-irene-on-us-nuclear-energy-facilities/.

Obama, B. 2012. "Taking the Cyberattack Threat Seriously." *Wall Street Journal*, July 19. http://online.wsj.com/article/SB10000872396390444330904577535492693044650.html.

Office of Management and Budget (OMB). 2001. *Annual Report to Congress on Combating Terrorism.* August. http://www.whitehouse.gov/sites/default/files/omb/assets/omb/legislative/nsd_annual_report2001.pdf.

O'Harrow, R., Jr. 2012a. "Cyber Search Engine Shodan Exposes Industrial Control Systems to New Risks." *Washington Post*, June 3. http://www.washingtonpost.com/investigations/cyber-search-engine-exposes-vulnerabilities/2012/06/03/gJQAIK9KCV_story.html.

———. 2012b. "Understanding Cyberspace Is Key to Defending Against Digital Attacks." *Washington Post,* June 2. http://www.washingtonpost.com/investigations/understanding-cyberspace-is-key-to-defending-against-digital-attacks/2012/06/02/gJQAsIr19U_story.html.

Olson, M. (1971). *The Logic of Collective Action: Public Goods and the Theory of Groups*. Cambridge, MA: Harvard University Press.

Orosz, M. 2012. Project leader, Information Sciences Institute, Viterbi School of Engineering, University of Southern California. Interview and email communications with the author, July 9 and December 24.

O'Rourke, T. 2007. "Critical Infrastructure, Interdependencies, and Resilience." *The Bridge: Linking Engineering and Society,* 37, no. 1: 22–29. http://www.nae.edu/File.aspx?id=7405.

Osborne, D., and T. Gaebler. 1993. *Reinventing Government*. New York: Penguin Group.

Ostrom, E. 1983. "A Public Service Industry Approach to the Study of Local Government Structure and Reform." *Policy and Politics* 11, no. 3: 313–341.

———. 1990. *Governing the Commons: The Evolution of Institutions for Collective Action*. Cambridge, UK: Cambridge University Press.

———. 1998. "A Behavioral Approach to the Rational Choice Theory of Collective Action." 1997 Presidential Address, American Political Science Association. *American Political Science Review* 92, no. 1 (March): 1–22.

———. 2007. "Institutional Rational Choice: An Assessment of the Institutional Analysis and Development Framework." In *Theories of the Policy Process,* 2d ed., ed. P.A. Sabatier. Boulder, CO: Westview Press.

Ostrom, E., R. Gardner, and J. Walker. 1992. "Covenants With and Without a Sword: Self-Governance Is Possible." *American Political Science Review* 86, no. 2: 404–417.

———. 1994. *Rules, Games, and Common-Pool Resources*. Ann Arbor: University of Michigan Press.

Ostrom, E., et al. 1999. "Revisiting the Commons: Local Lessons, Global Challenges." *Science* 284 (April 9): 278–282.

Ostrom, E., et al., eds. 2002. *The Drama of the Commons.* Committee on the Human Dimensions of Global Change, Division of Behavioral and Social Sciences and Education, National Research Council. Washington, DC: National Academies Press.

Paganelli, B. 2012. "Interdependency—A Whole-of-Nation Approach." Read-Online.org, February 21. http://read-online.org/archives/1969.

Page, E. 2005. "Joined-Up Government and the Civil Service." In *Joined-Up Government,* ed. Vernon Bogdanor. Oxford, UK: Oxford University Press.

Paik, E. 2011. "Hurricane Irene Floodwaters Blamed for Chemical Waste Spill in Bridgewater." New Jersey Online, August 31. http://www.nj.com/news/index.ssf/2011/08/hurricane_irene_floodwaters_bl.html.

Panayides, P. 2004. "Maritime Logistics and Global Supply Chains: Towards a Research Agenda." *Maritime Economics & Logistics* 8, no. 1: 3–18.

Patton, C. 2012. "Lessons Can Be Learned from Derecho." *State Journal* (West Virginia), July 25. http://www.statejournal.com/story/19113320/lessons-can-be-learned-from-derecho.

Pearl, J. 1984. *Heuristics: Intelligent Search Strategies for Computer Problem Solving.* New York: Addison-Wesley.

Petraeus, D. 1987. "The American Military and the Lessons of Vietnam: A Study of Military Influence and the Use-of-Force in the Post-Vietnam Era." PhD diss., Princeton University, October. http://www.scribd.com/doc/34023090/Petraeus-Princeton-Dissertation-on-Lessons-From-Vietnam-1987.

Pfleeger, C., and S. Lawrence Pfleeger. 2006. *Security in Computing.* 4th ed. Upper Saddle River, NJ: Prentice Hall.

Pierobon, J. 2012. "Outage Outrage: Lessons from the Derecho Storm." The Energy Collective, July

10. http://theenergycollective.com/jimpierobon/92046/outage-outrage-lessons-derecho-storm-heed-worst-case-outcome.

Plumb, M. 2011. "Hurricane Irene Tests Resilience of Communication Networks." IEEE Spectrum, August 30. http://spectrum.ieee.org/tech-talk/telecom/wireless/hurricane-irene-tests-resilience-of-communication-networks.

Plumer, B. 2012. "Could a Port Strike Really Cripple the U.S. Economy?" *Washington Post*, December 27. http://www.washingtonpost.com/blogs/wonkblog/wp/2012/12/27/could-a-port-strike-really-cripple-the-u-s-economy/.

Polson, J. 2011. "Utilities Restore Electricity to 57% of Customers After Hurricane Irene." Bloomberg.com, August 31. http://www.bloomberg.com/news/2011-08-31/utilities-restore-electricity-to-57-of-customers-after-hurricane-irene.html.

The Port Authority of New York and New Jersey (PANYNJ). 2009. "New York City Office of Emergency Management and Port Authority of NY/NJ Host Multi-Agency Field Exercise at World Trade Center." Press release, May 17.

———. 2013. "The Port Authority of New York and New Jersey: Overview of Facilities and Services/History." PANYNJ website, accessed February 3. http://www.panynj.gov/about/facilities-services.html.

Porter, M., and J. Rivkin. 2012. "What Washington Must Do Now." Special edition: The World in 2013. *Economist,* November 21. http://www.hbs.edu/competitiveness/pdf/theworldin2013.pdf.

Pressman, J., and A. Wildavsky. 1973. *Implementation, The Oakland Project.* Los Angeles, CA: University of California Press.

Raach, G., and I. Kaas. 1995. "National Power and the Interagency Process." *Joint Forces Quarterly* (Summer): 8–13.

Radasky, W. 2007. "High-Altitude Electromagnetic Pulse (HEMP): A Threat to Our Way of Life." IEEE-USA Today's Engineer Online, September 7. http://www.todaysengineer.org/2007/Sep/HEMP.asp.

Rainey, H. 1997. *Understanding and Managing Public Organizations.* 2d ed. San Francisco, CA: Jossey-Bass.

Regional Catastrophic Preparedness Grant Program (RCPGP). 2012. *Mid-Atlantic Strategic Playbook: Regional Catastrophic Preparedness and Supply Chain Resilience.* FEMA Grant Program, March 23.

Reich, M. 2002. *Public-Private Partnerships for Public Health.* Harvard Series on Population and International Health. Cambridge, MA: Harvard University Press.

Relyea, H. 2004. "Homeland Security and Information Sharing: Federal Policy Considerations." *Government Information Quarterly* 21, no. 4: 420–438.

Romzek, B., and M. Dubnick. 1987. "Accountability in the Public Service: Lessons from the *Challenger* Tragedy." *Public Administration Review* 47, no. 3: 227–238.

Russ, H. 2013. "New York Lays Out $20 Billion Plan to Adapt to Climate Change." *Reuters.* June 11. http://www.reuters.com/article/2013/06/11/us-climate-newyork-plan-idUSBRE95A10120130611.

Sahagun, L. 2012. "Rival Ports Join Forces on Green Growth." *Los Angeles Times*, December 25. http://www.latimes.com/news/local/la-me-port25dec25,0,2837538.story.

Samuelson, P. 1954. "The Pure Theory of Public Expenditure." *Review of Economics and Statistics* 36, no. 4: 387–389.

Sandler, T. 2004. *Global Collective Action.* New York: Cambridge University Press.

SANS Institute. 2011. "Australian Defence Signals Directorate Wins U.S. National Cybersecurity Innovation Award." National Cybersecurity Innovation Conference, Washington, DC. October 24. http://www.sans.org/press/australian-defence-signals-directorate-national-cybersecurity-award.php.

Scharpf, F. 1997. *Games Real Actors Play: Actor-Centered Institutionalism in Policy Research.* Boulder, CO: Westview Press.

Schlager, E. 2002. "Rationality, Cooperation, and Common Pool Resources." *American Behavioral Scientist* 45 no. 5: 801–819.

Schleifer, J. 2010. Translation of *Democracy in America*, by Alexis de Tocqueville. Indianapolis: Liberty Fund.

Searle, J. 1990. "Collective Intentions and Actions." In *Intentions in Communication,* ed. P.R. Cohen, J. Morgan, and M.E. Pollack. Cambridge, MA: MIT Press, pp. 401–415.

Sharp, T. 2012. "Superstorm Sandy: Facts About the Frankenstorm." LiveScience, November 27. http://www.livescience.com/24380-hurricane-sandy-status-data.html.

Simon, H. 1957. *Models of Man.* New York: Wiley.

Skjøtt-Larsen, T., P.B. Schary, J.H. Mikkola, and H. Kotzab. 2007. *Managing the Global Supply Chain.* 3rd ed. Copenhagen, Denmark: Copenhagen Business School Press.

Smith, E. 2010. "Communication and Collective Action: Language and the Evolution of Human Co-operation." *Evolution and Human Behavior* 31, no. 4: 231–245.

Spicer, J. 2011. "Wall Street Expected to Open Monday." Reuters, August 28. http://www.reuters.com/article/2011/08/28/us-irene-wallstreet-idUSTRE77R1UE20110828.

Sreenivasan, S. 2012. "Japan Earthquake Anniversary: Digital Media Lessons We've Learned." CNET.com, March 11. http://news.cnet.com/8301-33619_3-57394975-275/japan-earthquake-anniversary-digital-media-lessons-weve-learned/.

Stephens, K. 2011. "Social Media and the Japan Earthquake: What We Can Learn." idisaster 2.0, March 12. http://idisaster.wordpress.com/2011/03/12/social-media-and-the-japan-earthquake-and-tsunami-what-we-can-learn/.

Stewart, G., R. Kolluru, and M. Smith. 2009. "Leveraging Public-Private Partnerships to Improve Community Resilience in Times of Disaster." *International Journal of Physical Distribution and Logistics Management* 39, no. 5: 343–364.

Tennessee Valley Authority (TVA). 1940. *The Norris Project: A Comprehensive Report on the Planning, Design, Construction, and Initial Operations of the Tennessee Valley Authority's First Water Control Project.* Technical Report No. 1. Washington, DC: U.S. Government Printing Office.

———. 2009a. *Design for the Public Good.* http://www.tva.com/heritage/design/index.html.

———. 2009b. *Norris Reservoir.* http://www.tva.gov/sites/norris.html.

Terkel, A. 2011. "FEMA Praised by Governors for Response to Hurricane Irene." *Huffington Post,* August 28. http://www.huffingtonpost.com/2011/08/28/hurricane-irene-fema-response_n_939545.html.

Twenty First Century Communications (TFCC). 2011. "Case Study: Hurricane Irene's Impact on Electric Utilities." Columbus, OH: TFCC. December 28. http://blog.tfcci.com/Default.aspx?app=LeadgenDownload&shortpath=docs%2fHurricane+Irene+Webv+0811.pdf.

United Press International (UPI). 2012. "Lights Back On in Most of India." UPI.com, July 31. http://www.upi.com/Top_News/World-News/2012/07/31/Lights-back-on-in-most-of-India/UPI-25311343733417/.

USA Today. 2013. "Hurricane Sandy, Drought Costs U.S. $100 billion." January 24. http://www.usatoday.com/story/weather/2013/01/24/global-disaster-report-sandy-drought/1862201/

U.S. Congress. 2001. *Uniting and Strengthening America by Providing Appropriate Tools Required to Intercept and Obstruct Terrorism (USA Patriot Act) Act of 2001.* 107th Congress, P.L. 107-56. www.gpo.gov/fdsys/pkg/PLAW-107publ56/html/PLAW-107publ56.htm.

U.S. Department of Energy and U.S. Department of Homeland Security. 2012. *Electricity Subsector Cybersecurity Capability Maturity Model: Version 1.0 (ES-C2M2).* May 31. http://energy.gov/sites/prod/files/Electricity%20Subsector%20Cybersecurity%20Capabilities%20Maturity%20Model%20%28ES-C2M2%29%20-%20May%202012.pdf.

U.S. Department of Homeland Security (DHS). 2003a. Homeland Security Presidential Directive 5 (HSPD-5): Management of Domestic Incidents. February 28. https://www.hsdl.org/?view&did=439105.

———.2003b. Homeland Security Presidential Directive 7 (HSPD-7): Critical Infrastructure Identification, Prioritization, and Protection. December 17. https://www.hsdl.org/?view&did=441950.

———. 2003c. Homeland Security Presidential Directive 8 (HSPD-8): National Preparedness. December 17. https://www.hsdl.org/?view&did=441951.

————. 2008. *National Response Framework (NRF).* Washington, DC. January. http://www.fema.gov/pdf/emergency/nrf/nrf-core.pdf.

————. 2009. *National Infrastructure Protection Plan (NIPP).* Washington, DC. http://www.dhs.gov/xlibrary/assets/NIPP_Plan.pdf.

————. 2012a. DHS Cybersecurity Overview. http://www.dhs.gov/cybersecurity-overview.

————. 2012b. DHS Daily Open Source Infrastructure Report (DOSIR). October 30–November 9. http://www.dhs.gov/dhs-daily-open-source-infrastructure-report.

————. 2012c. *National Preparedness Report.* March 30. http://www.fema.gov/library/viewRecord.do?id=5914.

U.S. Department of Homeland Security (DHS), National Protection and Programs Directorate, Office of Infrastructure Protection. 2011. "Hurricane Irene Analysis Summary: Advisory 24." August 27. http://info.publicintelligence.net/DHS-HurricaneIrene.pdf.

U.S. Department of Homeland Security (DHS), Office of Inspector General (OIG). 2005. *Challenges in FEMA's Flood Map Modernization Program.* Report No. OIG-05-44. Washington, DC. September. http://www.oig.dhs.gov/assets/Mgmt/OIG_05-44_Sep05.pdf.

U.S. Department of Transportation (DOT). 2006. *Pocket Guide to Transportation.* Washington, DC: Bureau of Transportation Statistics. http://www.rita.dot.gov/bts/sites/rita.dot.gov.bts/files/publications/pocket_guide_to_transportation/index.html.

U.S. Department of the Treasury. 2012. *A New Economic Analysis of Infrastructure Investment.* Report prepared by the Department of the Treasury with the Council of Economic Advisors. Washington, DC. March 23. http://www.treasury.gov/resource-center/economic-policy/Documents/20120323InfrastructureReport.pdf.

U.S. Government Accountability Office (GAO). 2006. *Information Sharing: The Federal Government Needs to Establish Policies and Processes for Sharing Terrorism-Related and Sensitive but Unclassified Information.* Report to Congressional Requesters, GAO-06-385. Washington, DC. March 17. http://www.gao.gov/products/GAO-06-385.

————. 2007. *Critical Infrastructure: Challenges Remain in Protecting Key Sectors.* Testimony before the Subcommittee on Homeland Security, Committee on Appropriations, U.S. House of Representatives, GAO-07-626T. Washington, DC. March 20. http://www.gao.gov/products/GAO-07-626T.

————. 2010. *Critical Infrastructure Protection: Update to National Infrastructure Protection Plan Includes Increased Emphasis on Risk Management and Resilience.* Report to Members and Committees of Congress, GAO-10-296. Washington, DC. March 5. http://www.gao.gov/products/GAO-10-296.

————. 2011a. *Cybersecurity: Continued Attention Needed to Protect Our Nation's Critical Infrastructure.* Testimony before the Subcommittee on Oversight and Investigations, Committee on Energy and Commerce, U.S. House of Representatives, GAO-11-865T. Washington, DC. July 26. http://www.gao.gov/new.items/d11865t.pdf.

————. 2011b. *Homeland Defense: Actions Needed to Improve DOD Planning and Coordination for Maritime Operations.* Report to Congressional Requesters, GAO-11-661. Washington, DC. June 23. http://www.gao.gov/htext/d11661.html.

————. 2011c. *Maritime Security: Federal Agencies Have Taken Actions to Address Risks Posed by Seafarers, but Efforts Can Be Strengthened.* Report to the Ranking Member, Committee on Homeland Security, U.S. House of Representatives, GAO-11-195. Washington, DC. January 14. http://www.gao.gov/products/GAO-11-195.

————. 2012. *Critical Infrastructure Protection: DHS Could Better Manage Security Surveys and Vulnerability Assessments.* Report to Congressional Requesters, GAO-12-378. Washington, DC. May 31. http://www.gao.gov/products/GAO-12-378.

U.S. Navy Department (USN). 2007. *The Cargo Tracking Handbook.* Washington, DC: Office of Naval Intelligence.

Viteritti, J. 1982. "Policy Analysis in the Bureaucracy: An Ad Hoc Approach." *Public Administration Review* 42 (September–October): 466–474.

Waggoner, M. 2012. "Nine Months After Irene, People in North Carolina Still Suffer." *San Francisco Chronicle*, June 7. http://www.sfgate.com/cgi-bin/article.cgi?f=/n/a/2012/06/07/national/a134349D25.DTL&type=science&ao=all.

WebWire. 2011. "Contaminated Water from Hurricane Irene Causes Boil Water Alerts." Press release, August 31. http://www.webwire.com/ViewPressRel.asp?aId=144790.

Weimer, D., and A. Vining. 2005. *Policy Analysis: Concepts and Practice.* 4th ed. Upper Saddle River, NJ: Pearson Prentice Hall.

Welch, W. 2012. "Millions Brace for Worst of Monster Storm Sandy." *USA Today*, October 29, 1A.

White, R. 2012. "Union Walkout Cripples Ports of Los Angeles and Long Beach." *Los Angeles Times,* November 29. http://articles.latimes.com/2012/nov/29/business/la-fi-ports-walkout-20121129.

———. 2013. "Container Traffic at Los Angeles, Long Beach Ports Up Slightly in 2012." *Los Angeles Times*, January 17.

The White House. 1998. Presidential Decision Directive 63 (PDD-63): Critical Infrastructure Protection. Washington, DC. May 22. https://www.fas.org/irp/offdocs/pdd/pdd-63.pdf.

———. 2003. *National strategy for the Physical Protection of Critical Infrastructures and Key Assets.* Washington, DC. February. http://www.dhs.gov/xlibrary/assets/Physical_Strategy.pdf.

———. 2004. National Security Presidential Directive 39 (NSPD-39): U.S. Space-Based Position, Navigation, and Timing Policy. Washington, DC. December 15. https://www.fas.org/irp/offdocs/nspd/nspd-39.htm.

———. 2005. *National Strategy for Maritime Security (NSMS).* Homeland Security Digital Library, September. http://www.hsdl.org/?view&did=456414

———. 2006. *National Strategy for Combating Terrorism (NSCT).* Washington, DC: National Security Council. Full text available at http://www.asksam.com/ebooks/releases.asp?file=Combating-Terror.ask.

———. 2010. *National Security Strategy (NSS).* Washington, DC: National Security Council. http://www.whitehouse.gov/sites/default/files/rss_viewer/national_security_strategy.pdf.

———. 2011. Presidential Policy Directive 8 (PPD-8): National Preparedness. Washington, DC. March 30. http://www.fas.org/irp/offdocs/ppd/ppd-8.pdf.

———. 2012. *National Strategy for Global Supply Chain Security (GSCS).* Washington, DC. January 23. http://www.whitehouse.gov/sites/default/files/national_strategy_for_global_supply_chain_security.pdf.

———. 2013a. Exec. Order No. 13636: Improving Critical Infrastructure Cybersecurity. Washington, DC. February 12. http://www.fas.org/irp/offdocs/eo/eo-13636.htm.

———. 2013b. Presidential Policy Directive 21 (PPD-21): Critical Infrastructure Security and Resilience. Washington, DC. February 12. http://www.fas.org/irp/offdocs/ppd/ppd-21.pdf.

Whitwell, L., and T. Durante. 2011. "Travel Chaos Looms for Entire Country as Northeast Shuts Down Transportation Systems and Airlines Cancel Hundreds of Flights to Prepare for Irene's Havoc." *Daily Mail* (UK) , August 26. http://www.dailymail.co.uk/news/article-2030220/Hurricane-Irene-path-2011-New-York-City-SHUTS-DOWN-transportation-system.html.

Wilson, D., and B. McCay. 1998. "How the Participants Talk About 'Participation' in Mid-Atlantic Fisheries Management." *Ocean & Coastal Management* 41: 41–69.

Wilson, J.Q. 1989. *Bureaucracy: What Government Agencies Do and Why They Do It.* New York: HarperCollins.

Yamagishi, T. 1986. "The Provision of a Sanctioning System as a Public Good." *Journal of Personality and Social Psychology* 51, no. 1: 110–116.

Yin, R.K. 2009. *Case Study Research—Design and Methods.* 4th ed. Thousand Oaks, CA: Sage.

Zetter, K. 2012. "DHS, Not NSA, Should Lead Cybersecurity, Pentagon Official Says." Wired.com, March 1. http://www.wired.com/threatlevel/2012/03/rsa-security-panel/.

Zolli, A. 2012. "Learning to Bounce Back." *New York Times,* Op-Ed, November 2. http://www.nytimes.com/2012/11/03/opinion/forget-sustainability-its-about-resilience.html?pagewanted=all&_r=0.

Zolli, A., and A.M. Healy. 2012. *Resilience: Why Things Bounce Back.* New York: Free Press.

About the Author

Dane S. Egli (PhD) is a national security senior advisor at The Johns Hopkins University Applied Physics Laboratory in Laurel, Maryland, and a career Coast Guard officer who served on the White House National Security Council staff from 2004 to 2006 as a director for counterterrorism and as the president's advisor on hostages and global counternarcotics. He holds master's degrees from the George Washington University and National Defense University in National Security Studies, along with a doctoral degree from the University of Colorado–Denver in public policy, with a concentration in Homeland Security. Dr. Egli served as the senior maritime advisor to the combatant commander at USNORTHCOM from 2006 to 2008 and speaks nationally on homeland security, maritime security, national preparedness, and resilience issues.

Index

Italic page references indicate figures.